The —————
PROPHETIC
BOOKS *and their*
THEOLOGICAL
WITNESS

The
PROPHETIC
BOOKS *and their*
THEOLOGICAL
WITNESS

Odil Hannes Steck

TRANSLATED BY **James D. Nogalski**

Chalice Press®
St. Louis, Missouri

© Copyright English edition 2000 by Chalice Press
Original edition © 1996
Die Prophetenbücher und ihr theologisches Zeugnis: Wege der Nachfrage und Fährten zur Antwort
Published by Verlag J.C.B. Mohr (Paul Siebeck)
Wilhelmstraße 18 D-72074 Tübingen

All scriptural quotations are the translator's rendering, unless otherwise marked.

Publisher's Note: The publication of this work was made possible through the assistance of INTER NATIONES, Bonn. / Die Herausgabe dieses Werkes wurde aus Mitteln von INTER NATIONES, Bonn, gefördert.

Art Director: Elizabeth Wright
Cover: Scott Tjaden
Interior design: Wynn Younker
Cover art: Detail of painting of old, robed, bearded man (feature of the Arch of Apocalypse in St. Mark's Cathedral, Venice, Italy). ©1999, Randy Wells, Picture Network International, Ltd.

This book is printed on acid-free, recycled paper.

Visit Chalice Press on the World Wide Web at
www.chalicepress.com

10 9 8 7 6 5 4 3 2 1   00 01 02 03 04 05

Library of Congress Cataloging–in–Publication Data
Steck, Odil Hannes.
      [Prophetenbücher und ihr theologisches Zeugnis. English] The prophetic books and their theological witness / Odil Hannes Steck ; translated by James D. Nogalski.
          p.   cm.
      ISBN 0-8272-2957-7
      1. Bible. O.T. Prophets–Criticism, interpretation, etc.   I. Title.
      BS1505.2 .S79   2000
      224' .0663–dc21   99–050530

Printed in the United States of America

That which the words say does not endure.
The words survive,
because the words are always the same,
but what they say is never the same.

Antonio Porchia

Prophecy that was necessary for later generations
was written down,
and that which was not necessary
was not written down.

Babylonian Talmud, Megillah 14a

Table of Contents

Preface to the English Edition

The publication of this book in English has been expanded at several points. These insertions are marked with square brackets thus: [ ]. These insertions update bibliographic references to literature that has appeared since the publication of the German edition and offer several clarifications of the content. At several points, the reader will notice that for the sake of clarity, the German words are placed in parentheses beside the English translation. For example, the German has been noted in cases where technical terms appear that make the translation difficult (for example, *Wirkungsgeschichte* or *Rezeptionsästhetik*) or where the German term carries broader connotations than can be expressed in a single English word (for example, continuation for *Fortschreibung*).

I would like to thank Dr. James Nogalski, who has published his own outstanding research in this field, for the skilled translation. I would also like to thank Dr. Konrad Schmid for working through the translation and Dr. Jon L. Berquist of Chalice Press for publishing this book.

Zürich, January 1999
Odil Hannes Steck

Preface

Books claim to transmit something essential. As a rule, one first recognizes that which books want to or should transmit only when one reads contemplatively from beginning to end, not when one scans the works. These works affect the readership only when this contemplation occurs. This trivial insight has increasingly fallen into the shadows in the efforts to research the books of the Hebrew Bible. Prophetic books are no exception. The reason is simple. These writings do not constitute books in the sense that we commonly mean by the term. They do not constitute books with a single author who wishes the reader to follow his trail. To be sure, prophetic books go by the name of a prophet, but by all appearances, they are not simply created by that prophet. Instead, they acquire their current dimensions over a rather lengthy period. We encounter these works as developed works of tradition, not the literary product of a single author. Only the oldest material comes into consideration as a record of the work of the prophet whose name is associated with it. However, the extent of that prophet's work is unclear. Other questions also remain open. Where does the more recent material originate, that material which one finds undesignated in the very book bearing the prophet's name? How, when, and for what purpose does it enter the book? With respect to the author, we thus have a very different type of book, but we still know very little about its character.

Innovative prophetic stimuli that gave rise to this book development appeared to be the most valuable for an intellectual culture that is still operative today, one that primarily orients itself toward brilliant solitary figures. These stimuli were also the most valuable for a biblical theology that orients itself toward an inspired kerygmatic work stemming from individual figures. It is thus understandable that research, and subsequently the sermon and teaching based upon it, has focused upon the oldest material *in* the books. One seeks to find the original prophetic figures in order to make visible their message, work, and time and to traverse the radical change in the perception of YHWH for which they stood. This desire has thus primarily resulted in a wrestling match over precisely what can be considered part of the oldest original prophetic textual material. The more recent text material, once isolated, inevitably became less interesting. The book itself appeared only as a receptacle for the very valuable and the less important textual material.

In the meantime, however, we have reached a turning point in the discipline. One should certainly not abandon the question of the prophets themselves or the question of differentiating older material from more recent material within prophetic books. However, swift access to the prophet and the marginal evaluation of the books are no longer taken for granted. The idea continues to gain momentum that overzealous interest in the prophet himself skips the essential first step on the path toward finding the prophet. This dominating interest neglects the available book in association with other prophetic books, which is all that we have. It also unsuspectingly underestimates the value of the only thing provided, specifically prophetic text material in the form of books. No one has proven that these books are really only the packaging for many formally marked individual texts and stories from various periods. These books could also have intentions as books. The form of these works, even their final form, can also present a message intentionally and purposefully.

This suggestion is, of course, not obvious. Anyone who reads the prophetic books from Isaiah to Malachi with care and concern for the whole as well as the parts can only be confused at first by the multiplicity of statements, images, rebukes, and viewpoints. One is also confused at first by contradictory material and material that appears mutually exclusive. The search for fashioned units of meaning in this conglomeration of statements within the books appears to be a lost endeavor. That being the case then, only clarification and didactic authority from outside can form the redemptive embankment from which the whole can be viewed as a material unity from a suitable distance. Judaism and Christianity perceived this idea, but so did Israel in the late antiquity of the first and second centuries B.C.E. The prophetic commentaries from Qumran already demonstrate as much.

Nevertheless, the impression that the prophetic books as a whole do not intend to present something cannot be the final word. Despite manifold efforts in recent times, investigations into this field are just beginning. The question of intentional meaning in developing prophetic books as a whole should finally receive its due. In an extensive shift, prophetic books should be declared a conventional focal point of research. This shift means that the search for the original work of the respective prophet must proceed more peacefully and more slowly. Once one ascertains, where possible, the meaning of the book-forms of the prophetic transmission, then the path back to the question of the original work of the prophet can only proceed with caution from the latest presentations of meaning back to the oldest presentations from which everything started. Only then can one seek the prophet behind these oldest presentations, at the beginning of a reception process that has been adapted for meaning, that led to the growth of the books. In other words, a lengthy, productive process of tradition could come to light behind the current prophetic books. This process shows a growing reception and adaptation as the book grows. This process could itself have theological weight and a typical character which can no longer stand in the shadow behind the question of innovative original logia. Indeed, the process corresponds to the transmission and adaptation of the biblical message through the ages.

Efforts concerning the prophetic books as books have recently been undertaken in many places. Nevertheless, at this time they are still isolated attempts with very different points of entry. This current work intends to contribute by exploring, explaining, and affirming this newly emerging field. It is still far too early to harvest incontrovertible, comprehensive conclusions. We are just beginning, and even the type of approach must be contemplated and prepared. First, looking anew at that which we have and at appropriate approaches must take center stage. That is already difficult enough. Nevertheless, we hope that, in the course of this work, we can produce preliminary, foundational observations concerning the theological character of prophetic tradition in ancient Israel.

For many years, we, along with others, have concentrated upon initial glances into the world of prophetic books as books via numerous individual studies in the area of Isaiah and the Book of the Twelve. We have sought traces of the particular theological intention that these books present. This current volume stands in conversation with various starting points of the discipline. It seeks to be an interim contemplation in the flow of these endeavors. It provides an up-to-date status report with a current summary of suggestions (my own and others). This summary does not contain hard and fast conclusions that cannot be averted. Rather, the summary presents suggestions in the sense of practically achieved impressions regarding how one should work with the question of prophetic book transmission. It also presents noteworthy findings that these initial inquiries into this area have produced.

The first part of this volume, "Transmitting Prophetic Books," is published for the first time. It is dedicated to the approach, to the search for paths that will result in drawing closer to the profile of the prophetic book. It is directed foremost to those who work professionally in the field, but at the same time it provides a glance for a more widely interested readership into that which is most pressing for current prophetic research.

The second part, "Prophetic Exegesis of the Prophets," is dedicated to initial investigations into the world of prophetic books, to the trails that one can already see. It derives from an essay in the context of a Zürich lecture series honoring Gerhard Ebeling. It was first published in the collection of essays edited by H. F. Geißer, and others (*Wahrheit der Schrift–Wahrheit der Auslegung*, Zürich, 1993, pp. 198–244). I have revised the composition somewhat for reprinting in this volume because of its lecture character. The opening was changed so that it no longer reflects the original occasion. It derives from a guest lecture to the theological faculty at the University of Erlangen. It also has an expanded conclusion that further sketches the hermeneutical results of this finding in very brief fashion. Otherwise, the composition is printed here essentially unchanged. From the outset, as a lecture before the general public, it also addresses a wider readership. It attempts to provide insight into the theological treasures that can be cultivated from the transmission of prophetic books. These treasures are less concerned with the typical use of prophetic writings, namely, for addressing sections of prophetic pericopes that should concern the individual. Instead, these treasures of insight, based on the text sequence across entire books, encompass humanity's universal and temporal context. In this breadth, the insight wants to clarify meaningfully and to orient one to the origin over a lengthy period, current existence, and the outlook for the future.

The title of this volume relies upon the scriptural interpretation of the intertestamental book of *Jubilees*. If we are correct, shortly after the closing of the prophetic canon of the Hebrew Bible, this book used the term "witness" to convey the theological unity and continuing significance of the prophetic books in particular as synonymous, powerfully oriented instruction in the lengthy path that God and God's people walk together in the sphere of the nations. This "witness" burdens with guilt, but at the same time liberates with hope. As a result, this witness meaningfully clarifies the experience of the present time.

The text of the first motto for this book simultaneously contrasts and parallels the reception process of prophetic books as well. It is taken from the Argentine poet Antonio Porchia, from the collection of poems entitled *"Voces Nuevas."* The collection was published under the title *Antonio Porchia, 'Voces Nuevas,' Neue Stimmen* (translated into German by T. Burghardt, Edition 350, Dürnau: Kooperative Dürnau, 1995). The quote is taken from p. 24.

My heartfelt gratitude goes to Professor Dr. T. Krüger who took the time to read the manuscript and helped me with additional clarifications and refinements. I also thank Professor Dr. R. G. Kratz, and my assistants, Dr. Konrad Schmid and Peter Schwagmeier, for their efforts in reading and critically evaluating the manuscript and helping with corrections. I am also grateful to my student worker, Martina Oswald, for helping with corrections and to Philipp Stoellger for critical counsel with the systematic ideas in the concluding sections of the second chapter. I am grateful as well to my secretary, Ruth Funk, for typing the final manuscript and to Siebeck publishers for their friendly care.

Zürich, February 1996
Odil Hannes Steck

Abbreviations

AB	Anchor Bible
ABD	*Anchor Bible Dictionary,* David Noel Freedman, ed.
AOAT	Alter Orient und Altes Testament
ATD	Das Alte Testament Deutsch
AUSS	Andrews University Seminary Studies
AzTh	Arbeit zur Theologie
BBB	Bonner biblische Beiträge
BEAT	Beiträge zur Erforschung des Alten Testaments
BEATAJ	Beiträge zur Enforschung des Alten Testaments und des antiken Judentums
BEThL	Bibliotheca ephemeridum theologicarum lovaniensium
BEvTh	Beiträge zur evangelischen Theologie
Bib	*Biblica*
BIJDR	*Bijdragen*
BK	Biblischer Kommentar
BN	*Biblische Notizen*
BThSt	Biblische-Theologische Studien
BWANT	Beiträge zur Wissenschaft vom Alten und Neuen Testament
BZ	*Biblische Zeitschrift*
BZAW	Beihefte zur *Zeitschrift für die alttestamentliche Wissenschaft*
CBC	Cambridge Bible Commentary
CBNT	Coniectanea biblica, New Testament
CBOT	Coniectanea biblica, Old Testament
CBQ	*Catholic Biblical Quarterly*
CRINT	Compendia rerum iudaicarum ad novum testamentum
DBS	*Dictionnaire de la Bible, Supplément*
DiKi	*Dialog der Kirchen*
DJD	Discoveries in the Judaean Desert
DSD	*Dead Sea Discoveries*
EThL	*Ephemerides theologicae lovanienses*
EvTh	*Evangelische Theologie*
FAT	Forschungen zum Alten Testament
FLGP	*Forschungen zur Geschichte und Lehre des Protestantismus*

FOTL	Forms of the Old Testament Literature
FRLANT	Forschungen zur Religion und Literatur des Alten und Neuen Testaments
FZB	*Forschungen zur Bibel*
HK	Handkommentar zum Alten Testament
HSM	Harvard Semitic Monographs
HTR	*Harvard Theological Review*
ICC	International Critical Commentary
Int	*Interpretation*
ISBL	Indiana Studies in Biblical Literature
JAC	Jahrbuch für Antike und Christentum
JBL	*Journal of Biblical Literature*
JBTh	*Jahrbuch für Biblische Theologie*
JQR	*Jewish Quarterly Review*
JSOT	*Journal for the Study of the Old Testament*
JSOTSup	*Journal for the Study of the Old Testament* Supplements
JudChr	Judaica et Christiana
KuD	*Kerygma und Dogma*
KHC	Kurzer Hand-Commentar zum Alten Testament
LXX	Septuagint
MT	Masoretic Text
MThZ	*Münchener theologische Zeitschrift*
NSKAT	Neues Stuttgarter Kommentar zum Alten Testament
NBL	*Neues Bibel-Lexikon,* ed. M. Görg and B. Lang (Zürich and Düsseldorf: Benziger Verlag)
NICOT	New International Commentary on the Old Testament
OBO	Orbis biblicus et orientalis
OTES	*Old Testament Essays*
OTG	Old Testament Guides
OTL	Old Testament Library
POT	*De Prediking van het Oude Testament*
QD	Quaestiones disputatae
QpHab	Qumran Pesher of Habakkuk
RAC	*Reallexicon für Antike und Christentum*
RevQ	*Revue de Qumran*

SBB	Stuttgarter biblische Beiträge
SBLDS	Society of Biblical Literature Dissertation Series
SBLMS	Society of Biblical Literature Monograph Series
SBLRBS	Society of Biblical Literature Resources for Biblical Study
SBLSP	Society of Biblical Literature Seminar Papers
SBS	Stuttgarter Bibelstudien
SJOT	*Scandinavian Journal of the Old Testament*
StTDJ	Studies on the Texts of the Desert of Judah
ThB	Theologische Bücherei
ThLZ	*Theologische Literaturzeitung*
ThR	*Theologischer Rundschau*
ThW	*Theologische Wissenschaft*
ThWAT	G. J. Botterweck and H. Ringgren, eds., *Theologisches Wörterbuch zum Alten Testament*
TRE	*Theologische Realenzyklopädie*
TSAJ	Texte und Studien zum antiken Judentum
TThZ	*Trierer theologische Zeitschrift*
TU	Texte und Untersuchungen zur Geschichte der alttestamentlichen Literatur
TUAT	Texte aus der Umwelt des Alten Testaments (Gütersloh: Mohn Verlag)
UB	Urban Taschenbücher
UTB	Uni-Taschenbücher
VF	*Verkündigung und Forschung*
VT	*Vetus Testamentum*
VTSup	*Vetus Testamentum* Supplements
WBC	Word Biblical Commentary
WMANT	Wissenschaftliche Mongraphien zum Alten und Neuen Testament
WUNT	Wissenschaftliche Untersuchungen zum Neuen Testament
XII	Book of the Twelve
ZAW	*Zeitschrift für die alttestamentliche Wissenschaft*
ZNW	*Zeitschrift für die neutestamentliche Wissenschaft*
ZThK	*Zeitschrift für Theologie und Kirche*

Part 1

Transmitting Prophetic Books: Steps toward an Approach

1

The Prophetic Word and Prophetic Book as a Historical Problem

The Starting Point

Historical work operates within the framework of the possibilities and the limits of posing problems and solving those problems. This type of historical work has the task of separating early material from later material and then understanding the respective material as such. Historical understanding attempts to control critically one's own approaches to the question that are in fact determined by present concerns. Historical work attempts to perceive the material in its own time and in its "otherness," using source rationale as the basis for reconstruction. Only in this way can one preserve the character of the material that has been transmitted. Only in this way does the material's own weight and life remain in order to build a bridge of understanding, of appropriation, but also of evaluation from a distance. This otherness should by no means be perceived as negative or positive confirmation of present-day options, even according to a modern perspective. Rather, responsible inquiry represents this otherness as a dynamic expression of life on its own terms. In this clarity, that which was transmitted from an earlier time can appear to us as something special. It can provide contexts or discontinuity for that which comes later. It can also be stimulating by itself. This transmitted material can possibly even remain insightful precisely because it offers something that our time does not know (any longer), but that we should still know if we are to survive.

As with other cultural material from earlier times, this is true for the prophetic books of the Hebrew Bible, especially within communities that consider these books as holy writings that are still instructive. Anyone who takes the time to allow these books to work on her or him, and who attempts to see that they combine a text and a way of life from the past, can even today perceive their essential character from reliable translations. An image appears of the persons whose names these books bear. Also, an image of great intervals of time appears, over which these persons transmit their books. What impressions do these images leave behind?

Prophetic activity first makes itself known in this strange mixture of statements by the way the books transmit individual utterances and appearances within the framework of the constellations of that time. This prophetic work bears consistent lines of thought. Looking from the outside, experience from an earlier time is bound with traditional material using words and stories. Also, actions from an earlier time that are oriented toward attainable benefits become severely disjointed. From this standpoint, unrest, contradiction, relentless appraisal, unmasking of current practice, and the sober correction of high-flying or stagnant hope appear. Their claim of decisive clarification for life appears very near in the experiential world. Unrelentingly, they bring reasons and results into play for that which has been experienced or that which is feared. This perspective of a higher attitude points toward severe, but also hopeful, prospects that the addressees of Israel's prophets must know. Nevertheless, they still have not experienced these prospects because life's success is not at the disposal of a person or a people in this time or in the future. Even though Israel and churches now prefer ancient holy writings over new, current revelations, the unchanging meaning of reality transmitted by the prophets of these books is undeniable. The unchanging meaning mixes incorruptibly where the experiential world of humanity is encountered directly. The moving fantasy of these prophets continues to impress today. It sees life from outside, not with abstractions, but concretely. The courage, the unceasing push toward soundness, and the substance of meaning require attention. The disturbing and yet holy unrest of the prophets toward meaningless activity in everyday life illuminates the lack of an orientation to life that did not just exist at that time.

A second impression appears along with the first. Consider the image of the people of God in the course of world history that develops when entire prophetic books are read in sequence. Anyone who does so is taken along the lengthy chronological path of Ancient Israel in the realm of the world powers. The reader will find the apparent place, judgment, meaning, and goal in this flow of time across centuries. The reader thereby encounters an experientially sensitive nearness to historical currents and constellations, but also encounters a bewildering sobriety that is not addicted to the political powers whose time and end can instead be seen. The reader becomes aware of the particular world of the people of God, to see Israel's national self-determination. This view does not conceive election as Israel's own quality and achievement. Rather, it connects election with the continual, characteristic history of guilt, while it also waits upon goals of hope. From there, the reader encounters a purposeful experience of a lengthy history that points to the limits of humanity with an unparalleled sense of worldwide political reality. This experience does not exclude the people of God in their historical path.

For a curious, interested, or even a contemplative readership, the direct effect of reading the prophets can be grouped in this manner (or similarly). This readership exposes the character of the textual material from the distant past for the present generation. However, this readership stumbles upon all of this material embedded in the verbiage of entire books that encompass more than one-fourth of the Hebrew Bible. It is contained in a flood of unfamiliar formulations, images, and relationships to historical processes about which one can only conjecture today without more detailed research. Strange presuppositions hinder a better understanding. One would have to know much more in order to coordinate one's impressions from reading and concrete textual findings. One would need to know what the statements mean specifically, from whom they actually originate, about which time period and which experiential constellation they speak, and why they are formulated in this way and not in another. One would have to know how the individual text and the whole book relate to one another in these books. What is actually written? In what context does it appear literarily and with regard to its experiential framework? Only when such things are known can these impressions, even for a much later time period, offer a genuinely corroborated enhancement that can lead to evaluation, appropriation, or limitations. Only then can the clarifying effect of the earlier material and the strange material come to life in our time. Only then can one attempt to decide that which is passé and that which continues to stimulate. Only from such knowledge can a chasm or a bridge arise. Such knowledge can communicate to the world today that people's contemporary tasks will not be solved without the insights of earlier generations. Conversely, this knowledge communicates that the transmitted prophets must take a different form for our later times, even in the formulation, if the quality of their work is to be carried over and maintained. Who deduces this knowledge? With books from an earlier time, it first becomes the responsibility of historical inquiry to find the key to that which is strange and different, even when the subject is nothing less than the biblical God made known in the distant past. Historical inquiry must open the door to the character of these prophetic books so that understanding may grow from this knowledge.

However, all of the traditional certainty has broken down in Old Testament research, including the area of the prophets. The return trip to the final text of the prophetic books as we have it stands alongside the still dominant search for the original prophet. The historical question about the time of origin for the textual material determines questions about the formulation, shape, growth, and literary contextualization by the response to intellectual and political challenges. Alongside this question, one also finds structurally oriented attempts of ahistorical internal investigations which avoid the confusion of historical research into the meaning and development of prophetic books. Keys for understanding this transmitted textual material are currently offered from various directions. Whether they are appropriate appears to be largely a matter of opinion. The amount of knowledge that can be known with certainty, to which a majority of researchers would agree, becomes ever smaller. Also, the presumed knowledge presented in an abundance of starting points and investigations lacks consensus. This lack of consensus has its reasons. The subject itself becomes more blurry because it is processed to the point of excess with preconceived questions. Such is already the case in the area of historical inquiry that allows the prophetic books to be what they are—texts of antiquity. In the prophetic books, by whom, when, what, and in what context was something first put into words? What experiential framework takes effect, and what original meaning is connected with the current process of formulation and transmission as the books develop? These questions are more open than ever. The prophet at the beginning of the tradition and the question of the growth of this tradition into the final phase of the books are also beset today with this irritating uncertainty. The uncertainty in light of the whole burdens the understanding of the parts. The historical task of clarifying strong impressions from the prophetic writings for today's understanding appears to lack consensus and therefore success. Anyone not wishing to give up faces the challenge of finding anew the gateway and the pathways in this uncharted land. Above all, that person faces the challenge of winning over the scientific world. Research must therefore begin again in a higher sense, even in the area of prophetic texts. Though it has already been sufficiently discussed, research must approach the field of the text as if it is new territory.

This current challenge for research grows from the increasingly inescapable insight that the prominently investigated subject is more brittle than we thought. For too long we have wanted to acknowledge the poetic, kerygmatic, socio-revolutionary prophets. Concretely: it is difficult to grasp the prophet providing the name and his work respectively from prophetic books. It is harder than we thought, and our attempts are more subjective, more trendy than we admit. We do not encounter persons who are like us, but greater, with whom we need only identify. Instead, we encounter written material intended to be read. We have not yet detected how the two relate to one another. With respect to the books, we have something in our hands, but we do not yet really know what it is. In the ancient self-presentation of the prophetic books, everything is unambiguous. The self-presentation connects the statements of the book with the prophetic figure. However, in contemporary historical inquiry everything is open, because one finds unavoidable indications that one must distinguish between the prophet and more recent transmission material. This much is clear: The prophet is only provided in the superimposition of a relatively lengthy process of tradition that may have played a more or less active role. This process results in the prophetic writings.[1] This situation means that the book stands in front of the prophet.[2] Anyone wishing to find the prophet must first go through the book. In contrast to the long-dominant quest for the prophetic persons, the most pressing task now is an illuminating inquiry into the prophetic books. One must inquire into the self-presentation of the prophetic writings that stem from a time that does not yet know historical inquiry in our sense.

The Literary Prophetic Image within the Prophetic Book and the Return Path to the Prophet

This path cannot be shortened. Seeking the prophet directly, alongside the development of the book, results in highly divergent conclusions for determining the prophet's statements and message, in spite of an impressive abundance of isolated observations. The respective authentic image of Isaiah in recent times illustrates this diversity. In their respective commentaries to Isaiah 1–39, Wildberger[3] reaches his image of Isaiah with too much confidence in the prophet himself, and Kaiser[4] reaches his image of Isaiah with much skepticism and more confidence in later anonymous input and editors. It is no different with the image of Jeremiah, Ezekiel, or Amos. Contrasting examples from current scholarly contributions can be multiplied. The frequently studied Immanuel text of Isaiah 7 serves as a good example. Anything can be done to a single, defenseless exegetical specimen in the question of genuine or fictional Isaiah logia. Anything can be done if one forgets the literary frame that the text provides, or if one forgets what the text demands in terms of approaches. It is no wonder that theology, church practice, and cultural public opinion get the impression from the flood of investigations that the scholarly world is largely preoccupied with itself when dealing with prophetic texts.

It appears to us that this scholarly confusion ultimately relates to the fact that, as a rule, the concrete material we possess in literary sources continues to be overshadowed by the suggestion of the self-presentation of the prophetic books and by the force of conventional approaches. One works in one's own way, directly upon what one seeks. One does not work on that which one has. Thus one loses the ground beneath one's feet with respect to sources. The prophetic book is normally seen as the contributor of material to analyze, material which comes ready-to-use without considering the approaches. The book is not considered at the beginning. Instead, if it is considered at all, it only receives a little attention at the end. The interest concentrates upon isolated literary layers, but especially upon the original beginnings of the transmission, whether one seeks it with the prophet or in a later period. Behind this situation stands the self-evident assumption that a prophetic book is nothing more than the simple recording of sayings of the prophet for whom the book is named or the sayings of later anonymous prophets. Apparently, this assumption is justified by texts like Isaiah 8:16–18 and 30:8, or by scenes of prophetic appearance (like Isaiah 7–8; Jeremiah 7 and 26) or by the picture of transmission in Jeremiah 36. Additionally, one acknowledges varying numbers of isolated additions or actualizing individual continuations of these recordings along the broader path of transmission. If necessary, these continuations are connected with suggestions of a thoroughgoing revisional layer within a prophetic book whose profile overwhelmingly concerns only those new formulations. As an entity that possibly possesses its own material profile and its own message, the prophetic book itself remains obscure for historical inquiry. However, the prophetic book should be the next subject of historical inquiry.

Still, how reliable is the current presupposition from which so much scientific diversity of opinion arises? How reliable is the presupposition when one finds this diversity irritating, and when it massively hinders the transfer of well-grounded knowledge? Is our knowledge of the tradition-process in the prophetic books really so precise and so certain that one may simply proceed from the presumption that the prophetic books as such have nothing more of substance to contribute? Does it really suffice to concentrate on prophetic books, text unit by text unit? Does it really suffice to proceed on the basis of this postulation about original prophetic logia in order to analyze, to arrange, and to separate the traces of editorial work? Actually, to this point we possess no satisfactory insight. By moving directly to the search for logia, we bypass the literary transmission process and the inquiry into its own productive elements. The customary opinion is anything but self-evident that small units of proclamation can be isolated from the prophetic books without difficulty. Also, one stops too infrequently to question whether the use of a genre and formulaic work leads directly to the prophet or to question where one finds indicators of later literary shaping.

The actual situation is different. A prophetic writing presents a literary image of a prophet, perhaps even in constitutive association with a series of prophetic writings. This literary image stands before the aesthetically oriented search for the image of a brilliant, creative, original prophetic personality. This literary image stands in front of the kerygmatically oriented search for the image of a theologically innovative preacher figure. Form criticism only appears to open the door directly to the works of proclamation of this figure. The view of the prophet as speaker that dominated in the era of form criticism can no longer serve as the starting point for the question. The received location of prophetic messages in descriptions (!) of speaking situations is primarily not a speaking situation that can be immediately reconstructed. Instead, the received location is a book. We only possess the book, and only the book is the ground upon which we can pose our questions. Like the prophetic book itself, this prophetic image that the book presents has received little attention. This image could look quite different from the original prophet.

Our treatise in this study does not concede defeat in the matter by saying that, at any rate, the original prophetic figure and that figure's work remain irretrievably lost to the burden of tradition.[5] We would also not renounce inquiry into the prophet. However, everything must be done at the appropriate time and in the proper order. There is much to be learned on the literary side of the phenomenon. If the original prophets can only be encountered in the received transmission of prophetic books, then one must begin with the investigation of these received sources, and suspend the question of the original prophet. One must first utilize the image that these sources offer and the lines of origin that they suggest. Until the opposite can be demonstrated, one must also assume that the goals of shaping material belong to the process of transmitting the books, whether that material is independent material, material related to the book or to the transmission, or material that provides meaning. These elements as such are worthy of historical inquiry in their own right. This idea should be self-evident, but for a long time the field of prophetic research has not drawn the necessary conclusions for the approach and direction of the question.

Our treatise thus opts for the necessary reversal of the paths of inquiry and even challenges prophetic research at last to begin with that which we have before us (and as we have it before us). It challenges us not to begin with that which the search for the supposedly unique splendor too quickly prefers. The treatise thus offers the task of beginning with the prophet transmitted in the book in the sense of an ideal type of working program that is methodologically conscious and controlled. From that point, it returns step-by-step to the beginnings of the transmission, without deciding in advance.[6] Before a working program is undertaken too hastily in this direction from the end to the beginning, and before it has led to sufficient clarifications and consensus formulations, one cannot say, or allow to be transmitted, much that is reliable about the prophetic figures themselves and their work in general. To what degree it represents a gain to separate these figures from their book transmission is, by far, not yet determined.

It appears to us that the book as such should remain in view with this procedure whose substance is offered without hesitation. If so, then the frame of the investigation must be unavoidably expanded in contrast to the traditional usage. The path into the background of the transmitted material that we possess can no longer ignore that which is given. It can no longer proceed in the narrow framework of a distilled preparation of individual pericopes as well. This preparation yields the oldest individual logia of a prophet by means of literary-critical, load-bearing tests upon the smallest area by subtracting later materials, until the oldest logia appear. One must be cognizant of the limits of traditional methodological practice. Literary criticism is unavoidable in the preliminary segmentation of a concrete research procedure. However, seen as a whole, this limiting of literary criticism to the framework of individual pericopes signifies a source of error of the first order if it remains in this narrow framework. It also errs if it too quickly orients itself toward sayings of the prophet it has supposedly rendered instead of the prophetic book that is actually provided. Impressions from this process have their place as a necessary, partial analysis of an individual text. These impressions may push one toward younger and older material for reasons of linguistic and/or material content. However, they are essentially only impressions. They merely possess preliminary value when seen in isolation within the work under discussion. These impressions must be constantly reevaluated with the findings of the larger literary whole.

In the sense of the change of direction that we advocate, the working procedure is presented differently. The push into older backgrounds of the transmitted book can today only be accomplished via a return path through that which is transmitted (as we have it). It must be the path of investigating the given form of the book as a whole[7] and its literary stages back to indicators for reconstructing the work of a plausible prophetic figure (in most cases). This prophetic figure is the core and impetus of the book's transmission, although broken by the act of recording (*Verschriftung*).[8] The given shape of the book and its literary stages have to carry their own right and weight as a scientific subject. No longer can they be only a by-product of procedural determinations of the transmission of ostensibly genuine, and thus more highly evaluated, prophetic material. One may thus conclude the following: Today, if the guiding criteria are not the subjective assessment and the personal outlook of the exegete, then determinations about the original prophetic figure can no longer be the presupposition. Instead, only at the end can they be the result of investigations into the book's shape. In other words, we must first far more decisively consider what we really know and proceed from that which stands indisputably at our disposal.

We will prefer to use the book of Isaiah to provide examples in our deliberations.[9] In the case of the book of Isaiah, this consideration has the following implications. One can no longer self-evidently begin with the traditional constructs,[10] in which Isaiah arose from three separable, independent writings (Proto-, Deutero-, and Trito-Isaiah), or at least from two independent writings (First and Second Isaiah). Recent investigations still do so.[11] It has not yet been determined whether the inclusive shape[12] of Isaiah 56–66 leads to a literarily independent entity or to a section which is only materially independent within Isaiah, but whose understanding is necessarily prepared in the existing parts of Isaiah, and belongs with it literarily. In this respect, one must begin (again) by observing Isaiah as a whole. Commentaries on Isaiah in its entirety (before Duhm) thus take on new significance, such as those of Franz Delitzsch or A. Dillmann. No less significantly, those commentaries of the precritical period with their observations in the framework of the prophetic book as a whole take on new significance.

The same holds true for an independent isolation of Isaiah 40–55 as a previously existing literarily independent entity.[13] Even here, observations about Isaiah 40–55 within the framework of the whole Isaiah corpus must stand in the forefront, before convincing suggestions regarding possible older entities of Isaiah 40–55, Isaiah 1–55, or 40–66 can be submitted.

Also, when one segments the entity of Isaiah 1–39 within Isaiah, one experiences clearly that Isaiah 39 does not form a plausible conclusion for an individual book.

In these observations within the framework of the given source findings of the prophetic books in series, a treatment of Isaiah must also be associated with Jeremiah and Ezekiel, and with parallel manifestations in the developing Book of the Twelve.[14] The source phenomenon of the *Nebiim* even requires that one not lose sight of Joshua-Kings along with the Torah that precedes it.

Works that only concentrate on Isaiah 1–39, 40–55, or on partial connections of these entities, thus have the character of preliminary studies that treat previous investigation. Recent contributions correctly stress that these works disregard a great deal within exegetical practice. Seen as a whole, one must begin far more basically. In the current book of Isaiah, Isaiah 1–39, 40–55, 56–66 constitute two or three book parts within a single Isaiah book. However, the appropriateness of this type of synchronic segmentation, and even the diachronic deductions, today require new examination in the overlapping horizon of the entire book as we have it. The questionable acceptance that one or several individual prophets must stand behind Deutero- and Trito-Isaiah, because an individual prophet stood behind Proto-Isaiah, is no longer permissible as such. This classic expectation of Isaiah 40–66 is only one of several historical possibilities from which a renewed investigation of the entire book of Isaiah must produce the most plausible decision.[15] And we can add: Even the expectation is no longer self-evident that, primarily, many shorter individual logia or texts stand behind Trito-Isaiah, and that these logia/texts were later combined and integrated into Deutero-Isaiah and/or the Isaiah book. In the face of a very high degree of uncertainty in current research regarding the authorship of Isaiah 56–66, only an investigation of the Trito-Isaiah texts in their literary framework within the Isaiah book can lead to a decision whether this traditional image is confirmed or whether other, unfamiliar possibilities better explain the origin of these texts.

In other prophetic books, the situation is essentially the same. One can no longer presume without qualification the fact that portions of the book were previously independent literary entities. These portions include the confessions, the so-called "Book of consolation for Ephraim," and the series of foreign nation speeches in Jeremiah; the cycle of nations in Amos; and Zechariah 9–11 and Zechariah 12–14. These presumptions rest upon options for separate individual writings in the sense of reconstructed "sources" before the only source provided (the prophetic book as a whole) has been sufficiently taken into account.

In other words, even in the case of prophetic books one must be more determined than usual to ascertain how the given sources were transmitted, and the character of those sources. One must determine these elements before one makes deductions concerning older components or deductions concerning the work of a prophetic figure.

The Given Prophetic Book: Its Original Authorship and Readership

These sources are nothing other than the transmitted final versions of the (series of) prophetic books beyond which these writings can no longer be substantively changed or expanded. Sirach, the Dead Sea texts, and the Septuagint (LXX), when critically examined, provide the earliest attestation that at a certain point in time these final versions reached a certain size, arrangement, and position in the series. To this extent, they were a historically limited phenomenon. Thus, only historical investigation can clarify what this phenomenon intended to present and how it came to us. Anyone wishing to approach this phenomenon of antiquity must look into this historical environment. The same holds true for the question of the purposes of meaning which were associated with the formation processes of the final hand, whether that hand was preserving or even accentuating the material.

The question is no less historical regarding how one should imagine the author and the intended readership of the prophetic books in this time. From the outset this question receives an unusual answer. We (still) have no independent perception of the origin of the prophetic books from the framework of the sociology of literature with which we can begin the historical reconstruction of the development of the book. We can only draw conclusions based upon the literary discovery that we have received inside the books themselves. This discovery must bear the burden of proof. However, it appears to us that this finding, as such (!), is conclusive enough for the question concerning who primarily shaped these books for whom. According to everything we can see, based upon the internal reception processes in the state of the assertions in the (developing) books, the productive tradents and the immediate recipients of these entities were identical in the formative phase of the prophetic books until the final formations. One should accept similar ideas for the internal realm of transmission of legal and priestly knowledge. The second part of this volume will show more clearly that the prophetic writings primarily treat internal text material of assurance within the same professional framework. Without the acceptance of tradent schools and tradent schooling that was occupied with the care of prophetically transmitted material, one cannot account for the eminent knowledge of detail about the text's flow and the text's statements that prophetic books present in reference to the whole. Nor can one account for the construction and the reception suited to the intention if one seeks a plausible location without accepting these schools. On the other hand, it is not disturbing that prophetic books could be, and were, received differently by these places of maintenance within tradent circles of priestly or wisdom knowledge of tradition. With respect to the character of the prophetic sources, one must thus take into account the fact that, from the beginning, prophetic books were not shaped in light of a public, or even a private, reading culture[16] and its instruction for reception. One may consider that this public or private reading culture exists once the Nebiim were formed after the second century B.C.E. (Compare the following: Ps 1 as the opening of a psalter intended to be read; the prologue of the Sirach translation; 1 Macc 1:56f; Baruch?; scroll productions in Qumran; Acts 8:28). One notices, however, how much value was placed upon an authoritative (!) interpretation of the biblical reading material in this late period over against the possible free associations of reading (Dan 9; 1QpHab I–II; VII; Luke 4:14–30; Acts 8:26–40).

Our approach is directed toward the historical investigation of the development of the book from the prophetic transmission to the final hand of the processes of formation. Deriving meaning from the prophetic writings beyond this limitation[17] thus stands outside the consideration of this essay,[18] whether this meaning is provided by the external receptions, later Jewish or Christian adoption, or even today's reading perspective stimulated by an ahistorically oriented study of literature. One should differentiate between adaptation of transmitted material inside the books until the conclusion of the book's formation and later external adaptation of the transmitted books after the formation is concluded. The same is true for certain reading directions and reading paths in recent research. We do not contest the value and achievement of these new synchronic reading insights and approaches for our approach (whether they be methodological in nature or whether they evoke current themes). Nevertheless, even for literary science an adaptation also necessitates the transformation of criteria into an increasingly conscious historical approach which does justice to the character and peculiar features of the sources. In addition, one should include the fact that text-worlds should not be perceived as closed intellectual realms, but should be perceived in reference to historical worlds of experience. We do so in order to grasp the challenges that aid in understanding why prophetic transmission had to be continued in the first place and in understanding which texts provide the orientational horizon and which ones do not. We should not concern ourselves with the question of how one can read a prophetic book from then to now (the possibilities are legion). We should instead concern ourselves with how a prophetic book should be read according to the desire of those who shaped it during its formative period. This reading determines the formation as a historical process in its time. It is a question of the signals placed in the book itself and a question of the processes of reworking that were conducted and received in the book itself. Hence, in our method the only observations of indicators and interrelationships that play a role are those in which the text of the book itself (as a historical entity at the time of its formation) signals how it wants to be received using the configuration and assertions of its vocabulary. It is self-evident that slightly later external prophetic receptions (those still in close chronological proximity) can sharpen the perspective of the historian, including Qumran, intertestamental writings, LXX sources (*Vorlagen*), early targumim, early Christian texts, and graphic signals[19] in the oldest manuscripts. Naturally, this statement presupposes that one sufficiently investigates each of these entities as totalities in their own right, and that one recognizes the danger of incorrect decisions based upon selective comparison. One can really only learn about the character of older reception processes in the development of the books from interpretive differences in the text and the composition of the earliest manuscript transmission.

The following will sketch successive steps of an ideal working process that will enable one to approach the transmission process of prophetic books historically.

2

From the Book to the Message: Procedural Steps

The Given Prophetic Text as Starting Point

Ascertaining the Oldest Textual Foundation

Proceeding from the transmitted final versions means, first, clarifying the textual foundation of the prophetic books. This foundation has become less certain since the findings of the biblical manuscripts from the Dead Sea (Qumran, Wadi Murabb'aat Naḥal Ḥever). These manuscripts also stimulate the question of the old Hebrew textual versions behind the LXX. This foundation already demands the formation of a historical decision concerning the oldest attainable text version of a prophetic writing or even simultaneously transmitted textual versions before working with a standard text that lies beyond the final formative phase of the prophetic books.[1] Confirming the source of the oldest attainable text today requires a particular investigation and then a comparative investigation of the textual versions.[2] One must consider the consonantal (!) text of the prophets in the Masoretic Codices. One must also consider the reception of the prophets in the receptions of the New Testament, Targum, Apocrypha and Pseudepigrapha, Qumran, and LXX. One must pay particular attention to the prophetic manuscripts and quotes[3] from Qumran, which in the case of an Isaiah corpus means that a large portion of Isaiah 1–66 can be placed paleographically into the second century B.C.E.[4] The finding is similar for other prophetic books that are only preserved in fragments.[5] Divergent text versions were transmitted simultaneously in the oldest attainable manuscript examples. In the case of Jeremiah[6] and the Book of the Twelve (XII)[7] these examples even indicate differences in the macrostructure of the prophetic corpora. Facing these divergent versions requires that one form a decision about the time before the standardization of the text. This decision must connect text-critical investigations on the one hand and exegetical investigations on the other that oscillate between text criticism, literary criticism, and redaction criticism. One must first decide how this apparently inoffensive textual pluralism can be clarified historically with respect to the Qumran find. This finding shows that, after the formation of the Nebiim, the prophetic books have left the special framework of the care of the tradents of prophetic books. Do indicators provide the structure and size that a prophetic book had at its last formative act or even with concurrent final versions? Or do indicators provide a time when different versions continued to develop from a common stock? Even the question about how the order of the individual books was situated belongs in this context, especially in the case of the Twelve. Thus today, beginning with the given as the starting point means that one must first, again, ascertain the source foundation.

The Frame Spanning Individual Books in the Oldest Text Transmission

But that is not enough. In view of the source-foundation, one must also ask about the larger literary frame in which the text transmission of a prophetic book stood at that point. Alongside the state of the text of an individual book, one should ascertain the contextual size of the text at the time of the oldest attainable sources. Without detriment to the more practical nature of individual scrolls of the prophetic books and the important primary position of Isaiah as the first book in the series of prophetic writings, the individual books did not stand in isolation in this time. Rather, in the second century B.C.E., as suggested by Sirach, the individual scrolls stood within a larger frame of Isaiah-Jeremiah-Ezekiel-XII and in an even larger frame including Joshua-Malachi in connection to the Torah.[8] This finding deserves attention because this type of broader frame of the text transmission spanning the individual books could already have been operative in the phase of the last formative shaping of the book or even earlier. This broader frame could have been recorded in the shaping of the transmission as the reading-context and the reading-order that were taken into account. The macro-shaping of the final formation of Jeremiah in the MT version (with its characteristic placement of the oracles against the nations at the end), along with its prehistory, is also difficult to understand without considering Jeremiah's position in a series of prophetic books. The larger contextual frame of Joshua 1 / Malachi 3 also places markers for the reception of Jeremiah.[9] The question of the "canonical shape"[10] as a perspective transcending the book, but still operating within the book-formation of a series of books and individual book shapes, should thus be brought into play as a historical (!) question for this late period. However, in view of the possible preexisting forms, it should also be examined for earlier forms.[11] One should also consider possible indicators providing meaning by book connections and book chaining.[12] One should consider them in the sense of a higher material unity of the prophetic transmission itself, where prophetic books can be seen in sequence without additional internal intervention. Above all, this sequence receives essential material accents at its beginning and end. The manuscript situation shows that at the time of the oldest attested text transmission (manuscript finds from the Dead Sea, LXX) they still had the freedom to a limited degree to undertake different orders of prophetic books. Here too, one should consider this situation historically and inquire into the particular intentions of meaning. This task also requires that one clarify the question regarding which sequence was considered when the books themselves were formed. However, notable rearrangements of whole portions of a book can be demonstrated with the manuscript finds only with Jeremiah (MT, LXX).[13]

Finally, Qumran already shows, and the LXX allows one to deduce, something else about the oldest attainable entity in the second century B.C.E. At that time, the state of the text was apparently seen as a fixed entity that was essentially no longer expandable. One cannot demonstrate augmentations from additional books or insertions of larger texts from the time of Antiochus IV or later. This condition differs from insertions in the writings of the Torah and *Ketubim*, perhaps with the exception of the summary writing of Baruch as an appendix to Jeremiah.[14] Despite the prophetic quality of Daniel and David in Qumran, Daniel and the Psalms do not enter the picture as original continuations of the Nebiim after Malachi, in the face of the macro-literary inclusion between Malachi 3 and Joshua 1. The fact that these two books were related to the existing Nebiim framework is noteworthy, but it is a different problem.[15]

To summarize this first procedural step, prophetic research must slow down and reflect upon that which it really possesses with respect to sources. The Old Testament discipline cannot avoid the fact that, thanks to the Dead Sea findings, the course of ascertaining the prophetic source foundation in the future first has to acquaint itself with the time from which the oldest biblical text sources stem. It has to acquaint itself with the late period of ancient Israel that could have still influenced the latest formations of the prophetic transmission. If the Old Testament discipline wishes to investigate prophetic books as books, then it must again learn from the analogies of reception of the late period. The discipline of Old Testament must utilize historical imagination to learn how one should read such a book without diachronic hypotheses and reconstructions, specifically because, at the time, it would have been read that way and not some other way. One must make the step consciously, because recent historical inquiry, with the aid of sources of historical inquiry, serves to distinguish the self-understanding of the sources. Now we have reached the second section of our essay.

The Given Prophetic Book and Its Signals as a Starting Point

The Task of the Historical Synchronic Reading of Prophetic Books

We can accept that the textual foundation was clarified in the procedural step from section one (pp. 14–15) or will be clarified in the course of the following avenues of investigation. This textual foundation was attained from the transmission of an entire book in conjunction with the prophetic books in the second century B.C.E. and is the foundation for any further investigation. This further investigation turns at this point primarily to the shape of the individual prophetic book provided by its sources, despite more far-reaching literary connections to a prophetic writing. These connections must be kept in view as a larger literary horizon. The book must therefore be read in sequence, logically and precisely, from beginning to end. One must investigate textual contexts that extend across the book, and even across books! The task is more precisely a historically inquiring synchronic reading of the entire book. It seeks to investigate signals that show how this entity was intended to be adopted in its time. The historical framework for this inquiry remains vague at first. It is determined from unambiguous indicators in the text and from the oldest source-witness.

Where can the investigation begin? We will stay with the example of the book of Isaiah and first mention the approaches that one should consistently avoid as premature at this level of inquiry. If one wants to understand this entity historically with respect to the construction and the possibly-intended meaning it conveys, then one cannot begin with apparent certainties for dating the core transmissions and later material. At first, one cannot be certain how far back one should trace the existence of the text. For example, how far back should one trace Isaiah 1–66 behind the source-witness in the second century B.C.E.? The deutero-canonical book of Baruch also bears an ancient name, but stems entirely from the second century B.C.E. One can only say so much about limiting the framework for the origin of the book of Isaiah as we have it. The obvious lack of consideration of the events of Antiochus IV and the attestation in Sirach point to the beginning of the second century B.C.E. as the latest boundary. The specific reference to Cyrus in Isaiah 40–55 points to the late Babylonian–Early Persian period as the earliest boundary. Isaiah 1–39 should even be seen within this framework at this point in the investigation. Only in later procedures can one eliminate the possibility that the image of Isaiah presented in Isaiah 1–39 was first created in this time frame, as with the image of Baruch in Baruch 1. One can also not begin with the question of "authorship." It is also uncertain how one should conceptualize the more or less productive bearers and recipients of this literary entity that is only attested, source-wise, in the Hellenistic period. One can only conclude so much if the insights into the receptional-development of the prophetic books even appear to be correct. Namely, as already mentioned, the bearers and the recipients must be treated as professional entities in the milieu of scribal tradition.[16] One must admit that current preconceptions about the time, author, and addressees of the book should not too quickly close the actual gaps in our knowledge that exist in this area. Disinterest in these questions has long hindered relevant knowledge. With these statements we are not slighting the accomplishments of previous research. Rather, we are recognizing the fact that today the consensus on this matter has broken down and that elementary questions have not been considered and are therefore not being processed. Anyone staying with what we really possess and what we really know must first observe the wording and the flow of the transmitted book. The investigation must refer to this book and nothing else.

The Book's Presentation of the Person, Chronological Perspective, and Linguistic Procedures of the Prophet

Very elementary observations directed toward the entire textual state of the book stand at the beginning of this investigation. They provide initial explanations of the framework. These observations can note the overt material of the book's self-presentation. The macro-genre of prophetic books still awaits illumination, despite the tablet collections of Neo-Assyrian prophecy. Even so, the manner in which one should understand the entity of Isaiah 1–66 is clear enough if one considers the book's oldest transmitted text in the course of these explanations of the framework of the given vocabulary and the flow of the text.[17] Namely, the book is a whole that wants to present the work of the eighth-century Isaiah initiated by YHWH in its entirety.[18] (See Isa 1:1; compare the chronological order of Isaiah, Jeremiah [Jer 1:1–3], and Ezekiel [Ezek 1:1 and following] in Sirach [48:22–25; 49:6 and following, 8]). One can include in this observation the inquiry into whether or not certain chronological and thematic highlights of the prophetic books, as well as the position in sequence of books, are related to the chronological constellation in which the prophet worked according to the tradition. Are the position, prophet, and message of the book related? Moreover, many prophetic books pursue successive life-situations in the life of the prophet (Isaiah, Jeremiah, Ezekiel, Haggai, Zechariah). How are their messages related to these situations? Anyone paying attention to this fact becomes accustomed to reading the books differently than in traditional exegetical practice. That person must abandon the constant mixture (so typical for the discipline) of historically and genetically reconstructed prophetic images with the literary prophetic images presented in the sources themselves, and be determined to ask about the given sources historically. At first, that person must concentrate only on the literary images presented in the sources. One must, for example, without hesitation read statements like Isaiah 58:1, 59:21, 63:7–14 as though related to Isaiah. In the perception of this late period, the received prophecy that is intended to be read is the proclamation of God transmitted by the prophet in the form of books. In various ways, as one reads, the flow of the book shows the manner in which the prophet is presented. The flow of the book wants to be seen as a book first, and it wants to be seen in its entirety. It demands that one abandon all previous knowledge brought from outside that immediately isolates the book into components of diverse origin, namely into small units and additions, as well as genuine and non-genuine passages.

In the sense of the first explanations of the frame, the book's presentation of the prophet can be more precisely stated by observing two aspects of this presentation.

A first aspect of this type of holistic reading concerns the prophets and time. Isaiah by itself and the series Isaiah-Jeremiah-Ezekiel and the XII by itself are arranged according to the historical epochs of Israel in the context of the ancient world. Anyone who notes this arrangement attains an image of the chronological perspective that the book assigns to the prophet. If one follows the flow of the book (remaining with the example of the book of Isaiah), then the Isaiah of the book appears in his own time (the Assyrian period). However, the Isaiah of the book also anticipates the more distant periods of the Babylonians and the Medes from the time of Cyrus to the universal judgment and completion of salvation at the end time.[19] One recalls the advantage of reading Daniel in the book of Daniel. Often, inquiries back to a historical Isaiah and anonymous prophecies (or those made anonymous) in Proto-, Deutero-, and Trito-Isaiah are guided by preliminary opinions. Instead, we should primarily inquire into the comprehensive image of the far-reaching works of Isaiah from the late period of Old Testament, an image which incorporates Isaiah 1–66 as its given entity. We should inquire into this comprehensive image as the formative image of the book. Then we find that in Isaiah 1–66 we have a book concerned with Isaiah in its entirety. In this book, according to the superscription of 1:1, the eighth century B.C.E. is the chronological point of reference for the divine insights and the prophet's statements and actions. Even the presentation of the prophet's lifetime is often considered in chronological sequence in the book's flow in those places where the prophetically relevant processes are to be situated with him. The chronological realms to which he speaks run successively from his own period (the Assyrian period) to the time of Cyrus. The chronological dimension to which the prophet speaks is utterly comprehensive. It reaches from the creation of the world, to Israel's journey from the ancestors and exodus, into the future, which contains a final judgment and completion of salvation in a new creation of the world. Thus, in the book's shape, a prophet works in his own limited lifetime but also speaks far beyond his lifetime in chronological realms that occur centuries later. In so doing, the prophet opens perspectives that lie far behind him and perspectives that reach their completion far into an absolute future. This aspect exposes the chronological framework to which the prophetic activity relates according to the book's message. Like all other lines of thought belonging to the prophetic character according to the book, this chronological aspect requires further precision and comparison with corresponding statements from that late period during the process of historical synchronic reading. One should particularly observe the chronological perspective in the composition of the book of Daniel. The chronological perspective requires further precision in order to attain the prophetic image that the book conveyed at that time.

A second aspect concerns the book's presentation of the recorded linguistic processes in poetry and prose as they connect with the prophet in the book in question. Occasionally, these processes combine with narrated prophetic actions and experiences. The work of the prophet in the book is shaped and communicated with respect to the cause but also with respect to the performance. The prophet's work is also situated biographically, either directly or indirectly. Thus, the flow of the whole book must be considered separately, even with respect to the voices and addressees who are introduced. Who speaks at any given point: YHWH, the prophet, or others? How far does this speech extend according to the introductory and concluding signals? In which (thematically corresponding?) situation is the speech positioned? How does the flow of the book present the chronological perspective of the prophetic stations or the addressees? How does the book appear with respect to the transmission formulas? How do the YHWH speeches and the prophetic statements relate to one another in the book's structure, theological aspects, and image of the prophet they present? Does one find any recognizable arrangement in this setting and organization of the prophetic work in the book? Or, does one find a comprehensive arrangement, or more precisely, an arrangement of the prophetic work that has been superimposed? Could this arrangement be of importance for the prophetic image that is repeatedly presented in the book? Consistent observation of the book's context is demanded in this historical inquiry.

That which we suggest for Isaiah in the book of Isaiah also holds true for the prophetic images of the other prophetic books, in sequence as well as individually. From which time and from which chronological epochs does the prophet of a book express himself? What is the extent of the chronological dimension in which the prophet of a book expresses himself? What is the content and the communicative shape of the prophet's message according to the book's vocabulary? Each of the prophetic books must first be viewed in this manner, and each must also be considered in its position in the series. Only in this way will one receive an initial overview concerning that which the prophetic book itself wants to convey and, possibly, what it should convey in light of the neighboring books during the course of a comprehensive reading. Comparing the final form of the various prophetic books under this question shows, for example, that notably only the first of the prophets (Isaiah–Cyrus; but see also Ezek 38 and following) and the last (Zechariah/Malachi–Yawan) of the prophets in the series of prophetic books speak specifically within periods historically subsequent to their own epoch in world history. Comparison with understandings of prophets and prophecy in this late period also provides clarification.[20] This comparison will quickly, but with rationale, suggest that the prophetic books could not have first arisen in the time in which the sources are first attested. It will also quickly suggest that the series of books now before us did not exist in this form from the beginning. Too many concrete references in the shaping and vocabulary of the books remain unintelligible for this late period of origin. One need only consider the lack of all concrete biographical references to the person of Isaiah in Isaiah 40–66, or the stylistic mixtures and differences in Jeremiah, and of the signals structuring Isaiah, Jeremiah, Ezekiel, and the Twelve that have been superimposed on the books. This comparison also arouses suspicions of possible later shaping-influences from this late period. The task presented here has hardly been put into action to this point.

Questions about the Character and Intention of the Book's Presentation of the Prophet

How does one move forward from these first framing explanations about the book's presentation of the prophet and the prophet's activity to questions of the character and intention of this presentation? Also, continuation of the work requires that one recognize the lack of knowledge and admit various possibilities for the prophetic book's intention and purpose. These possibilities can then be eliminated or qualified by text findings. Protagonists of Isaiah research, especially in the last decade,[21] have guarded themselves against brittle presuppositions about who Isaiah, Deutero-Isaiah, Trito-Isaiah, and the other writing prophets were, and about what one can possibly say, or not say, about these entities. They have suspended diachronic insights that were thought certain, and they have taken the entire book as we have it as the manifest starting point. For a long time, we also applied ourselves to the agreements and complexities inside Isaiah as a whole before we came forward with suggestions about the latest formations of this writing, especially in the area of Isaiah 56–66.[22] However, the question remains open regarding what the final formation of a prophetic book like Isaiah wants to do, and what it could or could not do in its time. No comprehensive investigations yet exist that function as a model for the presentation of the prophet within a prophetic book as a whole. At this point, the attempts to conceive the historical shape and the conspicuous meaning of prophetic books, especially for Isaiah 1–66, are exploratory and generally partial.[23] They should all be welcomed as contributions to the discussion with methodologically diverse historical starting points. They all have the right to present the urgent historical task for understanding the given material in the time when it received its shape from the latest hand. However, they all have to battle with the difficulty that we do not know the criteria in advance that would have been known at that time regarding the manner in which the whole would have been intended to be read and applied in that time. The formation of the other prophetic books is just as peculiar. Each requires special investigation.[24] The formation of one book cannot simply be transferred to another. Each book demands investigation of its own final form.

Foundational Observations on the Prophetic Book between the Extremes of Compilation and Redactional Work

With all of the prophetic books, however, one faces the fundamental alternative of whether the quality and intention of the final form have a compilational or a molded character. We will again limit ourselves to Isaiah. Thus, the final form of this book at its point of origin is again an open question as to which is more likely. Is the final form merely a book preserving transmitted material from which individual formulations should only partially legitimate newer assertions as the oldest external reception initially appears to show of the book in Sirach, Baruch, *Jubilees*, or the Qumran texts? Or, do the flow and statements of the whole of this writing, as we have it, establish a comprehensive meaning that the book itself makes recognizable? What are the signals inside the book that would help resolve these alternatives?

One can speak about a compilational work in the given writing (or possible preliminary stages) if the book's flow is both broadly and narrowly presented as a scarcely related series of judgment/salvation sayings or as a three-fold division of sayings about judgment, oracles against the nations, and salvation.[25] One may also speak of a compilational work if the material flow is presented as sections that are only similarly structured in a formal manner, thus occasionally indicating an arrangement of preexisting material.[26] This arrangement would have found its internal meaning especially in preserving the transmitted material and that material's division into the two judgment/salvation epochs of Israel. A compilational work such as this would have tolerated a high degree of material incoherence of the individual statements. Also, these statements were not entirely usable for the origin of a prophetic book as a writing, because in this case the material coherence of the particular stock of statements was not a goal of the presentation of the transmission. One should imagine the tradents of a work that arose in this manner as collectors and archivists. These tradents do not continue to write the texts given them. Instead, they occasionally combined this material, possibly for use as professional prognosticating knowledge. The fact that prophetic transmission concerned only this type of compilational work of older preformulated texts, however, is by no means certain or probable. It must be specifically demonstrated. One would also have to eliminate the possibility that the transmission was more concerned with conveying prophetic books as a whole and also as coherent, higher material unities in which the incoherency of essential threads was expressly considered and processed. No one has produced this proof by plausibly eliminating the alternative, either for Isaiah or the other prophets. Also, no one has yet proven that only a conglomeration developed from individual continuations (*Einzelfortschreibungen*) of older, compiled text material in the final form of these books. It remains unproven that an intended meaning was not associated with the shaping of the book. There are only assumptions without excluding the opposite, especially in the case of Jeremiah.

The other extreme of the intended presentation of a prophetic book would be a final hand's shaping of the book in which the writing was conveyed in such a way that it consistently demonstrates itself to be a meaningful unity in whole and in part. This hypothesis requires penetrating examination in the sense of preeminently acknowledged purpose. Are there clues that indicate more than a compilational arrangement, specifically clues that indicate a comprehensive meaning presented for the entirety of the prophetic book? And how does one find these clues? Among the sparse answers that research into the book of Isaiah has maintained, one should not really consider suggestions that want to understand the entire book from the external construct of a drama.[27] Also, one should be cautious with the exposition of the form-critical compositional structures of a book. Despite the orientation toward the content of the statements, it runs the danger of generalizations raised from concrete vocabulary and of readily claiming the exegete's own structures and abstractions for the comprehensive material intentions of the shape of the book as we have it.[28] We think one should proceed differently. Also, clues going beyond the initial framing explanations to a potential meaning of the whole must be sought within the originating frame of Isaiah 1–66. The originating frame was defined above, albeit vaguely and in need of precision. The clues must be sought only in the book itself as a historical entity, and as such, as a historically consulted entity. Thus, one should determine concretely and without deviation, not beyond but within the statement's very concrete wording, how the statements are positioned within the flow of the book, how they follow in sequence, and how they can be explained exegetically on the level of the final formation. One must make this determination by considering the macro-context and not preexisting, diachronic developmental hypotheses. There is no other way to trace a desired meaning of the whole than the wording and structural signals of the book itself! The meaning of a prophetic text manifests itself from its literary context in the book's formative phase by persistently reading the text of the book's shape sequentially. Only after the formative phase does the meaning manifest itself by external, interpretive, or additional revelation. We already suggested above that when seeking the meaning of the book's wording, one must also keep in mind the conveying of meaning that a prophetic book could have received from its position in the overlapping series of books (Isaiah-Malachi or Joshua-Malachi). This meaning could be based upon apparent clues from the frame, the book sequence, or the sequence of chronological realms and thematic accents.

Using historical self-evaluation, one must place one's self in the context of a precise reading process at the time of the final formation of the prophetic books. One must imagine that the book was read successively from beginning to end. One must imagine that the book possibly even appears in the framework of a series of books as a unity that God has bestowed and as a unified work of the particular prophet. In this unity, the flow of reading of later material presupposes that which precedes it. Problems left open in the earlier parts of the book also demand that one continue reading. These problems can also be clarified in the process of reading. One thus has to dedicate utmost care to determining that which necessarily carries the coherence of the flow of the book when reading in whole and in part. Also, one has to determine what unites, bridges, and balances the diverse material in the eyes of those from that time. Images attested elsewhere in the Old Testament, or in intertestamental sources, relating to Israel's historical self-understanding from the time of the final formation can provide clues shortly thereafter. These clues show how, at that time, one would have read coherently with respect to Israel's history, existence, and outlook. In other words, even the suspension of literary criticism in the historical synchronic reading requires the interdependence of the different methodological aspects of historical exegesis! On this level of inquiry, one must completely ignore the fact that this reading adjoins the original meanings of older material from different times that now stand together in the book. The recipients of the later period knew nothing about historically reconstructed, older contours of meaning of the text. They only had the book. The only thing to investigate is the received meaning of the text (often later and secondary) that the entire book (or series of books) showed in that late period, meaning that was embedded in clarifying literary contexts and determined by the theological-historical and the experiential orientation of the tradents and recipients of the final form. Thus, in the historical synchronic reading of the writing, as we have it, the investigation of specific statements should not be determined by the question of the original meaning of a text at the point at which it was formulated. Rather, the investigation should be determined by asking, How would this book component have been read in the framework of the book at the time of its reception? Just as importantly, one should not forget the late time period of Ancient Israel in which one should read. The Assyrians, the Babylonians, the conditions of the former Northern Kingdom, its destruction, Sennacherib's siege of Jerusalem, and even the catastrophe of 587 B.C.E. no longer claim immediate interest at the time. Instead, these elements are threads of a literary perception of effective historical antecedents, the reading of which concerns the reader's present time and its outlook. In the Writings, Daniel reads in this manner in Daniel 9. The pesharim interpreters of Qumran read in this manner, as does Jesus in Luke 4. Even their work must have brought tension, dynamic inclinations, and accentuation into the reading process of that late period. With this historical synchronic reading, one does not open the gateway and the door for every possible way of reading. One should investigate those ways of reading that are suggested historically for that time.

In the historical synchronic reading of the individual writing, as in the wider framework of literary transmission, one should also observe carefully that, instead of a preferential way of reading, one should seek the reading clues indicated, intended, and providing shape from the wording of the book itself. The age of these signals, according to the subsequent diachronic investigation, plays no role on this level of the book's synchronic reading. The decisive element is that these signals (still) manifest weight on the level of the final formation. The arc connecting Jeremiah 1:4–10 and Jeremiah 46–51 in the MT of Jeremiah would be one example.[29] In this procedural step, the investigation must concern itself with the signals of this wording in the existing book as book. Only on this basis (the given wording and the signaled structure of the writing's text flow) should one pose inferential questions about a potential meaning of the whole in the course of an internal exegesis of the given entity. One should not draw upon broadly generalized thematic correspondences nor the occasionally conspicuous details, but upon the assertions of the entire book. The material inclinations of the entire book as it unfolds specifically provide clarifying weight to the assertions at the end of parts or of the whole. Clearly signaled structural and compositional arcs, as well as significant cross-references, provide clues as to how the particular element stands within the framework of the whole. These cross-references include anticipatory references serving the reception and references backward. These elements also provide clues as to how a coherent adoption of the entire book could have been introduced in the service of the material reception. Or these elements provide clues as to whether, in the perception at that time, one also allowed incoherences in the whole to remain without reworking them. The fact that the entire book intends to be seen as a coherent whole requires explanation. However, until one proves the opposite, one should concede coherence to the book, despite our impressions to the contrary. Historical synchronic reading is thus primarily presumed to be the attempt of a historically coherent reading.

In a thorough exegetical investigation of the wording one should even inquire into the individual paragraphs from this perspective. One should inquire how a text could have been read within a book, not selectively, but into its position within the frame of the whole at the time of the final formation. Then, for example, one finds that a text like Isaiah 2:2–5, despite its prominent position in the book, does not remain operative as a statement of the final state of salvation in the flow of the current book as a whole with respect to the character and contour of the wording. Rather, the text remains operative in Isaiah 60 and following in a number of aspects, or, it remains operative in the book's flow only with considerable modifications related to the salvation status of the nations (Isa 51:1–8; Isa 66). We do not know how one copes with this observation. One must consider additional clarification, being prepared to revise, as to whether the measure of acceptance of Isaiah 2: 2–5 would have been differentiated according to different phases of salvation for the meaning of the final formation of Isaiah. (Is there a penultimate phase which proves true in the Persian period in Isa 60 and following as a result of the perspective on the nations in Isa 2:2–4 and a final phase, still to come in Isa 65–66, which overhauls this perspective in the sense of a judgment on the nations according to the connecting text of Isa 2:6–22?) These observations and questions must be asked repeatedly and must be processed with the expectation of unfamiliar results.

Until proven to the contrary, one must also proceed from the assumption that the final formation essentially saw the articulation of all the statements in the entire book as valid. Methodological clarification has the task of ascertaining the aspects and differentiations for the sake of a higher unity. This clarification involves signals of reception and closer inspection by historical exegesis into the existing shape of the book as a whole. The details of a prophetic writing's flow of assertions appear anything but linear from the perspective of recent historians. Statements also appear that seem to function as contradictions when compared with one another. These facts must not hinder this foundational procedural program even if, given the transmissional character of a prophetic book, one should not expect that everything one encounters in the process of the text-flow has been explicitly processed in detail in the reception. The aspects essential for the final formation are those that are explained.

Nevertheless, these aspects must first be noted carefully within the framework of the whole. In so doing, one must address the historical question of the agreement ascertained from parallel manifestations, and one must address the order within the framework of an ancient Israelite/late Israelite conceptual world. How can we know in advance whether the same elements disturbed the ancients and whether these elements appeared as irreconcilable to them as they do to us with our historically oriented genetic questions?

In the following methodological considerations, we will try to expand upon the attempts of the historical synchronic reading of a prophetic book that have been offered in recent research. We will attempt to prepare the ground for a potential consensus by sustained observations in the entire book. We will also attempt to avoid the danger of presenting conclusions too early, conclusions that must constantly presume more than we know for this procedural phase, or that generalize and ignore more than we should know for such a reading. We agree with those researchers who also inquire historically, with respect to the basic concerns and to the essential methodological principles. Nevertheless, these approaches should be expanded and delineated to include a search for material coherence for the existing, formative final version of a prophetic book (in a series of prophetic books) that may have been intended. We maintain this approach over against Seitz and the careful suggestion of Sweeney (see n. 47), but also over the recent treatments of Collins and Koch.

In our opinion, Collins (*Mantle*, pp. 11–16) works too quickly with a schematicized image of a three-staged development of a prophetic book. He does not reflect methodologically about the multiplicity of materials achieved, "the relationships that bind together into a new unity all the parts of the work." He also inserts far too much questionable, diachronic foreknowledge into the discussion of the individual prophetic books. Similarly, one could criticize De Vries (*Revelation*) where he inserts individual findings that have been disparately achieved or adopted into a redactional reading he has not covered.

We can agree with Koch's suggestion (*Profeten*, vol. 1) that we observe the opening passages of the prophetic book (pp. 27–31), and in principle with the reference to "the structuring markers of the book genre" (pp. 31–33). Nevertheless, in this regard, one expects investigation into the extent of the formulaic networks within the entire book and into particular structuring aspects that the book manifests in its entirety. One must doubt the fact that a book's opening passages and structuring markers already suffice to perceive the compositional structure, or better said, the intended structure of the whole. Koch's treatments at the end of his book (p. 274 and following) should be methodically evaluated, especially the "metahistorical" perspective that he also brings into play for the construction of the books. Without going into more detail about the material contents of a book's flow of statements, one will not find the trail of an intended structure. We are not so quick to throw in the towel over the question of whether or not the final formation of the prophetic books intends to convey a meaningful whole (see Koch, *Profeten,* vol. 1, p. 47 and following). To do so, we would need to know much more. The fear of statements whose contents always appear subjective (Koch, *Profeten,* vol. 1, pp. 27, 47–49; compare also the recent work of Schramm, *Opponents,* p. 21) can be countered by the historical methodological considerations posited below with exegetically secured historical perspectives and with corresponding concepts that are plausible tradition-historically and historio-theologically. One can see where the exclusion of the text's concrete contents leads to uncontrolled, imprecise, or abstracting characterizations of the text in structural and compositional schemes of the prophetic books, or their parts. Such schemes are currently offered in sufficiency.

In using an ancient empirical model of a different type of transmitted literature of prophetic books (Laato, *SJOT,* 1994, pp. 272–278), we prefer to emphasize boundaries and character. We also find that agreement exists with the foundational concerns of Laato. Prophetic research should proceed from the given prophetic books and should first historically investigate this whole as such (pp. 278–282). We can even concur with the methodological approaches (pp. 282–286). The questions about the "ideology of a book," about "intercontextural interaction," and "extracontextural interaction" can converge with the question of the image of history and its traditional and experiential associations that the book conveys. Two items correspond to our opening question about how the book's text was received in the final formation in comparison with known and presupposed elements close to the chronological framework of the oldest attainable source documents: the "intercontextural interaction" with the observation of interrelationships signaled in the book regarding structure and formulation and Laato's orientation toward the historical entity of a "religious reader" of the book. Differences exist, as this essay that grew from our own earlier works, independent of Laato, shows. These differences also include laying out observations and approaches, and also holding open various historical possibilities of the book's genesis, about which only the plausible book findings decide. Last, but not least, these differences include caution with respect to an ingeniously refined methodology of intertextuality. The given and demonstrable interrelationships of the book's text from inside and outside are authoritative for the book's intended profile, not the "(potential) referential worlds" (281). Our questions result less from a reader-response theory used historically. Instead, they are directed toward those persons who have shaped a book's formation to the corresponding reception by the intended readership.[30]

Book Signals for a Historical Coherent Reading

What has a signaling effect for the book as a whole and its intention? Only the elementary aspect to this question can be emphasized to this point. We have not yet gone beyond gathering observations and indicators that suggest that meaning has been given to the existing literary whole.

The most important indicators for an intended reception in the flow of reading are those that dominate the existing whole, those that subordinate other signals in the book, or even those signals that push others to the side. Specifically, these indicators include several elements. (1) The book's superscription at the beginning as a reading instruction for the whole serves this function merely because of its explanatory position, regardless of the question of its origin. (2) Material relationships are signaled between the beginning and end of the writing and illuminate the reading path as the thematic exposition and goal for the flow of reading.[31] These relationships can also potentially clarify the reading path with modifications in the course of this movement. These relationships can also show the direction and the inclination of reading in the flow of the book. Other items, in a nutshell, contain the material profile of the whole book comprehensively, or successively in parts: (3) literarily/materially marked blocks of statements enclosed by framing references (for example, the block of foreign nations speeches) or shaped compositions as parts of a material whole; (4) superscriptions for sections; and (5) programmatic texts as reading clues. These texts thereby shift one's perspective in the course of reading. They encompass and combine partial material. At the same time, they clarify overlapping material in the flow, and they potentially even continue by escalating and by completing that material. (6) Literarily and materially significant references and resumptions, primarily inside the same book, lead to signaled relationships, contexts, or modifications by the interrelationships of the formulations, identical topics, structure, or stylistic peculiarities. (7) Finally, prominently positioned concepts and controlling words stress the material perspective for the readership throughout the entire book. In all these things, the flow of the wording through the book remains the foundation of the observations. It may not be abandoned and should be completed as a continuous process of reading under the observational perspectives already mentioned.

> The phenomenon of interrelationships or cross-references requires particular precision inside the whole of a writing or, in a second line, potentially even within a series of writings (see the references in n. 115 and pp. 100–105). A constellation of criteria comes under consideration here, not every little item of which can be found using a concordance or an electronic search program. This constellation of criteria pushes one to descriptive findings intended for the formation of the book. For the version of the final hand that concerns us at this point (but also for its previous literary stages), one should proceed from the fact that the given literary entity is a reading whole in the concrete state and flow of the statements. The tradents have created this reading whole, and the literary leading of these tradents should move the recipients. In this framework, the literary entity potentially represents a network of internal literary references about which one should inquire, even primarily, within the framework of this entity itself.
>
> The synchronic reading will tell us whether the commonalities between the writing's text assertions really concern intended internal references, interrelationships, or cross-references, especially by combining (!) the following facts. (1) Agreements between statements using distinctive vocabulary. What is significant is not the number of common words, but the exceptional nature, quality, outlook, and peculiarity of the words, word ensembles, and occasionally stylistic correspondences. (2) Correspondences in the thematic content of these assertions. Later material potentially even considers the context of the earlier material. In so doing, the later

material relates entire passages to one another, beyond the formulated references. (3) The position of the passage in the literary
flow of the whole. This position raises the question of whether, in
the course of reading, these assertions suggest that they are materially determined signals explained in advance or afterward.
(4) The question of a recognizable material intention for the connection in the framework of the assertion's intention should be
expressed by its adoption in the flow of reading of the literary
whole. The established connection must not just serve as a repeti-
tive strengthening in the book. By reaching back to its position, it
can have a delineating, delimiting, expanding, surpassing, or some
kind of reactive intention with respect to material asserted earlier
in the book. If this reaction has a synonymous or complementary
character, this would suggest that the connections were created by
the same hand. By contrast, if it concerns a reaction that changes
the accentuation, then the reference appears to process older, preexisting material. (5) The question of intended lines of reading
and reading inclinations should lead through the literary whole
by cross-references.

Note several examples: No intended cross-reference can be
ascertained in Isaiah from "house," "horse," and many other atypi-
cal words by themselves. However, words occurring prominently
through the book, like "Jerusalem," "Judah" (1:1), "comfort," and
"light" do appear to have this quality. These words would also
include the "covenant" statements in Jeremiah, reference to judgment sayings in the salvation section or the "formulas" in Ezekiel,
or, especially, the "day (of YHWH)" in the Twelve. However, individual leading words are not to be seen in an isolated way. Rather,
they always appear in their literarily meaningful reading-context
with the signals from that context. Intentional interrelationships
of texts incorporated along with the context in the flow of reading
clearly include, for example: Isaiah 40:1–5//52:7–10; Isaiah 49:14–
26//*60; and Isaiah 34//63:1–6. Closer inspection of numerous
other passages raises the question of intentional interrelationships,
as Jeremias, for example, showed with the relationship of Hosea
and Amos, and as we have undertaken in our investigations, in
Trito-Isaiah. For the methodology, see the dialogue with Lau, in
Steck, *ThLZ*, 1995. For the question of historically diachronic cross-
references, see below, pp. 100ff.

This flow of reading adopts that which the prophet who is recorded in the book had received and conveyed one after the other during his lifetime (compare the dates in Jeremiah, Ezekiel, Haggai, Zechariah). Only the flow of reading determines, by exegetical clarification, whether the results of the observations are appropriate or not. These observations must remain in the text and not transcend it.

Several examples and remarks of these deduced questions for the historical reading of the given material are presented in the following for Isaiah.

First, a readership living after 587 B.C.E would have noted the formation of a framing arc that encompasses and aligns the whole with correspondences between the beginning and end of the book. In so doing, the readership takes account of stipulations and purposeful procedures that would have immediately affected this readership in the period of reception. What thematic focusing of the stock of assertions in the book as a whole is thereby achieved? It is not sufficient that this framing inclusion between Isaiah 1–2 and 65–66 has only been observed by itself. One must read the entire book with it and ask what the book wants to make of it and what has been illuminated in the first place within the book's stock of assertions.

Above all, one should grasp the above-mentioned observations for the book's frame of presentation and trace them further. What can one recognize from the book's flow about the origin of the whole from the work of YHWH through the Isaiah presented in the book? In this respect, what can one recognize through superscriptions, through the work of the revelatory formulas, and through statements related to the prophetic person? How does Isaiah 1–66 read if the whole book is seen as the recorded perception of Isaiah in light of the superscription of 1:1 and by observing the statements in which the prophet speaks about himself or in which YHWH addresses him directly? And more illuminating for the concrete and multifaceted whole, how does Isaiah 1–66 read if one allows one's self to be led by the explicit object of perception, "Judah and Jerusalem" (1:1; compare 2:1), when reading the flow of statements of the entire writing? The flow apparently takes account of these entities in a lengthy chronological condition from the Assyrian period until the future completion of salvation. How is the book's flow presented if the Isaiah of the eighth century looks into the near and distant future epochs of his people and thereby makes particular statements about this condition? Are there then epoch-specific flows and highlights to clarify this condition? Like the readership of that time, one would be led on this path by the statements themselves to a temporal image of the condition of Judah and Jerusalem, an image whose flow is imposed from the beginning to its goal. Of course, this image does not simply result from a nonlinear, superimposed flow of statements. And, one can ask further: What are the constitutive stations of this condition that the book exposes? (Is this why the "revealed vision of Isaiah" is to be seen as a prophetic look into the divinely decreed world of Judah and Jerusalem through the ages?) Also, how are the multiple streams of the literary text sequence related to one another so that they can be presented? Are there clearly marked sections in the text flow (like Isa 12; 27; 35; 39; 56; 63:7–64:11) that arrange a coherent reading flow of the whole in potentially compositionally shaped blocks with opening and closing hints for reading (like Isa 13//24–27)? How does one read these blocks, in whole and in part, as a composed, potentially inclusively shaped, materially coherent flow? And what would be a partial meaning of these blocks despite material overlapping in the framework of the whole? Does the meaning combine with the intended stations of the state of Judah and Jerusalem, upon which the Isaiah of the book also concentrates? Does it mean that in Isaiah 1–11(12) the prophet speaks from his time (1:1) to the Assyrian Epoch with an anticipatory glance about the condition until the completion of salvation in 13–27? Does the prophet also speak a parallel in 28–35 (39), connecting the Babylonian-Median epoch to the Assyrian epoch? Does the prophet continue to speak about the salvific goal of the condition? Does he continue to speak in 40–55 to the Persian Period as the end of the Babylonian epoch with an anticipatory glance at the return of all those in the Babylonian *golah*? And, after the final message to go forth (55:12 and following), does he continue to speak in Isaiah 56–66 to the Persian epoch regarding God's people in the land with an anticipatory glance at universal judgment, at the completion of salvation, including the return of the diaspora and the homage of the nations?

However, within Isaiah 56–66, statements about the restitution and completion of salvation in the land create problems for a materially and historically coherent synchronic reading,[32] because of the specific, modifying, double movement in 56:1–62:12 (63:6) and 63:7–66:24. Should these texts be read as identical or as sequentially appearing stations along the way for God's people in the framework of the entire writing? Should one suppose that Isaiah once again starts anew and speaks about the catastrophe of the temple, Zion, and cities of 587 B.C.E. with respect to the time of Cyrus in 63:7–66:24, and then in Isaiah 65 and following broadens the perspective into definitively future elements? Can one even recognize a signaled meaning in the final eleven chapters for the flow of the whole (!) of Isaiah 1–66 or for a series of prophetic books (compositionally and redactionally inherent)? Or can one not recognize such a meaning (compilationally inherent)?

One must also pay attention to the successive threads of the macro-structure in Isaiah. In large blocks, the book's text-flow from Isaiah 1–66 holds to a chronological sequence of epoch stations for God's people. The Isaiah of the book also looks specifically toward these stations in 1–11, 13–27, 28–39, in 40–55, and in 56–63:6 (66:24). Is this sequence only an accident, or occasionally the result of sequentially adding separate, smaller complexes? Or should this sequence have meaning for the final text? How does this remain virulent for Judah and Jerusalem through the time periods in the flow of reading? What should one deduce from this consideration? One gains the impression that the expounded epochal situations of Judah and Jerusalem (the Assyrian, Babylonian, and Persian periods, and the completion of universal judgment and salvation) also correspond to specific, material aspects of the condition which are connected and which refer consecutively to one another.

The question of expounded hints for reading is of great significance for an intended, coherent reception of the presentation regarding the condition of Jerusalem and Judah in different chronological and material aspects and in different flows that are literarily parallel and successive. These hints preserve the material perspective in the succession of the blocks of statements in Isaiah 1–66. Is there a material inclination in the course of reading the whole as well as by looking at the blocks? Does this inclination point especially to material inclusions between the beginning (as the perspective opening the book) and the end (as the perspective of the writing's goal)[33] that form a framework for the statement-flow of the whole that is directed toward a goal? Reading back from Isaiah 65 and following, do Isaiah 1–12, 13–27, and 28–66 (divided into 28–55, 56–66) prove to be organizational blocks of the final formative shape of the book? What significance is it that these kinds of inclusions backward to Isaiah 1–2 are already found among previously positioned statements of the book about the goal of salvation?[34] Are there multiple, complementary, or directed programmatic perspectives of the goal in the poetic realm at the end and in the transition of the blocks? For example, are there aspects of the recurring thematic ensemble of final judgment, the return of the diaspora, and the completion of salvation in Zion (compare Isa 10–13; 24–27 [and following]; Isa 34–40 [and following], 51:1–11 [in context], Isa 60–63; Isa 63:7–66:24),[35] that accentuate the goal toward which the message of the book of Isaiah runs? Do expounded formulations function as anticipatory references and references backward that serve the material context or that, at this stage, combine and compare apparently contradictory statements?[36] Are there poignant concepts, for example, "comfort,"[37] that contribute backward from Isaiah 66 to the network that carries the meaning of the whole book as one reads? Be careful, however, of a proliferation of synchronic discoveries! In the framework of a historical synchronic reading of Isaiah one should ask about reading signals for the literary whole that also would really have been placed for the final formation of the whole prophetic book. Also, the extent to which individual concepts belong, and the identity of these concepts, is not provided by the concepts that today's exegete favors or in a current theological conversational setting. Instead, these concepts are only provided by the textual finding of the literary entity itself. Heuristic investigation and historical literary findings are not the same. In other words, one should not trace the abundance of possible readings, but one should trace the reading instructions of the final hand. It will thus depend upon whether expounded concepts also recur at positions and in statements of the book that apparently wish to structure the whole materially. It will depend upon whether, in the course of reading the whole, certain statements are recognizably networked and point forward or backward within these concepts. Finally, it will depend upon whether these concepts show themselves to be the consolidation of an aspect of a thoroughgoing concept of the whole that wants to present a prophetic writing in the final formation. "Comfort" is meaningfully placed in Isaiah and is such a concept. Also, as Rendtorff demonstrates,[38] the same can be said for other concepts. Whether the same can be said for the concept of "Torah" in Isaiah must still be investigated in light of the work of Lohfink. However, one must first attain method-ological clarity that he omits.[39]

Also, as mentioned, a glance beyond the book's boundary shows noteworthy material and raises the question whether a prophetic book, in its current form, is consciously shaped in consideration of a series of prophetic books so that its meaning intends to go beyond itself into this wider literary framework.

The position of the series Isaiah, Jeremiah, and Ezekiel also appears to carry material accents beyond the chronological order of these prophets. Is Isaiah 1–66 shaped with material consider-ation of the following books? Isaiah briefly offers the demise of the Babylonian kingdom (Isa 13 and following; 21; 43–46). Jeremiah offers it extensively (especially Jer 50 and following). Ezekiel has not a single oracle against Babylon. Isaiah offers uni-versal final judgment several times. Jeremiah has it only briefly in Jeremiah 25:27 and following (compare 45:4 and following). In Ezekiel, one finds universal judgment in chapters 38 and follow-ing (compare 38:17 and following), and perhaps as a receptional reading in 7:2, 7 and 21:9. Further, the meaningful positions at the end of Isaiah and the Twelve make it understandable that the in-ternal problems of the current time of the tradents, of postexilic Israel, are treated extensively at that point (Isa 56–66; Hag-Mal). At the same time, Jeremiah, Ezekiel, and also Hosea-Zephaniah were read primarily as prophets of the exilic judgment and its salvific turn. The fact that the Greeks are only indirectly treated in Isaiah, while they are openly treated in Zechariah 9, may relate to the fact that Isaiah speaks into the time of Cyrus and includes the Diadochoi kingdoms in the outlook of the end time. Haggai and Zechariah, however, speak in the time of Darius where the Helle-nistic period can now be openly attached. And finally, why do Jeremiah and Ezekiel actually offer the catastrophe of Jerusalem in 587 B.C.E., while Isaiah hardly mentions it? Or, at least, Isaiah mentions it only in 63:7–64:11, but only by taking up salvation statements from Isaiah 33 and then only in connection with Isaiah's view of the Persian period.

Are particular epochal highlights, by shaping or sequence, arranged for the series Isaiah-Jeremiah-Ezekiel[40] to which the prophet also expresses himself with purpose statements? For the final formation of the series of Isaiah-Jeremiah-Ezekiel does Isaiah represent the whole? Does Jeremiah (MT) especially represent the nations-Babylon theme because of its macro-framework that is fulfilled in the Persian period? Do the Assyria-Babylon-foreign nations statements in Isaiah form an anticipatory reference to this theme? Does Jeremiah 30–33 form a reference backward to the salvation statements in Isaiah and an anticipatory reference to those in Ezekiel? Does Ezekiel especially represent the question of the salvific presence of YHWH for which the כבוד sayings in Isaiah 60 and 66 form an anticipatory reference? And should the framing watcher-sayings in Ezekiel 3 and 33 be taken as a reference back to the warnings in Isaiah 56–59? It is no accident that Ezekiel 33 takes up the sign of Isaiah (Isa 58:1).[41] In this perspective of the series Isaiah-Jeremiah-Ezekiel, is the thematic macro-structure of Isaiah (judgment-judgment against the nations-salvation) reflected in Jeremiah (judgment-judgment against the nations) plus Ezekiel (salvation) by the placement of highlights of the time? Was the Twelve seen as a series of books that was especially parallel to the comprehensive image of the prophetic viewpoint that Isaiah presented?[42] The formation of inclusion frameworks that are found in Isaiah (*40–52; *40–61,62) and, as already mentioned, in Jeremiah indicates that even earlier stages of the *Nebiim did not create isolated individual books. Rather, this formation more likely shows that epochal sections were connected with specific prophetic persons inside a series of books, as is the case for Isaiah 56–66 inside Isaiah. The situation was initially different for Jeremiah (LXX), where a prophetic book was apparently formed later in such a way that it now compares by itself to the books of Isaiah and Ezekiel in three parts (judgment on the people of God, oracles against the nations, salvation for the people). Thus, three individual prophetic books are shaped in parallel fashion, and three literary presentations of prophets arise which are similar to that extent. Is the image of the LXX operative there?

Thus, it would be essential for the desired internal coherence of a prophetic writing (or series) if a contoured material perspective was conveyed to the readership that simultaneously presented the transmitted and ongoing summation of the prophet's work. One must thus examine whether we are provided with a consistently clear, hopeful, and instructive image of YHWH's plan for Israel in the realm of the nations over a lengthy period. Is this image provided if one does not read the prophetic book selectively (and in connection with the other prophetic books)? Or is this image provided if one reads the prophetic book directed by reading instructions in the wording and construction in the entire existing text? One should investigate whether such reading brings us closer to a potentially intentional, comprehensive statement for the book.

In the course of this investigation of a coherent reading of Isaiah 1–66, one naturally comes constantly upon noteworthy elements in the textual order as well as in the contour of material sayings. These noteworthy elements look like disturbances of the coherence. One must still discuss these elements with respect to questions about the final formation as a compilational work left incoherent or about coherent wholes on the final stage and before. Nevertheless, one must remember that one must differentiate. Incoherences exist that have only come to light with recent historical approaches but that were not considered in the construction and wording of the prophetic book itself. In contrast to today, the successive development of the book was not a topic of discussion in ancient times. However, incoherences also exist that already occupied the tradents producing the book. One can see these incoherences in receptionally direct efforts (cross-references) and indirect efforts (material inclinations in the flow of reading) to mediate and to balance elements within the book itself. These efforts deserve precise consideration. Thus, the question of the possible comprehension of incoherent material as part of a comprehensive image of coherence conveyed at the time of the book's formation stands in the foreground as the foundational procedural step of a historical synchronic reading of prophetic books. Correspondingly, one should search for literary and material connections in the book itself and search for reading directions that potentially serve a consciously constructed coherence of the whole. Inquiring into this image of coherence as a historical entity of the final text formation is by no means hopeless from the start, despite all the complexity of the prophetic books. In order to trace the given shape of the book in a historical investigation, one must keep in mind the ways in which the current prophetic book itself provides guidance for this exegetically unusual access and how it was presented as a dominant means in its time. In the following discussion, we want to focus upon what belongs to these apparently fundamental aspects using Isaiah as an example.

The View of the Prophet in the Given Prophetic Book

THE PROPHET AND THE ENTIRE BOOK

The entire book, including Isaiah 40–66, concerns the image of Isaiah of the eighth century B.C.E. The book concerns the image that one obtains in the late Israelite period about Isaiah's prophetic knowledge of God, his prophetic activity, his life under the kings, his representation of God, and his time. [Note that post-Isaianic developmental stages are not marked in the book's transmission. In the mind of the prophetic tradition, everything in Isaiah stems from or treats Isaiah.] Sirach[43] and the Qumran references also see the book in this way.[44] And from the other side, only in the shape of the book does one encounter the prophet.

THE RADIUS OF THE PROPHET'S WORK AS PRESENTED

In the book, Isaiah mainly addresses Judah and Jerusalem with the neighboring nations, the world empires, the world of the nations, and even heaven and earth. He sees these entities in the surroundings of his own time but also predicts about them well beyond his own time into the distant future, into every essential subsequent epoch, including the Persian period, down to the purposeful processes of universal judgment and the final completion of salvation. He brings this entire image to bear in the framework of successive epochal highlights, to which he speaks in the macro-flow of the book.[45] The prophetic image is comparable to Moses in the final chapters of Deuteronomy and *Jubilees*, or to Daniel in Daniel also with multiple parallels in the course of the vision from the Babylonian time to the completion of salvation. To this extent, the chronological and epochal frameworks of Isaiah in the book, as we have it, are to be taken completely literally for an intended reception of Isaiah 1–66.

THE PROPHETICALLY INFERRED CHRONOLOGICAL ORIENTATION OF THE BOOK

Isaiah dispenses divine orientation for Judah and Jerusalem over time, as can be seen from the conceptual world of the book in its wording and flow, not from elevated abstraction and research reflecting a search for structure. However, one does not merely see historical facts or historically reconstructed history when observing the lengthy time span or when presenting an image of the flow of history. This image is neither a precisely recalled path of historical events after the Assyrian period nor its literarily sequenced presentation in the concrete flow of the text. Rather, one glimpses the previously envisioned observation, the material judgment, and the steering that exists on YHWH's part regarding how Judah and

Jerusalem fared over a lengthy time, together with their worldwide environment. This observation is not completely imparted to the prophet in a single revelation. The observation is presented several times in succession, according to the contents of the book in individual lines, and determined by the text flow. As YHWH decided in his disclosures relative to the people of God, this knowledge was communicated to Isaiah and conveyed in the book of Isaiah. Time is thereby adopted, critically explained, deepened, and concentrated as the lengthy realm of the existence of God's people. Time is not just an arsenal of historical facts in divine significance, upon which the recent historical approach gladly concentrated its finding. Rather, time is, more comprehensively, the experiential realm, extended and observed in the present from current concerns. This experiential realm includes a lengthy, changing qualification of events and an uninterrupted sequence of events. It includes the lengthy qualification of fears and prospects that YHWH provides with meaning. Also, the references backward to the Davidic, tribal, and exodus periods, and to creation, and the anticipatory glance at the final consummation are included in this lengthy chronological perspective. This lengthy chronological perspective is indebted to the reception of tradition from the occasionally prevailing experiential concerns. The wording of the book's assertions leads to this image if one reads it in the flow that is introduced by the realms noted in 1:1. In this flow, the works in Isaiah designated to the lifetime of Isaiah should relate to the lengthy, chronological, material series of references to the condition of these two entities: Judah and Jerusalem.

As we saw, this insight encounters a succession and an inclination with respect to the surveyed whole that the prophet observes in an insight granted with the eyes of God. The succession and inclination occurs in an essentially selective, purposeful series of the essential stops along the way *sub specie dei* (from the perspective of God). In large measure, the goal of the succession and inclination is then ultimately uniqueness and definitiveness. This arrangement into the successive epochs of God's people was thoroughly understandable at the time. The fact that the Assyrians, Babylonians, and Persians followed one another as world powers was elementary historical knowledge for Israel that could be placed into the prophetic transmission to arrange the series of statements chronologically and materially.

Nevertheless, in this view of things, one does not find an irreversible flow of history meaningfully conducted. Prophetic books are not history books even in this perceptional depth. Rather, prophetic books announce YHWH's historically related intentions, characteristics, and actions. YHWH personally and sovereignly decides and affects these elements. Therefore, the prophetically conveyed outlook for the entire path of Israel *sub specie dei* is not simply a glance into a series of unrepeatable events. This exposed perspective also encounters actions typical for YHWH and humans. Namely, one encounters these actions in the historical time span that still provides correlation and context for later generations in the revealed flow of epochs (for example, between judgment on Assyria, Babylon, the nations, and the entire world). Also, one encounters these actions in the corresponding historical constellations of a later period where one can observe the recurrence of divine and human action that the prophetic transmission of the word already stated for the earlier period. For example, on the basis of this perspective, the given book of Isaiah readapted, or further adapted, the threats from Assyria to the threats from Babylon. And threats from Assyria and Egypt in the lifetime of Isaiah can reflect these entities through the Diadochan period, at which point they transform into world judgment (for example, compare Isa 10:5 and following [23!]; 13:1 and following; 29:1–8; 30:1 and following, 27–33[!]; 31:33,34; 51:1–52:6). The same is true for the sins of God's people according to this perspective. The current grievances from a later time period were seen in correspondence to those of earlier generations transmitted in the prophetic writings for the preexilic period. Using current modifications, these grievances are again adapted in the foreseeing eyes of God with which the prophet sees as the references back to prophetic accusation allow one to recognize (for example, in Isa 56–59; 65–66).[46] Thus, beyond the actualization presented in the final formation, the prophetic book also preserves a basic openness for even later orientations of Israel within the framework of Israel's enduring, revealed, comprehensive path. Then, of course, these orientations should be, and were, externally fixed, as late Israelite prophetic receptions in Qumran, Ethiopian Enoch, *Jubilees*, and other texts show.

One may thus generalize on the basis of this finding in Isaiah. With their books, at any rate, the prophets convey a glance into the lines of thought for a perspectively exposed, lengthy, calculated, and comprehensive concept of the will and intention of YHWH for Israel in the realm of the world of nations. Later experiences were observed in this light and arranged as they corresponded to this comprehensive concept. These experiences were clarified from this concept using additional explication. Thus, revelatory content and a time period of revelation appeared in the prophetic activity transmitted in the book. These elements can also include and explain all later experiential constellations within the book. The recipient is convinced that the essential place of Israel in the recipient's own time can only be determined by looking to YHWH, who conveyed the entire plan (!) for Israel in the prophetic transmission. The recipient should see the challenges of current experience as a question about YHWH in the present. If so, the "surplus value," the transmitted prophetic material pointing beyond the original situation, becomes understandable. This surplus value constantly allows one to turn back to this text material. It also attracts a productive new reading and an innovative continuation of the explanation. In so doing, the transmitted message of the book does not limit the version[47] of the sayings to concrete, unique, and thus unrepeatable situations and addressees of the past. Rather, the transmitted message encompasses the initial, divinely prophetic reference and historical impulse and leaves open multiple validations and multiple relationships. Also, the message leaves open the lengthy, potential actualization of the wording. The wording is repeatedly, characteristically, poetically formed and formulated, thus making it more open to reference. Even for the pesharim from Qumran, contemporary interpretations show the same hermeneutical premises.

All of this presupposes that one sees the ontic *prae* (prior existence) of YHWH's works in the journey of Israel's essential experiential pathway through time in the message of the prophetic books. That which God intends, performs, and brings to fruition in this lengthy stretch of time is uncovered here. Just as God once acted inside this comprehensive framework, so God can again act in a corresponding constellation. The prophet of the book accordingly offers glimpses into the past perspective, opinion, and intention of YHWH over a lengthy time period. As a result, in the perception of the tradents, the prophet need not speak about anything and everything in chronological succession in the book's flow. Instead, the prophet speaks from a deep sense of YHWH's intention concerning the essential stations of meaning for God's people and for the nations as they have been made known. Thus, "Isaiah" speaks from the beginning of the judgment on Assyria in his time to the completion of salvation, where the historical dramatization of meaning stops because endlessness belongs to the completion of salvation.

One could object that this divinely generated image of history for Judah and Jerusalem that one encounters in Isaiah, is, as such, seldom presented, and that it is offered only in individual aspects that repeat and overlap one another. As a result, one could object that this image of history as a whole equates to an abstraction of the exegete. However, the structuring of the book's flow in general, as shown by the macrostructure of Isaiah, Ezekiel, and the XII, is not the only thing that argues against this objection. For example, under the direction of Isaiah 1:1, one must only read once what is said for Judah and Jerusalem in the book's flow. Then, as if by itself, an image of history with essential stations over a lengthy time reveals itself as the content of the exposed vision of Isaiah for the addressed readership that, while reading, asks wherein this vision consists. The flow of the book certainly implies qualified lapses of time, as shown, through conscious reference backward, for example, by the very well-known dissolution of judgment sayings from the front part of the books into complementary salvific sayings in the latter part. These flows reflect a time span of divine activity with Israel revealed in stages and realized in historical movement. Further, the wider theological frame of reception as it existed at the time also speaks against the objection mentioned above for the final form of prophetic books. The great stations of meaning for God's people from the preexilic period to the completion of salvation were undoubtedly common theological knowledge since the Persian period. They appear alongside texts like Deuteronomy 28–30, and especially Deuteronomy 32. They also appear in historical psalms. They form the background for the particular view of prophetic books. Also, for the tradents and the readership of these books, these stations of meaning can lay out the journeys through the individual thematic aspects and overlappings in the presentation of the view of history. At this point we must guard against distortions stemming from the isolation of specific research subjects that come only from our questions but are not led by the book itself. Once it is precisely highlighted and exegetically presented, this image of history presented by Isaiah primarily provides the grounds for considering the following question: How does this image relate to historical presentations that were literarily available at the time in Genesis-Kings and Chronicles-Ezra-Nehemiah? And how does it relate to historical images in this late period as well, especially for the image shaped by the late Deuteronomistic perspective in the sources of the second century B.C.E.?[48]

Similarly, the view of the prophetic figure of the book certainly took its direction from outside. The image of the prophet that directs this presentation of divine history revealed can already be compared with the image of the prophet in Isaiah 44:26; Jeremiah 29:10 and following; and Amos 3:7.[49] As previously mentioned, references exist to the comprehensive, divinely determined world as a source of all the essential processes in the experiential world of God's people on earth. According to this prophetic image, prophets received knowledge of this source. Also, the prophetic books provide a glimpse into the exhibition and message, thanks to the received foreknowledge of these prophets. Thus, using Isaiah as an example, we can illustrate what Judah and Jerusalem have experienced on their way. We can illustrate how they have failed (and can fail again). We can illustrate where they currently stand, what they should fear, and for what they can hope. In this opinion, one can explain what happens later only if one sees one's self in the mirror of Isaiah's divine knowledge preserved in the book of Isaiah.

Thus, one must ask how the flow of reading prophetic books is presented under this divine intention, an intention arranged according to a lengthy chronological perspective directed toward the divine, deep dimensions of the history of events and experience. To what extent does the flow of the book repeatedly bring this lengthy chronological perspective to light in its entirety from partial aspects? How is this material movement through the book's flow correlated with the phases of prophetic activity that the book's flow shows by historical situating and dating? Is there any material significance to that which is revealed to Isaiah under Hezekiah in Isaiah or to Jeremiah under Zedekiah in Jeremiah?

We will call this perspective a metahistorical perspective in this sense following the important insights of Koch. It is thematic "history" led by tradition that is seen, experienced, viewed, and desired *sub specie dei* (from the perspective of God). However, we do not call this perspective "history" in the sense of a hereafter, separated from the history of events, or even limited to the final eschatological event.[50] This perspective specifically includes the experience of a lengthy time span by selection, concentration, depth of meaning, and order of meaning, as these elements correspond to the perspective, plan, and activity of God–the higher point of view mentioned at the beginning. This perspective surveys the entire path of God's people, in aspects of the diverse elongation and detailing of epochs. This path is present in the background, or more precisely, in the foundation of the center of divine action. This center determines its meaningful course in the sequence of time. It appears to us that, if one follows the macro-structural book signals, then Isaiah (like the final form of prophetic books in general) wants to be read from this perspective, focused upon the reader's present time, and against the background of the comprehensive intention of YHWH as the true author of prophetic books.[51] Like the other prophetic books (by themselves and together), Isaiah should first be processed from this perspective if one wants to consider a meaning for this literary entity as the wording of the book at times manifests.

We remain with Isaiah. Can one recognize that, in the presentation of Isaiah, the epoch since Cyrus thus transitions into the final events (Isa 40–66) without appending the Greeks (unlike Zech 9:9 and following)? Does it do so because the epoch since Cyrus is the fundamental, continuing time of change when that which was begun by YHWH at that time will be metahistorically completed salvifically for Judah and Jerusalem? Does the Greek world power not need its own epoch because it will fall in the imminent universal judgment? In the final text, one must ask whether one should read Isaiah 13, 24–27, and 34 in a metahistorical perspective in which Isaiah's knowledge shows the following: With the end of Babylon (Isa 13) and the threatening neighboring power of Edom (Isa 34), YHWH thinks even further in advance about the end of all non-Israelite human power in a future universal judgment about which Isaiah 24–27 deals specifically.

The peculiar text series Isaiah 33–35, 36–39, and 40 is a particularly difficult problem for a coherent historical reading of Isaiah because of its constitutive placement of Isaiah 34 and 35[52] alongside one another in light of their recurring themes in the continuation of the book. Nevertheless, Isaiah 1–27 expounds reading clues that suggest that Isaiah 33–39 are logically arranged inside the text flow of the book, especially within Isaiah 28–66. After Isaiah 24–27, Isaiah 28–31 should be read as relating to the Assyrian threat against Jerusalem. Isaiah 28–31 should be read with an opening for the salvation of the city and judgment against Assyria/universal judgment. Isaiah 32–34 should be read as relating to the Babylonian danger to Jerusalem (33:1 and 33:1 and following after 32:7 and following) with an opening for judgment against Babylon, salvation for the city (33) and universal judgment (34). Both aspects reappear in Isaiah 36–39 and in the subsequent statements. The Assyrian element reappears in Isaiah 36–38, which is continued in Isaiah 40–66 with respect to Zion and the people of salvation. The Babylonian element reappears in Isaiah 39 with respect to the end of Babylon, universal judgment in Edom, the return of the deportees, and the return of the treasures. It also continues similarly in Isaiah 40–63 (66:24). One should observe that, for the intended perception of reading in the final form of Isaiah, Assyria-Babylon-Edom stand in a metahistorically lengthy flight line of the typical intention of YHWH for the goal of universal judgment and the completion of salvation for Zion and Zion's people.

In this picture, Isaiah 35 also has its contemplated place. The return of the diaspora noted at the end (11:11–16) of the Assyrian judgment and salvation in Isaiah 10 and following, and the return of the diaspora appears in Isaiah 24–27 at the end of universal judgment (27:12 and following). It also appears at the end (Isa 35) of the universal judgment of Assyria-Babylon-Edom in Isaiah 28–34. The dominance of the theme of return in Isaiah 40 corresponds to this prominent position of the diaspora return after the Assyria-Babylon judgment in Isaiah 36–39, together with the continuations of these two thematic aspects in Isaiah 41–66. Guided by Isaiah (1–)10 and following and 24–27, Isaiah 28–35 and Isaiah 36–39 (40 and following) represent parallel presentations of divine intentions for God's people over a lengthy time span from the Assyrian period into the completion of salvation. In so doing, parallel manifestations converge in view of God's intention with the nations. Compare the notable correspondence of the end of Assyria in Isaiah 10, the end of Babylon and the end of the nations in Isaiah 13–27 with the end of Assyria in Isaiah 28–31, the end of Babylon in Isaiah 32–33, the end of the nations in Isaiah 34 on the one hand and, on the other hand, the end of Assyria in Isaiah 36–38, the end of Babylon in Isaiah 39–47, and the end of the nations in Isaiah 51; (63:1–6; 66:15 and following). The following correspondences may have provided an essential confirmation of these lines of reader-reception giving coherence to the continued reading: Isaiah (40:12–41:28;) 42:12 and following / Isaiah 34; Isaiah 42:11–18 / Isaiah 35; 42:22–25 / 36–39; and Isaiah 43 (the first statements of the worldwide collection) / Isaiah 40–66.[53]

Does the side-by-side placement of Isaiah 34 and 35 particularly show the perspective (in the sense of a historical synchronic reading) that YHWH already reveals to Isaiah in Isaiah 27:12 and following, and again in Isaiah 51:1–11; 62:10–12; 63:1–6; and finally 66:5–24? Does this placement show that YHWH even cares about the salvation of the returning diaspora at the universal judgment? Should not the anticipated salvation in the middle of the judgment context in Isaiah 1 and following and 28 and following also be read in such a manner that YHWH's encountered intention is made known from the beginning? When read in succession, Isaiah 10:5–27 already shows this intention on a small scale. Information coming through Isaiah from his book concerning that which YHWH intended over a lengthy time frame, from that time forward, unifies the complexly transmitted flow of the book on the level of the assertions. It also manifests coherence.

CONSEQUENCES FOR THE BOOK'S INTENDED READERSHIP

Correspondingly, one must present the intended reception of the reader for the entire book. The books present divine knowledge and divine activity through the named prophet. To this degree, they do not exist from the insights and intentions of scribes/authors. Rather, the books exist from manifested proclamation and external effects. Therefore, they have no primary interest in prophetic biography. They contain divine knowledge connected with the prophet, and they keep it lively by literary conveyance. This knowledge should be adopted reader-receptively without specifying an immediate intention of the tradent in light of the current readership. Direct address, in advance, of the prophets' contemporaries who are expressly encountered in the prophetic books occurs far less frequently than one might expect. When it does happen, as for example in Isaiah 56–66, or in Zechariah-Malachi, then, as we have seen, this address characteristically occurs in positions which are metahistorically (!) leading (but not directly chronological) in the flow of the books into the immediate present tense of the recipient. Rather, for the most part, the books offer another image of the presentation of the transmission.

The reason lies in the fact that the professional tradents and recipients of the prophetic books now more likely expect the use of reflection related to the present in a broader historical span, with respect to YHWH's presence. They are less likely to expect an attitude directed only to the actual behavior of the readers' generation. Above all, reading prophetic books demands dialogue with the experience of the respective historical constellations. For this reason, reading prophetic books occasionally attracts productive new readings.

However, as already suggested, this image has deeper reasons. Prophetic transmission in books should not apply just to individuals nor just to individual generations in light of their own current limits. Prophetic transmission in books views God's people at the time of reception in their extended chronological existence (!). Indeed, this transmission views God's people from the beginning of the Assyrian judgment by references backward into the period of the ancestors and creation and by references forward into subsequent time periods. These later periods bring judgment and change. Finally, time flows into the completion of salvation. There are indications[54] that professional recipients (in the narrower or broader framework of a culture of professional tradition) may also read the prophetic book transmission in order to function in a manner that correspondingly orients itself toward and admonishes the population. If so, then these professional recipients should record that this transmission speaks of the entire people of God not as a punctilliar entity, but as an entity over a lengthy time span in its entire existence. This entity is the intended subject of the prophetic books, not in the sense of an immediate readership, but according to the content.

Reading prophetic books awakens God's people's experience of the lengthy time span that is determined by tradition. This experience is also metahistorically explained through the message of the books. In so doing, the "now" of the time of reception can be seen as it appears in God's eyes through the prophetic transmission with respect to where it came from and where it is going. Consequently, in accordance with the wide perspective of revealed meaning, one should not conclude that the intended readership, both direct and indirect, explicitly identifies itself with the addressees of the prophetic period transmitted in the book in every respect. Naturally, later recipients should learn something from what they have read and heard in the prophetic transmission. However, this learning need not take place simply by immediate and thoroughgoing identification with the addressees of the past. Only with the *pesher* hermeneutic of Qumran can we grasp that change. Rather, later recipients should see themselves included in a far-reaching historical context as the path of God. In so doing, they should also observe what lies in the past, indeed the past itself, as an event that has led to the present and will lead to the future goal of completion. Or spoken theologically, later recipients should learn that the present situation in which they live lacks in salvation because of events in the long-past monarchic period. YHWH used Isaiah, Jeremiah, and the other prophets associated with the preexilic period to put in motion an event, a historical process, through the prophetic word based upon the behavior of the addressees of that time. As a result, one must experience the effect of this process. One can identify its effect as the continuing action of YHWH specifically with the help of the prophetic word issued at that time. This action should also be observed in light of the prospects for the future of God's people that are displayed in the prophetic books.

In addition, reading prophetic books will lead to thematically selected observation of the currents of history, to concentrated observation upon that which is meaningfully operational in the currents of history, and to those existing prospects that YHWH has established for the future. The diffuse and multifarious pathway of events is therefore composed of certain epochs of meaning. Above all, for the present one should learn to illuminate the present experienced situation from events in the past history of YHWH's decrees, reaction, and performance. One should also learn to illuminate the present experienced situation from prospects that lie before them from YHWH. Reading prophetic books allows one to determine the present from the standpoint of the historically prophetic time span based upon the interplay between prophetic transmission and experience. Prophetic books also display the future that exists meaningfully on YHWH's part for a long time according to the outlook of the prophets.

Theological thought over the large span of history from the eighth century until the present, along with its meaning for the future, guided by the prophetic activity currently explained and presented, was thus especially required of the readership familiar with written prophetic transmission in light of God's people. Above all, one also certainly read Isaiah, Jeremiah, Ezekiel, and the other books of the preexilic prophets as the divine foundation of a great truth process in light of the experience of the historical time span and the salvation-deficiency of the present. They also carefully differentiated between that which was apparently fulfilled and that which still lay in the future. That which was apparently fulfilled incorporates much of the formulational aspects that materially unite the experience of history for 722/720 and 587 B.C.E. Prophetic books correlate the experience of history with past prophetic impulses of YHWH that have created this experience. In so doing, prophetic books also confirm the power of the prophetic word of YHWH in the future outlook anticipated therein. The one supports the other, and both open the comprehensive movement of events that also incorporates the present, the movement of YHWH's past and future work for God's people. Historically determined chronological processes are explained as meaningful events of God and humanity. Correspondingly, these processes capture the state of the prophetic words of YHWH in the times of the prophets, in the sense of the initial nature of a divinely prophetic impulse effective over a lengthy period. The settings of time in the superscriptions and the datings that increasingly appear after the exile (e.g., in Jeremiah, specifically in Ezekiel and Zechariah 1–8, and especially strikingly in Haggai, which is now conceived as a chronicle of the temple construction in the past) are probably also connected with this feature. Prophetic transmission is adopted as YHWH's self-affirmation of his path with the people of God.

That which the transmission offers for past material therefore carries a double connotation from the standpoint of later recipients. On the one hand, one can observe that events come into view that initially occurred in the past and that potentially reappear as acts of God or human behavior according to the measuring rod of corresponding constellations of experience. Thus, these events can be encountered again directly in the time of the recipients before the proceeding perspectives of the definitive completion of salvation. We have already spoken about the fact that the transmission's statements open a revalidation and a repeated validation. We have also spoken about the fact that the transmission no longer concretely elaborates the original historical circumstances and addressees in characteristic concentration. The transmission no longer even directly addresses God's people in many texts of reflection. Prophetic books convey YHWH's entire chronological sequence of action and constellations of activity typical for YHWH within that sequence.

On the other hand, however, in the absence of current, corresponding constellations of experience in the recipients' time, the transmission will then really present the material lying in the past chronologically as something in the past. This material no longer directly affects the present, but, in fact, continues to have consequences, and it must be known by the current recipients in order to explain the existence of God's people over a lengthy time span. In so doing, shaping the transmission also concerns resistance to direct appropriation for the current period. The texts of the prophetic books are thus largely stripped of the original communication between prophet and listener. The path is cut off to the immediate adoption of the truth of these assertions by the substitution of the later persons in the roles of addressees. The reason for this other perspective that the prophetic transmission also bears is probably twofold. First, the texts do not invite later persons to identify with people from the time of the particular prophet that lies in the past. Rather, the texts invite later persons to observe God's earlier activity in these prophetic texts. However, this activity still operates now as it did then. Second, later persons should see themselves as belonging to the people of God who are addressed, but not in timeless coexistence. Rather, they should understand themselves as members of God's people, a people who traverse a historical path. Not everything encountered as Israel in the present is pertinent for later persons as direct addressees! At this point, historical inquiry into what once happened does not decide about the coming repetition or past nature of events addressed prophetically. Instead, historical inquiry decides about what is typically experienced for the prophetically revealed God. Thus, one must continuously inquire to correlate experiential constellations with YHWH's intention as the reason of all meaningful events as YHWH is construed in the prophetic books.

The finding shows that the later adoption of prophetic transmission did not continually flow through personal identification of a single generation and through direct actualization of every individual statement. Instead, it runs through a contemplated, hermeneutically theological process which reflected upon the historically constituted identity of the whole people rather than erasing it. This kind of thinking, which repeatedly connects the experience of the lengthy time span and the current time in the prophetically revealed activity of God, appears to have been the particular intellectual challenge of the prophetic tradents. Using the prophetic insights into the way of God transmitted in the book, the question is continually raised: What is true for whom when, and what is true now? Or, expressed in more flowery terms: Where does God's world-clock stand now for us? The prophetic reception in Qumran and also in the New Testament still show this challenge quite clearly.

From the perspectives of the book, one can bring together that which unifies the literary whole in the final version in the image of history and that which has provided the view of the intended readership of the prophetic transmission in the initial, briefly sketched considerations that remain interested strictly in the given book. If so, one should then primarily accentuate the following. At any rate, after the Persian period Israel is granted direction for understanding itself as a people and as a nation in the sense of an entity that existed over a lengthy time span. The historical transmission of Genesis-Kings provided Israel with direction with its comprehensive perspectives on the whole way of God, especially in the final chapters of Deuteronomy. The transmission of the prophetic books does the same. Israel is also offered an image of identity in this body of tradition. This image encompasses a flow of history under the perspective of YHWH's favor about decline and purpose, with splendor and distress, with guilt and salvation.

The theological shaping in all of these transmissions is, of course, not always precisely the same in the individual prophetic books. It is not even limited solely to the Deuteronomistic perspective that the different version of the guilt of YHWH's people shows. Israel, without diluting and without disguising it, movingly maintains its guilt in all its images of identity. The changing effects and limitations between different intellectual streams of the postexilic period also differ over the question of the length of guilt and signs of current presence of salvation. These intellectual streams should be investigated more precisely from the perspective of the history of theology with respect to the way they shaped the prophetic transmission. One should also investigate more precisely the conclusion that, in fact, diverse groups of tradents worked to shore up diverse perspectives that exclude one another. Not just the later finding of the complexity of tradition and theology in Qumran, but also the realities in postexilic Jerusalem and Judah as well, suggest that the protagonists and the tradents of different concepts of identity did not exist in impervious division. Rather, they existed alongside one another with permanent contacts. They influenced each other interactively according to their own options with critical reservation. Thus, they acquired diverse influence and external effect. The authoritative tradition-material was perhaps alternately more well known and, as such, less contested, than it appears to us today in efforts to reconstruct a postexilic history of theology. Instead, what was contested was the reference to the current time and the application, especially with respect to the theological qualification of the present and its forthcoming outlooks for the eschatological completion of salvation. Also, the thematic fields that they processed were different. One should mention several things here. First, one should mention the explication of the law (*torah). Second, one should mention the theological diagnosis of time for Israel among the nations (*prophetic books), and third, one should mention reflections about the order of the human world in general that do not depend upon concrete, changing historical constellations for proving the world dominion of the kingly God of Zion, especially in the framework of the life of the individual (wisdom). Despite receptional combinations of the basic approaches, the intellectual lines of scribal prophecy and wisdom run alongside one another for a long time, as shown first by late connections at the beginning of the second century B.C.E.[55] These lines occur in tension, especially concerning whether or not the prophetic outlook about an eschatological change in the future should first question YHWH's turning to the world and individuals within time. Likewise, differences could have existed between the prophetic tradents themselves and wisdom recipients in the system of the receptional reading method of prophetic transmission (the illumination of which is really just beginning).

Prophetic books represent that transmission area that most sensibly and most precisely opens the historically experienced political processes in metahistorical screening. Above all, this transmission area, led by its authoritative, protected tradition, processes that which concretely occurred with respect to God's people in the course of time. In its prophetic books, the transmission area also offers truth on God's part in this respect. It offers that which is valid, but mediated over a lengthy time span, and that which is directly valid in the current transmission time. It offers what one should do and what appears as hopeful. Diachronic findings will show that prophetic books continually explain this aspect and present it anew in the transmission movement that these books include.

For Israel, these historical images provide identity. They are orientational, metahistorical images supported by revelation and experience. In the preceding text, we accented the fact that these images were effective in perceiving the complex flow and linguistic shape determined by the transmission. They directed the reception process from the whole structure, the thematic blocks, and the thematically superimposed and repeating vocabulary of the prophetic books in light of historical experience. They did so from the abundance of sayings with a grand view of the essential. They did so by learning the stations and threads of God's coherent, comprehensive action with Israel. They did so even if, on the one hand, the literary flow of the wording is not identical with the multiplicity of individual formulations that diverge and that cannot be unified receptionally. On the other hand, they also did so, even if the metahistorically successive flow of this activity is not identical with the flow of the wording because of how the books developed. Anticipating the diachronic finding, the books grew over a lengthy period and were not continually reformulated from the ground up so that they might be shaped anew linguistically.

Therefore, the orientational, comprehensive image of God's ways with Israel must first be provided by contemplative reading in the search for God's plan and the position of Israel at the time of reception. One should contemplate while reading the transmitted prophetic book as a literary whole that comprises the entire book (or relatedly, the series of books). With respect to a comprehensive image, it is no different for Genesis to Deuteronomy/Kings or for Chronicles-Ezra-Nehemiah. These works reach from the beginning and go beyond the exile. Transmitted entities, whose text flow is not primarily conceived with a presentation of metahistorical flows, offer the opportunity to place the comprehensive image compactly in a special position. For example, such is the case for Deuteronomy 32 and Nehemiah 9. Such is also the case for Daniel (1)7–12 with respect to the characteristic sequence (not in a linear order, but in a thematic order from Daniel to the current world rulers). Such is also the case for Tobit 13 and following. Later writings composed after the Torah and Nebiim that want to shape the authoritative tradition in this respect are free to make the comprehensive image their own subject of transmission, as one can see in Sirach 44–50, in the image that Baruch presents, and especially in *Jubilees* 1, *1 Enoch* 85–90, 4QpsMos, 4QpsDan, or *As. Mos.* That which is revealed in one place in these references was first unveiled over time for the prophet through YHWH's speech in the developing works of transmission of the prophetic books in the sense of the tradents. And it can be derived from the flow of reading the books in this complex shape.

MODIFICATIONS IN THE FLOW OF READING

We have investigated how the flow of a prophetic book (especially Isaiah 1–66) should be read under a unifying perspective whose literary signals are useful to observe. This investigation allows for the coherence difficulties that existed even at the reception of that time, and it allows for the possibilities that could have been resolved in a higher perspective of unity in Isaiah 1–66. However, one must pay no less attention to the extent that the inclinations of the book's statements also undergo conscious and clearly recognizable modifications. The inclinations appear in the (flow of the) book in such a manner that the prophet repeatedly expresses appropriately noted messages in subsequent acts of revelation. As a result, the earlier material (knowledge of the prophet) existing in the book is made more precise by later material (knowledge of the prophet). Or from the opposite side, the earlier material existing in the book offers the broader perspectives that the later material encompasses and limits.[56] One can see this clearly in Jeremiah if one pays attention to the qualifications that have been placed on top of one another, qualifications that limit God's people for salvation in Jeremiah (MT) in the framework of the series of books begun with Isaiah and continued by Ezekiel.[57] In Isaiah, one can note modifications with respect to the nations in the Persian phase and its transition into the final events, or with respect to the limitations of a complete world judgment. However, as suggested above, one can also note modifications with respect to the final realization of Isaiah 2:2–5.

> Are there potentially two phases of universal judgment for the given book of Isaiah in the sense of the final formation, with one occurring in Edom (Isa 34; 63:1–6) and one occurring from Jerusalem outward (Isa 66:14–18, 24)? Or, were both judgments seen as identical because YHWH also returned to Jerusalem after judging Edom (Isa 63:1–6)? Does the concluding formation of Isaiah succeed with the complete world judgment (Isa 13; 24–27; 34; 51:1–8; 63:1–6) and the limited world judgment (Isa 66:15–24) in such a manner that the concluding statements in Isaiah 66 operate backward thanks to their position and thus argue for limitation? Or how does the phased return of God's people mentioned earlier appear in the advance perspective of the book according to the final version? Are the Babylonian *golah* and the children of Zion (population of Jerusalem) seen as being at home again until the phase in Isaiah 62:7 that would correspond to the image of the Ezra-Nehemiah period? And does one now expect the gathering of the diaspora from "Assyria" and "Egypt" and beyond?

The domains of statements at the literary conclusion of the final formations are especially important for explaining these incoherences in Isaiah and the XII,[58] but also in Ezekiel 33–39; 40–48 (Jeremiah differs in the ultimate, metahistorical statements of intention in Jer 30–33). These domains materially illuminate the literary whole by operating backward, and they expose a flow of activity intended to be divinely directed toward a goal. These fields explain what YHWH will do with God's people and the nations when he reaches the goal of his paths. They also provide direction for the receptional reading of existing statements that are materially parallel but divergent concerning the final event. The statements are modified as partial truths of this final event fixed at the end or as work of YHWH preceding him in the last time. Isaiah 66:5–24 is a notable example. There, explanatory cross-references in Isaiah 66 point back toward the beginning of the book[59] after the final comparison between the nations' participation in salvation in Isaiah 2:2–4; (40–55) 60–62 (in the Persian period?) and the comprehensive judgment of the nations in 63:1–6 has been carried out. Corresponding things are true for Zechariah 14 (nations) and Malachi (Israel) as statements of purpose in the flow of the XII. We must cease with these suggestions and examples. It is self-evident that in order to provide sufficient proof of intended coherence, a satisfactory synchronic reading of the prophetic books in the final formation demands extensive investigations that await further research into the prophetic books.

Review

The expectation of a metahistorical orientation for YHWH's people among the nations appears to us to be most important for the question of how the prophetic books should be read in the final formation by those who considered them to be authoritative. Therefore, the explanatory effect of the intended metahistorical perspective cannot be evaluated highly enough as a higher material unity for the reception of the literary and material complexity of the formulations of the book at the final stage (as well as earlier stages of the book's formation). This still holds true, even if the effect is completely foreign to today's emphatically analytical manner of observation for historically oriented exegesis of the prophets. Prophetic books as such, and as a whole, may characteristically provide meaning, and they may want to convey a coherent whole and a higher material unity with all of their assertions. If so, then it must be God's perspective that establishes this quality through its lengthy chronological extension and its typical lines of thought. The standpoint in which the prophets pronounce in advance YHWH's intention over a lengthy time span appears to us to be one of the leading presuppositions for shaping the book and understanding the book among the prophetic writings. YHWH authoritatively and effectively expresses himself about events through the writing prophets, as the experience of judgment in particular teaches. YHWH expresses himself in the concrete formulations and the presentation of the events of the book and the book's flow from the Assyrian period to the entire path of God's people still to come. YHWH also expresses himself about the nations through the book and the combination of books that are actually related to one another. This standpoint represents the direction, reducing the material complexity of the prophetic writing, in the sense of its overriding material inclination, by ordering the divergent statements in different phases (past, current, future) of the whole path of the one Israel as metahistorically observed by God. Inside this divine observation the assertions should be understood as materially identical, free of contradiction, and metahistorically synonymous.[60]

Seen diachronically, the cumulative transmission process among the prophetic books leads to a particularly complex literary shape with respect to the intention and effect of these entities. Even so, one may continue to recall in advance the heavenly, divine predisposition of events on earth that maintain the tables of fate and exceptionally accorded insights into the heavenly realities. The fundamental conviction appears to be that the prophetic writing contains only divinely validated material, but that not everything is valid for God's people at the same time. Several texts (Dan 9; 1 QpHab 2:1–10; 7:1–8; Luke 4:16–21; Acts 8:26–35; Heb 1:1 and following; and 1 Pet 1:10–12) show that this question represented the central problem of interpretation for the prophetic reception: To whom and to what time period do the statements relate?[61] The explanation relevant for the present in these texts beyond the prophetic canon henceforth requires its own externally powerful interpretation of the prophetic texts. In these external interpretations, direct access to the knowledge of heaven (*Jubilees* 1; *1 Enoch*) or the specially attained knowledge of the powerful interpreter (Sir 39:1; Dan 9; 1 QpHab 2, 7; Luke 4; Acts 8) plays an important role. It exposes the hermeneutical unity of the transmitted material whose written form is complex and already closed.

> Recently, in his essay on Proverbs 10, Krüger observes a formation of compositions in the wisdom transmission that are carefully compiled. They combine substantively disparate material, but do

not explicitly balance that material. Instead, they apparently prefer to leave the clarifying discussion to the reader while conceding a tendency and perspective. In light of this observation, we must raise the objection whether the same is intended with respect to the incoherences in the (final) formation of the prophetic transmission. Do authoritatively transmitted materials remain standing alongside one another in their disparity without balancing inside the book? Does this material continually demand to be kept open, despite a clearly indicated comprehensive concept for external clarification, perhaps with respect to the chronological relationship of the statements through the respective readership of the books? The productive process of tradition shows that this challenge exists *de facto.* However, have the prophetic tradents themselves occasionally also consciously refused to clarify the complexity inside the book, and have they left the respective unifying explanations to external processes of discussion about the book? This possible explanation cannot be excluded without foundational processing of the source material in historical synchronic reading. Nevertheless, this possibility should remain *ultima ratio* (a remote reckoning) if a comprehensive material unity of the details cannot be conveyed in the framework of the whole for the self-presentation of the prophetic books.

It appears to us, as suggested earlier, that the wisdom transmission and the prophetic transmission are different. As shown by external prophetic receptions which are only slightly later, the prophetic transmission is directed toward a metahistorical explanation of the time of the recipients that is clearly shown from the prophetically presented comprehensive image of the ways of God with Israel. An unambiguous message should therefore be conveyed from the book transmission. In our opinion, several things should be examined as hints to the readership: conveying the lines of YHWH's intention, the projected metahistorical framework, the differentiation of times and phases to which the validity of statements is related and limited, and the positioning and the inclinations of the metahistorical perspective in the flow of reading. These items show how to sort disparate text statements and to relate diverse material. Nevertheless, once differentiated, the text holds fast to the validity of *all* the statements of the book (or sequence of books) as God's messages.

The incoherences in the Torah potentially signify that the final formation wants to create a compromise work (see Steck,

Abschluß, p. 18), although one must also inquire more precisely about the signals of an intended material unity of the whole in the Torah. This fact must not mean, however, that the same was true in the framework of the prophetic transmission. The highly complex statements about the nations in the final formation of Isaiah and the XII could also have been received and transmitted as completely accepted and valid. This could be true if one considers that the divergences in Isaiah 60–62, 63:1–6, and 66 or in Micah 4, or in the Assyria statements in Nahum-Zephaniah (after Jonah), should also have been consciously read chronologically and sequentially as a metahistorical sequence and that they should have been read as a phased plan of YHWH. Especially the literary statements at the end with respect to the nations in Isaiah 66 and in Zechariah 14 could be more than a partially successful mediation between the pilgrimage of the nations and judgment of the nations in Isaiah and the XII respectively. One must take into account that the presentations of the final events for the nations that appeared separately earlier in the book now become more precise in the final statements. They become more precise to the degree that the final statements differentiate for whom they are valid among the nations, or that they were related to preceding phases of the final events whose finality then is the scenario at the end of the book.

We leave the aspects and examples to approach the unit of meaning which could have been provided to the prophetic book in the final form. Later, this heuristic blending of observations and determinations of the material profile of a prophetic book can and must be fundamentally and openly examined in additional working procedures for revisions. It contains unexplained material that is certainly still accidental but also clearly and recognizably bears meaning in the text's final form. This blending must be explained more closely and determined more precisely if measures are to appear more clearly upon the literary-critical and redaction-critical paths, in comparison to the preceding preliminary stages of the book, that shape the book by the final hand as a whole.[62]

Even if these measures await more detailed processing to become a plausible comprehensive picture, there are, however, apparently satisfying indicators that at least the given book of Isaiah was not presented and received solely as a compilational work in the formative final shaping. Rather, it was presented and correspondingly received as a meaningful whole, free of contradiction, all of whose statements are valid. (Hence, one can even see a corresponding higher unity in the framework of the series of all prophetic books.) Those responsible for this shaping thus wanted to convey a materially unified entity, or so it appears to be suggested until evidence appears to the contrary. In this entity, Isaiah (or more precisely YHWH, through Isaiah) continually explained, amplified, refined, and actualized. In this entity, in the minds of those responsible, there exists no reason for inquiring back to the prior literary stages of this final form, because the entire content is the work of the prophet who is commissioned by YHWH and whose name is provided. It is YHWH who continually seizes and protects the prophet and reveals ideas of divine activity. Also, for those responsible, there exists no reason for inquiring back to the prior literary stages of this final form, because, in their minds, divergences are partial truths of a whole, and concurrent material—indeed contradictory material—can be harmoniously arranged, above all through chronological relationship and limitation to partial phases of the metahistorical perspective of the entire book. One must examine whether the same is true with the other prophetic books. Many things argue that one also encounters entities in those books that were seen as materially coherent and correspondingly formed for the given final shaping and, in fact, for the prophetic series of books. If a historical synchronic reading also leads to a historically coherent reading, then the final formations of the prophetic books as such become meaningful wholes whose characteristic and particular witness seeks attention in this shape of the book.

The Question of Prior Literary Stages for the Given Prophetic Book

Reference Points for the Diachronic Investigation

Anyone who inquires about a prophetic book's prior literary stages brushes the given final form against the grain and evaluates indicators contrary to the self-presentation of the books. These indicators have only recently been widely noticed for historical understanding, but they are not specifically signaled by the book itself. They can be found in final form in the initial supposition of a lengthy diachronic growth of the books. Apparently they can be found only because older transmission material was preserved by the final formation. The final formation did not change its formulations, but received and processed them for the current period as authoritatively conveyed material whose wording and structure were just as valid then as before.[63] The effort of historical synchronic reading can lead to a conclusion for the final formative shaping of the book that indicates the inclination for the comprehensive coherence, the provision of meaning, and the conveying of meaning for the literary entity as a whole, even in the details. With the question of a prophetic book's prior literary stages, anyone who has reached such a conclusion thus faces a particular difficulty. References that want to and can be read coherently at this time, should simultaneously be taken as indicators for the book's prior literary history.

Undoubtedly, historical research on prophetic books encounters indexes in other writings as well as in Isaiah 1–66 that tend to strengthen the initial presupposition. As we have seen, the final formation of the given book of Isaiah, as well as in the final formation of the other prophetic books, is in all probability presented not just as a mere conglomeration of transmitted material or as a complex foundation for external discussions. It is also presented as an intended and receivable material unity. There is, however, no question that we have the work of a final hand, a higher unity, whose existence was expressly demanded and had been expressly created.

Reference points for the necessity of an inquiry behind the final formation, into its literary prehistory, naturally present themselves differently than with the problematic starting point of a preconceived image of the original prophet himself or the question of what should be attributed to this prophet and what should not. The reference points should now be sought in the character of the prophetic book under discussion and only in that book. The image presented by these books in their existing form, the image of text material originating from the lifetime of the prophet, does not withstand historical inquiry. Rather, this image should be replaced with the model of a lengthy development of the books. This fact is already suggested by comparing the writings of the late period. By contrast, one can see what writings without an inherent prior literary history look like in Israel of the second century B.C.E. One can also see how to formulate a harmonious metahistorical image in the internal coherence of a book like *Jubilees*, or as we believe, in the book of Baruch, as well as numerous other writings of this late period inside and outside of Qumran. The final form of the prophetic books offers another image. Complex overlappings in the structure, in the macrostructuring, and in the lines of composition indicate that one must inquire behind the final form step-by-step. In the area of a prior literary history, one potentially encounters well-arranged entities that are smaller in size that now stand inside the given book. Certain similar indices can be attained from concurrences in the determinations of purpose for God's people and the nations. They provide evidence that, hidden in the book, one finds even older, materially .climactic statements that are differently accentuated and that function as literary conclusions. The fact that the wording of the text reflects a development can be deduced from notable divergences in style between sectional blocks, but also in particular texts. Those signs in the book that have the greatest significance for diachronic inquiry are those that subsequently react to the textual material in the book and process this text material within the book from a different tendency (see above, p. 34, for the cross-references that are changing accents). These signs are based upon observations of openly contradictory material in texts. This material can only be explained by mediation in the literary context or by associations with a situation of the recipients. No less importantly, it also concerns modifications, compensatory bridge formulations, and cross-references for the same theme in the flow of statements. If one thus attempts to arrange a dominant tendency, one is pointed toward the chronological distance between the textual material that is adopted and that is received. This distance greatly exceeds the actual or fictive lifetime of the prophet. Also, historical challenges lead to a prior literary history of Isaiah 1–66 as plausible originating situations for texts such as Isaiah 7–8, Isaiah 22, or the sayings about Assyria and Egypt in Proto-Isaiah. All of these indices thus suggest that one must work with the model of a lengthy chronological transmission process for the development of the prophetic books. They also suggest providing space to presuppose that this model of reconstruction offers the highest potential for explaining the phenomena of the books. That which tips the balance must, of course, be the historical investigation of the given writing itself. With this changed starting point for the inquiry, we think that one can also follow the fundamental insight of historical research into the development of prophetic books. Isaiah and Jeremiah, as well as such apparently complex books as Amos, Micah, Zephaniah, and Zechariah, were certainly not recorded in a single formative act as we now have them. Existing literary material must have been integrated and processed, and upon closer inspection it becomes clear that not a single one of the prophetic books should be excluded from this appraisal.

How does one determine the transmitted material behind the final formation? Insights that build consensus for the closer determination of the literary development of the individual prophetic books are naturally not provided. Thus, one cannot lean upon reliable

presuppositions from the discipline. The suggestions are far too diffuse. It is no different with the traditional process of inquiring about
the (preliterary) origins from the final literary shape and then simultaneously permitting yet another glance at the development of the
books according to a presumed image of this field of the genuine,
original prophetic logia. Of course, in the narrow arena of particular texts, consistent—even poetically shaped—linguistic material can
continue to be plausibly differentiated in comparison to later adapted
material. However, these individual findings investigated in isolation do not allow one to recognize the transmission stage that one
encounters. Nor do they allow one to recognize whether one has
reached the beginnings of the book's development. In the discipline,
one sees as much in the high degree of divergent determinations of
original prophetic material that serves as the origin of the transmission of the prophetic books. In this process, essential framing stipulations are already blurred together in anticipation.

In order to avoid this blurring regarding the question of that
which was presupposed literarily for the final shape of the books,
one must start with the foundation. The consciously maintained framing stipulations of the entry points possible for us demand that the
inquiry back into the development of the prophetic transmission of
the given material must also move backward, from the end to the
beginning. Instead of beginning with original individual logia, that
is, beginning with preliminarily extracted passages that are presumed
certain, the correct starting point is the given final form, with its
literary and material contours. From here the path of inquiry moves
backward step by step to the next oldest literary layers of reception
and their characteristic contours. The given material characterized
the historical synchronic reading. One does not abandon it as the
starting point in the diachronic realm. Instead, one preserves this
starting point as the framing stipulation. With respect to the origin
of the text, nothing is decided in advance about the literary (!) layers
of reception encountered along the way that existed before the final
layer. However, with this successive journey backward into prior
stages, the question of the origins remains realistic. In the given finding one can rationally differentiate between measures of reception
and received material on every level. This step-by-step path backward will lead to origins entirely by itself when led by the question
of the beginning of the respective levels of reception. Thus, at this
point, we are pleading for a diachronic procedure that illuminates

the growth of prophetic books and that takes its indicators from observations into the entire book as we have it. This process pushes itself backward literarily into older transmission layers, but simultaneously, does not too hastily jump back into the apparently evident preliterary world of the original prophet himself.

Therefore, in the case of Isaiah (as we accented at the outset), a completely new investigation of the literary properties must be skeptical with respect to the traditional division into three or two formerly independent literary entities/sources and their later combination. In such a division, possible networks inside Isaiah would simultaneously be cut off. These networks could connect the entities and could constitute a comprehensive whole, potentially even before the final formation. In so doing, the insights of the Isaiah research since Duhm should not be depreciated. They should only be dissolved from their self-evident option for "sources" from which Isaiah was compiled, and critically incorporated today in a newly framed question.

There are already very elementary findings[64] that indicate that Proto-Isaiah, Deutero-Isaiah, and Trito-Isaiah, as macro-blocks, have something to do with the development of Isaiah. Thus one notes that these macro-blocks go together with layers of style, which are quite different among themselves. The Isaiah of Isaiah 1–39 speaks differently than the Isaiah of Isaiah 40–55, and the Isaiah of Isaiah 56–66 speaks differently still. Further, one notes that the apparently chronological reflections on the Assyrian period are concentrated in Proto-Isaiah, and the reflections of the Babylonian and early Persian periods are concentrated in Deutero-Isaiah. This fact further indicates a divergent origin of the textual material.

After these basic observations concerning the macro-blocks in Isaiah, if one looks at Isaiah 1–66 as a whole, one can hardly overlook the frictions that point toward various developmental levels of the book. The structure and the sequence of statements of the book are by no means indubitably apparent for the perception of the time. Dominant and superimposed[65] structural signals stand alongside one another in the book of Isaiah as we have it. Also, metahistorical concentrations of themes (e.g., in Isa 13–27 and Isa 56–66) preserved in the book and in the concrete literary flow diverge, as shown by the position of Isaiah 34 over against Isaiah 13–27 or the position of Isaiah 63:7–64:11 in contrast to the preceding material. At the stage of the final formation, these divergences require their own receptionally processed, meta-historically comprehensive perspective in order to present the entire text as a material unity.

As one can recognize in Proto-Isaiah especially, corresponding elements are provided when one observes that the macro-thematics of the book-parts are not reconcilable to the given contents. One can see these elements, for example, in the parallel nature of Isaiah 1–11 and Isaiah 28–35, or in the placement of Isaiah 22 in Isaiah 13–27, or in the position of Isaiah 36–39 after Isaiah 33–35. In addition, one can mention the particularly notable finding that the book's flow points toward different statements of purpose for the completion of salvation, one after the other, but each of them has its own point of culmination. One need only compare the overlapping in Isaiah 11:1–5, 6–9, 10, 11–16, or the concurrence of purpose statements like Isaiah 12 or Isaiah 33, with the new beginning in Isaiah 40:1–11. Or, one need only compare Isaiah 52:7–10 with Isaiah 60–62, together with Isaiah 63:1–6, or compare this finding with Isaiah 65 and following. Also, upon closer examination, one finds literary interrelationships within the book in which reaccentuations take place. These interrelationships point toward receptive transitions of growth. As examples, one can mention the reception of the servant of YHWH texts by Isaiah 60–62 or the reception of Isaiah 11:6–9; 40:1–11; and 60–62 by Isaiah 65 and following.[66]

And last but not least, the book adopts material understandings with respect to the metahistorical final events and purpose that are not only different and that amplify one another, but material understandings that actually contradict one another. By no means could all these material understandings be simultaneously original. A glance at the expectations that Isaiah fosters makes this statement self-evident. Jerusalem's completion of salvation can also include the nations in some passages (see, for example, Isa 2:2–5; 33; 49:14–26; 60–62 [66]), but in other passages Jerusalem's completion of salvation is bound with the downfall of these nations (Isa 13; 24–27; 30:27–33; 34; 63:1–6).[67] Isaiah thus by no means exhaustively considers the metahistorical goal with a universal judgment. Where universal judgment is mentioned, Isaiah can even foresee a different extent of this universal judgment. (See especially Isa 66 over against Isa 13 [in the book's horizon, judgment in Babylon as the beginning of a future comprehensive universal judgment in 13:9–13]; 24–27; 34; 51:1–8 [see 51:6]; 59:18

and following; 63:1–6.) The same holds true for statements that determine the boundaries of the holy community of God's people (compare especially Isa 56–59 on the one hand and Isaiah 65 and following on the other, contrasting striking statements in other parts of the book). The final version of Isaiah opens the complementary reading of these divergences by relating the concluding statements in Isaiah 65 and following backward to phases that metahistorically precede the final events of the completion of salvation, or, by modifying limitations that point backward. This complementary reading points to a receptive act of literary shaping, but not to one that is simultaneously original.

In Trito-Isaiah (TI), the problems for reading in the flow of the reading multiply themselves. Of course, on the closing literary level, one can and should read Isaiah 56–59 as making Isaiah 55:6 and following more precise, as the links show. However, the problems of the delay of salvation and participation in salvation, as Isaiah 56–59 perceives them, are not found in Isaiah 55 and in Deutero-Isaiah (DI). Not until Isaiah 56–59 (compare 59:20) does one know that an adequate repentance of the whole people of God will never occur. To this extent, a literary-critical break appears to be suggested between Isaiah 55 and 56, in spite of the relationship of TI to existing statements in the book.

Or consider Isaiah 60:1–63:6. The sequence of statements offers an image of the completion of salvation with insurmountable statements. For its part, it should also certainly be read on the final level with respect to the saved people, the saved country, and participating nations in light of Isaiah 65–66. Thus, it should also be read as making more precise all of the preceding corresponding material that already stood available, especially in DI. Numerous references back into the formulation and thematics also make this material recognizable. However, even if one leaves the question of authorship completely open, it does not concern an original context. Rather, it concerns a context that has developed only as the changed relationships and (no less importantly) the contrasting view of the final fate of the nations shows (note the perfects in 63:1–6 over against 60:1–16; 61; 62:1–7).

In the course of reading, the following is very difficult: Why does the prayer in 63:7–64:11 only appear at this point, when it sounds as though it first happened in 587 B.C.E., after all the full-toned salvific sayings of DI and Isaiah 60–62 that are situated in the time of Cyrus? Did the final layer think that, after the many salvific divine promises that had preceded, the Isaiah of the book now speaks? Did the final layer think that the Isaiah of the book expresses the contrast between God's care and the people's rebellion? (Does 63:7–14 take up 58:1–59:8 in the first-person singular?) And, according to the Isaiah of the book, do the people speak in the present with complaint, confession of guilt, and petition about the epochal situation of 587 that continues to affect them? (Does 63:15–64:11 take up 59:9–15 in the first-person plural?) The subsequent material does not contain a divine response, an encouraging "Yes" and "Amen" spoken about that which the people petition. Apparently, in Isaiah 65–66, one encounters another literary layer with a divine response that makes more precise the statements of the prayer and that which precedes it. Above all, it also limits in an enormous manner. For the final arena of the ways of God with Israel and the world, these final two chapters offer a completely different view with respect to the final judgment and to those overtaken by God with respect to the participants and the condition of the completion of salvation.

Isaiah 56–66 contains a complex flow of statements that one may apparently explain only by diachronic differentiation! The subsequent material's self-evident references backward to the existing material in TI itself, and in DI (but also references forward in Proto-Isaiah), argue against accepting that all of this would have simply come into being by accident and without a plan. Instead, the text-finding itself calls the discipline to find the tracks of this plan.

Even the above noted observations on Isaiah provide enough reference points so that we may now more closely consider the diachronic approach we suggested. The Isaiah book and the other prophetic books could each show something comparable. These books thus lead to the historical question of prior literary stages by themselves when one runs up against insoluble incoherences. When seen historically, these incoherences argue against seeing one and the same act of presentation. Especially when one proceeds from the given text, the prophetic books show such a high degree of complexity of shape and assertions for historical inquiry that one must consider developmental stages of reception inside the (series of) books. That is, one must consider an explanatory model of the literary growth of tradition. In this growth, older states of the text unfold the potential meaning by productive continuation or by rereading under later challenges. Thus, these older states attain additional aspects of meaning whose formulation increasingly allows the prophetic book to expand, to lengthen, and to become more complex materially.

With this judgment, we do not allow ourselves to be led by prior decisions of hypotheses already articulated. Nor are we led by a literary criticism with questionable criteria for what is genuine and what is original that is based upon processing only small, and thus shortsighted, portions of the book. Rather, we keep to literary and material observations in the area of the given final formation of the books. These observations have often been seen by the discipline, even if they are considered too seldom in the horizon of the entire book. These are the observations that also lead to the unavoidable impression of a book that has only come to its final form over time. As is the case with most of the other prophetic books (each with its own reasons), when it comes to the historical question of the process of origin, and the indicators of this process that can thus be perceived, at least this much can be said: The existing book of Isaiah is no original unity. Rather, it is a higher unity. Synchronism as a historical (!) approach to the given shape of the book must thus transition into historical diachronic approaches, if one wants to give the text of the prophetic book its due as an entity of its time in our historically trained eyes. These approaches seek to understand the current complexity of the transmitted material by its prior history. They seek to understand the complexity as the history of the transmission of authoritative texts that are continuously transmitted, preserved, but also enlarged. These approaches grope their way back to earlier entities literarily and materially grounded in persistent consideration of the spacious flows of reading and in the meaning potentially provided with the texts, the meaning of higher, complex units. Potentially, they do so in order to collide with prophetic logia previously delivered orally. This path back is inescapable if one desires to understand the origin of the concrete formulation and the shape of Isaiah and the other prophetic books, and if one is aware of the truth of the historical differentiation of originally precluded text-findings under the protection of the text's inherent chronological and transmission factors. So how does one take this path backward to draw near the process of origin?

Likewise, all diachronic efforts, as we have said already, must proceed only from the form of the book in hand, its concrete flow and vocabulary, its structuring signals, and its comparable presentation. In the process, one must continuously observe the statements' position in the book. One must make observations on the basis of the historical synchronic reading of the whole book already reached in order to step back to plausible, text-grounded suggestions for reconstruction with respect to the growth and the prior stages of the book. Traditional certainties thought to be apparent concerning the book's genesis or the character of the historical prophetic figure again become a source of error of the first order when they are brought into play as fundamental assumptions without questioning, especially on this level of investigation. These apparent certainties would construct a yardstick whose measurement one still would not know. In the diachronic procedure suggested in the current situation, these perceptions cannot be the starting point. Rather, they come only at the end, as potentially confirmed or modified conclusions with offsetting reactions to the already processed diachronic finding. In so doing, a modesty is required that is conscious of limits. The way the prophetic books arose can hardly be significantly illuminated internally from every angle, especially products as complex as the book of Isaiah or Jeremiah. One must limit one's self to clarifying several chief spheres. The most plausible solutions will finally be those that best explain the concrete text phenomena in the same book with respect to the large text blocks and their interrelationships and with respect to the different theologically metahistorical contours of events. Therefore, the proven starting point for the diachronic question is found in patient exegetical observations that continuously advance through the whole book with the aid of examined insights of research to this point.

Analytical Indicators for an Initial Layering and Sorting in the Given Prophetic Book

No options of specific diachronic models appear at the beginning of this investigation. Even the book redactional model, which will be considered more closely below (pp. 85–108), will not have the favorite's role from the outset. Options of models chosen too quickly by the exegete are without value when they do not spend time testing and excluding other historical possibilities. From the beginning, such predetermined models would limit what is open and what is known. They always stand in danger of finding only what they seek. At the beginning of such an investigation stand only potentially diachronically characteristic observations upon the prophetic book, as we have it. Thus, one begins with an initial viewing and sorting of the material of the statement, for example, of the given book of Isaiah, with respect to commonalities and differences in comparable areas of this book.

How should one proceed in this phase of initial observations? As examples, the following could be inferential questions in the large sphere of the book's flow of statements.[68] These questions must proceed with fundamental exegetical precision for the material profile of the individual statements in the horizon of the contexts (for example, with respect to the divergent presentations of the return, nations, judgment of God's people, judgment on the world of the nations).

(1) In the flow of the book's statements, are there oddities of coherence, in details and as a whole, that exist not just for modern reading impressions but also in the conceptual world of the time? Also, are the elements of these oddities encountered separately in other books? In other words, do certain manifestations merely appear problematic as a so-called reading disturbance? When seen historically, do these manifestations contrast with comparable material inside and outside of the literary entity under investigation in style, language, structure, and in the contents of the statement? Are they so massive that their material character would originally be excluded as focal points of statements and alignments of the book's statements? Does the book provide balanced, reconciled, or limiting signals that react to these divergences? As already suggested, statements about the nations in Isaiah offer abundant evidence at this point. For example, whoever formulated Isaiah 2:2–5, 49:14–26, or Isaiah 60:(1–16) and 61, did not have a final judgment in mind that involved all the nations in which the people who were saved survived completely or, at least, survived essentially alone according to the two final chapters (Isa 13; 24–27; 34; 51:1–8; 63:1–6; 65–66).

(2) Does the book as we have it, or even the transcending series of books, provide purpose statements potentially expounding the conclusion (for example Isa 33 and/or 34; Isa 52:7–10; Isa 62:10–12; and/or 63:1–6; Isa 66:5–24)? Specifically, does the book provide statements that are metahistorically contemporary, but whose content is substantively competing? Are these statements structured for continuation or literarily sufficient to complete the idea? Where do they stand in the book? If one looks at them from the book's context, how are they prepared in the book by corresponding, potentially graduated, anticipatory statements, frames, or contextual

compositions? And from the other side, if one looks at their position in the book, what do they presuppose as context, or from the context if need be? Are there correspondingly competing statements at the beginning of the writings? In this framework, certain questions have an important heuristic role. For example, how are the people of God defined at the completion of salvation? Who will encounter the final judgment? Who returns before the completion of salvation to constitute the people of salvation? We will address these "characteristic fossils" of the history of concepts below more closely.

(3) Does the final text, in whole or in part, provide superscriptions of different shaping[69] and macro-inclusions of competing breadth in terms of the literary position or content?

(4) Does the book provide competing transitions (for example, Isa 11:10, 11:11–16, and 12 point to Isa 13)? Does it provide comprehensive and partial references that one can recognize as intentional by corresponding words, style, and material (e.g., Isa 1–2 // 65 and following; Isa 1 // 11; Isa 1 // 33; Isa 13 // 34; Isa 40:1–5// 52:7–10; Isa 40:1–5, 9–11 // 60 and following; Isa 40:1–11 // 62:10–12; Isa 34 // 63:1–6)? Or, one should note graduated explanations of Isaiah 55 in Isaiah 56:1–8, 56:9–59:21, and 60–62.[70] Of great diachronic significance in this context are the compositional observations about the book that Jeremias presented for the literary shape of the book of Amos. These observations show that such book composition proceeds from older, more partially addressed material. They show that this material structures a prophetic book as a material unity, and that this structuring stands out from later accents of the formation of the book of Amos. Last but not least, these observations show that this finding about the (oldest) book of Amos cannot simply be generalized. Things are different in the book of Hosea.[71]

(5) Can a limited *range of similar interrelationships* be ascertained in a particular expression from formulations or from the same precise theme? Where do these relationships show a homogenous network? What contexts do they presuppose? Where do they react to existing material? Where do they resemble, accentuate, and shape a specific understanding for the text's flow? Can superimposed, signaled lines of reading be recognized by text connections? Which ones dominate and react? Which ones are suppressed, limited, and extended? Should these observations, combined with those already mentioned, lead to preliminary suggestions about competing book contours? And should one even infer a relative chronological sequence from these observations?

(6) Observations in partial text fields appear as compositional superimpositions that exclude themselves as original structuring (for example, in Isa 56:1–63:6). They join the first five observations that appear in the large arena of the flow of statements of the whole book as competing and divergent material with respect to references carrying the metahistorical perspective and with respect to the literary exposition, positioning, and contextual relationship of these references in the book.

(7) Preliminarily sorted observations for the smallest realm ultimately demand particularly intensive work. By themselves these observations must not too quickly claim presumed original logia. Rather, they treat the individual texts in the flow of the book. Indices for an initial grouping and sorting of these texts include formulas, addressees, rhetorical pauses between purpose statements, opening statements, and genre indicators. These indices are thus just as important as the question of whether their context or lack of context is (literarily or thematically) provided in the book's flow of statements. Also, in the positive case, how far does such an articulated context of a literary and/or metahistorical nature extend? References in a text that point beyond themselves across the book with respect to the parts or the whole deserve special attention. No less importantly, one should pay attention to commonalities and differences of language and style, to agreements and distinctions in the world of fixed concepts and concerning the same metahistorical situation. One should pay attention to these elements text for text, both internally and externally. Finally, one should record one's impressions regarding whether understanding one text necessarily presupposes another text in the book. Does one text take up another text by receiving it synonymously or by changing it? In this work, for example, one should note that Isaiah 1:2 and following and Isaiah 6 come very close to one another materially, and that Isaiah 28 and following contain intentional similarities to Isaiah 6 and following. One should note that Isaiah 11:6–9 functions like a (later) cancellation of Isaiah 1:3 and following, that Isaiah 60:1–16 functions like a continuation of Isaiah 49:14–26, and that Isaiah 63:1–6 functions like a stated completion of Isaiah 34. The observations of individual text passages in their position in the book must also keep the context in mind. Where does this context offer the materially necessary presupposition for understanding the passage being considered? Are these presuppositions identical to the intention that the original formulation of the passage manifests? Or can one observe that the text formulations deviate in meaning by their association with the

literary contextual level? If so, then a hint exists that an older text formulation potentially exists that is not changed at all. However, this older formulation is now read in another sense than the original meaning. It is now read as related to the book through new contextual images. From that reading, one can recognize indicators of the growth of transmission. Older text material is reread on receptional levels and becomes newly illuminated text material through new redactional contextualizing.

Initial Delimitations of Text Boundaries and Relative Diachronic Arrangements

After these and similar observations, one attempts initial coordinations and differentiations. What stands close to one another in the book's surface with respect to the style and linguistic shape, and what does not? What could belong together according to the material profile, exegetically explained by the history of tradition, the history of theology, and the conceptual world of the concrete sayings? And what could even form a literary connection and a material flow? In this respect, what is related but accented differently? What is completely different in this respect and with respect to significantly different, divergent historical challenges? Which text material is presupposed in the same layer? What functions like a later reception of older material? What lacks any relationships? From these separations, do any of the following elements parallel one another: characteristic networks of formulas and sectional, organizational, or compositional patterns that are superimposed and that were perhaps originally mutually exclusive? Textual and positional clues are especially important for further evaluation in the framework of the diachronic reading (for the large and small realm). These clues were already important for the synchronic reading (see p. 17 above) in a constructive sense. They show that preparing, bridging, processing, balancing, or clarifying elements are used to create book-relevant contexts and to highlight disturbances of coherence. Text passages like Isaiah 35 or Isaiah 51:1–16 appear to us to be striking examples in this respect.

In a further step, fluid observations and preliminary sortings of this type lead to initial delimitations of relative diachronic orders and literary boundaries of older material inside the prophetic book.

(1) Homogenous spheres of statements probably originally belonged together. Thus, in the sense of initial segmentings inside the

book's entire text, impressions of these spheres allow the question of the literary and material cohesion of these segmentings, the question of their arrangement, and the question of their size along with a constitutive beginning and ending.

(2) Initial evaluations of the literary character of these spheres can then be attached. Does the sphere of statements consist of text pieces that are not context-dependent? Does the sequential pattern just follow the same genres, contents, chronological relationships, and catchwords? Does the common arrangement limit itself to insignificant means of compilation and balancing elements? If these impressions about its character are confirmed as the work continues, then they provide a basis for accepting the collection of older discrete material.

(3) Or, does this evaluation show that the sphere of statements is preserved by its flow through materially profiled, compositional measures? Do these measures potentially even preserve inclinations and a purposeful direction in the text flow? In this case, the basis for independent, materially centered, literary measures is provided, even if this way means older materials without characteristic formulations serving the compilation are essentially only rearranged. Here, one raises a question: How do these profiled compositions relate to shapings across the entirety of the book?

(4) Or, does one encounter a sphere of statements with indices that proceed beyond the characteristics named to this point and that point to a far stronger processing of a text flow? Texts that serve this material processing for a larger text flow are especially important heuristically. These texts are thus determined by this context from the outset, supplied by it, and thoughtfully placed in its flow of reading. Which literary and material horizons inside the given writing indicate these texts? Alongside a profiled text-sphere of this type (for example, Isaiah 65 and following), are there also solitary statements of the same character in the given text realm (Isaiah) in a different textual environment or even in a conspicuous position? Or are there potentially even solitary statements toward the front of the text (for example, Isa 1:29–31; 12; 56:1–8) that could be considered as a signal to the reader for what follows?[72] Are there in fact several continuations of these statements pointing to one another as programmatic texts in the successive unfolding of a material perspective? Do these continuations encompass the remaining material, thus bringing a literary whole into line and establishing a

perspective for the reader? These literarily peculiar texts created a priori for relating to the book are diachronically powerful statements in a far-reaching text-flow when they shape changed perspectives for their context, another inclination for the flow, and characteristic accents of meaning. If so, then a reason exists for accepting that the existing material has been processed and that later measures are directed toward an older context. Divergences in literary signals, in compositional lines, in the materially metahistorical arrangement, and in the determination of meaning would strengthen this impression that different diachronic layers were laid over one another in the given text flow.

In conjunction with this impression, two carefully considered follow-up questions illuminate these initial diachronic insights into the profiled shapes of the book that have been thoroughly processed inside a prophetic book. First, are these literary layers of a type that accent integrated, older text material because of divergences and not homogenous continuations? If so, then here one finds the basis for accepting the character of the receptional processing of the given material. This material *eo ipso* reacts to something that is already provided literarily and again simultaneously inquires about this integrated, older material. Second, how great is the extent of this profiled processing of literary contexts behind the final formation of the prophetic book? If it limits itself to a text block inside the final form without contacting a broader book-context, then one may infer a particular development processed for a specific literary entity inside the book. The integration into the whole book would be a secondary act, characterized by compilation, or relatedly, by materially processed integration. Or do clues present the breadth of this processing in parts of the final form of a transcending network, for example, across the width of the entire book of Isaiah? If so, then one comes across literary layers that are already encountered before the final form in the realm of Proto-Isaiah to Trito-Isaiah. The question can be addressed, for example, also for the often conjectured "Book of Comfort for Ephraim" in Jeremiah *30–31.[73] Are its formulations without literary, material external relationships in Jeremiah, so that one may point to a later source? Or is the booklet constituted by literary material references to its context in Jeremiah, and should it be seen from the outset within more far-reaching contexts?

Once again, the starting point is not some type of preformed judgment that appears correct or incorrect to us, the modern readers. The starting point is not imposed, formally structured schemes, abstractions, or concepts of drama that one cannot really prove. Nor is the starting point some type of literary critical analysis and hypothesis of a traditional type in a small format. Rather, the starting point is found in the reciprocal convergence of the careful, historical observation of literary and philological signals on the one hand, and the exegetical treatment of material complexity on the other. This complexity potentially excludes the same original beginnings in the given literary framework of the wording of a prophetic book (or series of prophetic books) and the manner of perspective that dominates these works. No less characteristic are text phenomena that react to other texts in the book in the sense of a reception processed later. Initial, cautious evaluations of this path of observation are now possible with respect to differentiating older and younger textual material, as well as independent and dependent textual material. These evaluations, however, still have a very preliminary character that is yet open to revisions.

We thus now explain indices for a literary criticism of a particular type appropriate for the findings of prophetic books.[74] This literary criticism attempts to remain as close as possible to these findings as the starting point for everything. Also, it builds upon observations upon the book rather than seemingly certain presuppositions. This literary criticism does not limit its indices just to those things noted inside specific, isolated texts.[75] It knows that in so doing the larger literary context in which the text appears remains unconsidered. It knows that one may not omit examination from the opposite side to see whether the complex manifestation of this text, when seen by itself, could instead be literarily unified, not by diachronic layering, but regulated by this wider framework, intended for that framework, and supplied with thoroughgoing references that point backward or forward. The text could thus be explained within the continuing flow of reading. The investigation of isolated texts for the purpose of the search for individual logia in traditional literary criticism of prophetic literature too quickly leaves the foundation of the given, and fails to recognize that diachronic approaches must be directed toward a book, or even a series of books. It therefore acquires some type of allocations, which for the most part pass judgment prematurely. Nevertheless, when observed in the horizon of the book, oddities and discrepancies can be removed quite differently than when narrowly considering an isolated text. In this case, that which appears as disunity (for example, change of speaker and/or change of addressee) can consistently present itself as unified. This material is often broken into small fragments of text by analysis that is fixated in this manner. In reality these fragments instruct one another if one observes the alignment of this text with other texts in the same literary entity, and if one sees punctilliar irregularities as regulated by the denoted function of referencing the context (for example, Isa 51:12–16).[76] Instead of micro-directed literary critical explanation, one examines a plausible redaction historical explanation from the text's context and the growth of the book. However, the opposite is also true: Not everything that appears unified must be unified. Rather, seen contextually, a text can include contradictory material. Also, not every inclusion points to material that originally belongs together. Later material, recognizable by material differences, can also establish an inclusion with the help of existing material or reuse and extend an existing inclusion.

Upon what basis can a literary criticism of the type we suggest find support that is suitable for a prophetic book? Where does this support that proceeds from observations and initial evaluations achieve a more solid foundation for diachronic differentiation of the different text levels of a literary entity? If we are correct, then, as we have already suggested, two phenomena in particular converge where material changes in the written transmission leave behind literary traces.

First, one finds support by observing notable literary and philological realities in the text itself and in the book's text flow, or relatedly in potentially prior stages (for example, peculiar characteristics in the literary context, linguistic peculiarities that are not contextually qualified, indices of supplements, or a text's position and function in a literary context). Here the criteria of classic literary criticism come into play, but these criteria are reexamined for the phenomenon of the book's transmission, modified, and counterbalanced with the interdependence of methods.

Second, one finds support in those realities that were likely denied as criteria by a literary criticism pursuing exact results, specifically realities of the content profile of passages themselves: in the book's text flow, or its potentially prior stages. Here we mean conceptual (!) breaks, doublets, and tensions in the textual finding that suggest that they cannot be conceived as internal continuation on the same literary layer when seen historically in the chronological framework of a book's development. Rather, in all likelihood, these tensions originally exclude themselves and potentially even require their own adaptations, bridges, and modifications in the minds of later recipients so they may stand alongside one another and express a higher receptional material unity for later literary layers. These content and conceptual complexities relate to the same metahistorical times and stations of meaning. Their breadth and literary presuppositions of context in the given book in particular served as the "characteristic fossils" for our suggestions for differentiating late literary phases in the whole Isaiah corpus and in the Twelve.[77] In so doing, one should particularly observe which component concepts presented in the flow of the book form originally constitutive elements of a homogenous comprehensive concept for the respective book as a whole. Its coherence essentially coincides with the agreement of the outlined metahistorical perspective. One should also observe whether and how this type of concept is transmitted with diversely constituted conceptual references from the preserved, successively transmitted older form of the book and whether this concept was integrated into a higher level. The literary exposition and position of the concepts accompanying the growth of the book itself, and their building blocks in forming the whole text, were important for the reader's reception of a prophetic writing. Even though we differ in the question of the Zion texts,[78] Hermisson has explored, in a methodologically elucidating manner, the particular significance of these concepts for the question of the material coherence or incoherence as indicators of literarily diachronic elements for the prophet Deutero-Isaiah.[79] Hermisson and Kratz have extensively conducted this approach regarding the literary layering in Isaiah 40–55.[80] The example of the divergent ordering of the texts about Lady Zion in Isaiah 49–54 naturally shows that conceptual indices are only diachronically conclusive in the case of tension with a material, concept historical nature, or with reactive processing. If the relationship to other texts in Deutero-Isaiah is complementary in nature, as in the case of the Lady Zion texts, then one must bring other criteria into play for the question of simultaneous origins or non-simultaneous origins concerning Isaiah 40:1–2; 41:27; and 52:7–10 (for example, contemporary provocation).

The contents of these theological concepts differ from others. Seen from these contents, these concepts essentially concern the divinely generated course of events. Thus, these contents treat the concrete image of history for the path of God's people in the world of the nations as the respective prophetic layers of transmission present it. One must pose the question of the metahistorical perspective that a prophetic writing exposes. One must do so here, as well as for the final formation, in light of the material coherence of prior literary stages. It is also true that in the formative phase of the prophetic books themselves these concepts were not hard to overlook in the books. However, tradents as well as recipients took an interest in metahistorical confirmation of a position. This interest was apparently directed toward these concepts, as details of the continuations (*Fortschreibungen*) materially demonstrate (see preceding text, page 43 and following, concerning the prophetic view of history). By contrast, the historical work of modern persons is no longer acquainted with these interests and perspectives. Later work must first reconstruct the leading concepts, as with all sources. Above all, later work must expose that which was self-evident at the time. In so doing, one encounters the danger that determining these concepts relating to the flow of metahistorical epochs and stations of meaning can turn into abstract constructs that nullify the text profile. Instead, concepts must incorporate thematic highlights and concrete statements and ideas of the text as an image of God's metahistorical path. Concepts must be checked against tradition-historical findings that precede or coincide with prophetic tradition-historical findings.[81] These types of ultimately assured concepts presented by the book are diachronically relevant in their respective theological contour. Such is true no matter whether one treats them as synonymous findings that were conceivable as a homogenous development, as contrasts, or even as contradictions. The same is also true if these concepts concern findings that compare different orientations (for example, the pilgrimage of the nations and judgment of the nations in Isa 66 and Zech 14). As already suggested, observing conceptional statements of climax and purpose is important,[82] especially those that do not demand a modified continuation on the same level.[83] In our opinion, these conceptional findings of coherence or incoherence inside the same literary entity, in conjunction with literary-critically relevant indices, are ultimately sufficiently reliable to lead to historical, diachronic probes for approaching the subject in part and in whole.

At the end of this initial procedure of collecting and sorting diachronic indicators, one should have a preliminary image of the homogenous material that belongs together and that was arranged together. One should also have a preliminary image of material that is related to it and of totally different material. Naturally, this image is continually correctable. With this image, one can already distinguish material that is characteristic of the course and the inclinations of the statements of the final form from divergent, potentially older material. In so doing, one should particularly attempt to explain whether a writing's designated later material literarily presupposes the older material and is thus incorporated into the transmission for a reaccentuation. Or one should explain whether the later material treats external, independently formed material that is only secondarily inserted.

Ideally, but precisely, in a thorough investigation (taking initial impressions further) the next question is whether and how the material that has been separated and sorted can now plausibly be arranged into older literary stages for the prophetic book under consideration. Thus, the question about the constantly changing relationship of the methods devoted to the text's development (text criticism, literary criticism, redaction criticism) now transitions from the analytically attained findings to the problem of redactional syntheses. Of course, this procedure could also create revisions of the sorting of material according to the interdependence of the approaches. We also cannot proceed from anything certain in this respect (certainly not from datings of text blocks). For this reason, attempting to make these prior literary stages precise in the sense of objectively controlled, heuristic presuppositions of exegetical work requires playing with various historical possibilities of the book's genesis.[84]

Limiting the Historical Possibilities of a Prophetic Book's Genesis

Synthetically Determining Prior Literary Stages of a Prophetic Book by Playing with Various Historical Possibilities of the Book's Genesis

The game that should finally lead to reliable determinations of the prior literary stages of a prophetic book builds upon that which the preceding working process yielded with respect to historical synchronic reading and to the diachronically analytic sorting of various layers of the book's origin. It also presupposes corroboration and testing.

Ideally seen, this game should continue to operate in the realm of the whole of a given prophetic book within a series of prophetic books. One should consistently, step-by-step, inquire back into the respective preceding arenas of a literary prehistory. This challenge, however, pushes the limits of practical execution. If one limits the investigation to subjects that detailed research projects treat, then very different, combinable, partial working fields are also possible. These partial fields are based upon the unavoidable procedures covering the entire book. The development of the prophetic book as a whole may proceed illustratively from these partial working fields. In practice, both types depend upon one another: partial investigations within the book that keep an eye open for the whole book and comprehensive investigations of the whole book that incorporate the partial investigations. Together, they can approach productive determinations for the genesis of the transmission of the prophetic book.

The following examples of partial paths of investigation provide a certain preservation of the continuity of research while seeking to clarify the developing whole. (1) One can treat the relatively oldest texts and text fields after (!) executing the procedures already sketched by working backward from the whole book as we have it.[85] For the most part, these procedures are lacking in the following examples of research. These older texts and text fields were suggested by the procedure of sorting, striving for a plausible picture with respect to the literary beginnings of the book's transmission, and then continuing the search in the growth of the book and its markers up to the final form. In so doing, as we will see shortly, the expectation is not without justification that one can encounter not only the relatively oldest products of transmission, but also the initial impetus for the entire transmission process. Such is the case in the oldest relative text arenas, but also in the sense of the working program suggested here if this impression of small units suggests itself as the most plausible. Such is the case if the impression most likely points into earlier realms for reasons that are self-evident, context independent, and potentially even chronological over against later levels of the book and situations. Here, one would encounter recorded logia from the prophet who provides the name (or an anonymous prophet). Still (and this is what is new in our working program), this impression from processed insight must be critically controlled and cross-checked for the comprehensive, wider transmission process. Thus, the foundational entry must be brought into line with the given material. (2) However, in order to remain with the Isaiah example, one may also choose markedly profiled intervening layers[86] and pivotal transitions (like Isa 10–13, or the particularly difficult Isa 33–40)[87] as working fields to illuminate the book's genesis. (3) Or, working in reverse, one can remain with the supposedly latest layer, the now diachronically ascertained final version, and from there go back to the beginnings.[88] Such would be the suggested and materially indicated path. (4) However, the following fields of investigation on this procedural step could also be chosen, such as: diachronic indicators found in representative text blocks like Isaiah 1,[89] Isaiah 1–11,[90] Isaiah 56–66;[91] diachronic indicators found in the reception of particularly prominent text statements like Isaiah 6;[92] diachronic indicators found in chronological concepts and formulas (which would be particularly interesting for the prophetic view of history);[93] or diachronic indicators found in prominent themes like judgment against Assyria, Babylon, foreign nations, or a world judgment (which may be comprehensive or limited).[94] These fields of investigation can be chosen in order to inquire synthetically about a prior and a later literary history within the book (!) of Isaiah (probing the broader literary presuppositions and contexts). No matter which partial arena one chooses, it is imperative that one not obliterate the given comprehensive literary framework of the (series of) books. Rather, one continually considers the given literary framework that forms the work's horizon.

We do not know in advance how prophetic books arose. Rather, we have only what appears to be the best supposition: a lengthy development that contrasts the self-presentation of the books. For this reason, one plays with the various historical possibilities with the purpose of tracing the prior stages that affect the shaping of this type of book, or potentially even a series of prophetic books. Playing with these possibilities, above all, implies an openness to diverse models of the writing's formation and text growth in the prophetic transmission. In part, previous scholarship already has these models at hand, even though the models were too seldom, or methodologically too late, exposed to concrete testing upon the books as books. We do not yet know whence the macro-shaping of the written prophetic transmission in these books stems, or how the transmission processes occurred. As long as one does not yet know, even if certain types are more probable than others, one must as a rule consider all models of origin that are historically presentable and probable (or even suggestive) according to our knowledge of the material transmission of the book scrolls in antiquity (see the following). This openness must also extend to the fact that just one book could be affected by completely different models among the various prophetic books, but also among the phases of that book's development, phases that follow sequentially in relationship (!) to one another according to procedures already performed. The model one recommends for the respective layers of literarily diachronic reconstruction depends mainly upon determining that character of text fields in their homogenous literary context that could have belonged to the same developmental layer.

In a broad and comprehensive sense, we call the methodological approach that concentrates upon the growth phenomena of these writings the redaction-historical approach.[95] It is the historically synthetic testing of the unity or disunity of the text material as indicated literary-critically. The redaction-historical approach concentrates on the means and intentions, of whatever type, used with the creation of written, literary entities. It can encounter processes of the initial written recording of oral material or in works that existed in written form from the outset. However, it also includes processes that connect and expand existing literary material, whether these processes are large or small in scope. These processes may also concern collection, compilation, or reshaping in a specific type of book redaction (for a part or for the entirety). Only in this last-mentioned case does redaction history turn to the origin and productive growth of literary entities in the sense of a new presentation of a writing (or series of writings) created with literary means and material intentions that convey meaning as a whole. We introduce these diachronic, explanatory models in the following types. They come into question for the growth of prophetic books and their environments. We differentiate them according to the extent of their redactional measures.

Collections and Compilations

It is possible, but not necessary, that this extent could be comparatively small at the beginning of the (respective) transmission. If one explores this possibility, then an explanation of the redactional text levels is of particular interest. Additional growth processes of the text take their starting point from these levels according to the results attained by the probe. By no means must they be the initial material in the development of a prophetic book. It concerns a literary layer in which older material would first have been conveyed. If this proves true, then one stumbles here upon that which could most readily be conceived somewhat later as coming from the named prophet himself or anonymous prophetic figures.

Above all, one should expect to encounter the presuppositions of the transmission, especially previously independent logia or smaller texts, that are now completely processed into the written record. If this common expectation for a prophetic writing, as propagated, is to be demonstrable and not, as often happens, merely upgraded to an apparently certain presupposition, then this determination of small units at the beginning of the transmission processes must satisfy clear criteria that consider this type of text material.[96]

Negatively, one must eliminate the possibility that the formulation of this text material was instigated by literary dependence upon the context, by original book functionality, or by original text-genetic interlacing with a larger literary whole. Positively, for text material that is free from the horizons of (book) context and book functions, one must verify that the oldest core texts can be demonstrated from which the literary growth of the text began. By contrast, the widely preferred criteria of originality are better omitted. The same is true for revelatory formulas, communication formulas, and genre impressions as the decisive argument (in contrast to the euphoric high estimation of form-critical findings). None of these elements transmits unambiguous clues to independent logia that could also have served later tradents for shaping their own contributions. Criteria for the materially coherent homogeneity of this oldest textual building block for a prophetic book are measured by structure, style, distinguishing characteristics of linguistic shaping, and conceptual completion. These elements have their supporting correspondence in the respective original building blocks of the same or comparable prophets.

Still, in the framework of any redaction-historical confirmation that we seek at this point of the process, these oldest textual building blocks are not an independent subject of investigation by themselves. They are important primarily for their recorded form as the beginning of subsequent transmission. In the earliest text layers, one may likely encounter the recording and arrangement of those text elements along with compositional measures and insignificant compilational measures. If the finding exposes a smaller literary whole of this type, then one may assuredly speak of a collection (refer to the analytical procedure beginning on page 111). In this case, one can then inquire about its less explicit indices of meaning that are demonstrated particularly in the arrangement of the logia into a flow.[97]

In this procedural phase, one must once again check (and not exclude from the outset) whether the Isaiah book in general only arose from this type of loosely compiled collection. However, indices already mentioned above do not favor a purely compilational work.

Isolated Expansions with a Narrow Contextual Horizon

Another example of redaction is offered by those text layers that contain older material in the sense just mentioned but that show their internal growth in isolated expansions of a narrow contextual horizon. In this case, the extent of redactional work is even greater. If a text layer exhibits later isolated expansions of older text material as its own current contribution, then it could be integrating genuine prophetic logia which have been commented upon, or even anonymous logia. If so, then one may reconstruct a collection with traces of isolated growth. However, clustered insertions of sayings are more significant in the sequence of text layers presuming one another. In these clusters, the respectively older text material only persists in the immediate literary-contextual horizon, even though these insertions were context dependent upon a written entity from the outset. In this case, one is now assured of encountering isolated continuations in the growth of a writing, without meaning that one can and may speak about a book redaction of a literary whole in the complete sense.[98] However, the reception processes manifest themselves more directly here in contrast to the collection. Literary and conceptual growth criteria also yield clear diachronic layering in the narrow contextual horizon. This layering, together with the absence of book-wide contextual horizons and functions in a literarily developing entity of this kind, constitutes the decisive marker of this type of redactional process. Even in this respect, one must examine whether or not the Isaiah book continued to grow only in clusters by processes enlarging its immediate context. However, such expectations may not be just the pseudo-redaction historical flip-side of the narrow investigation of individual pericopes! One can concretely present this process of partial continuation, expansion, and commentary upon existing sayings, as the insertion of marginal and intralinear notations, as the addition of newly written material in an existing scroll, and, for somewhat more comprehensive textual material, as the affixture of larger material at the end or even at the beginning of the scroll.[99]

The Book-Specific Redactional Model

Along with others, we have concentrated upon a third redaction-historical model for the development and growth of the prophetic books.[100] In this model, the extent of redactional activity is the greatest. We call this type of book development the book-specific redactional model. It is that model that tentatively concedes that the prophetic transmission wants to create and to convey the meaning of comprehensive wholes with developing books. By a cautiously proceeding examination, indicators and corresponding findings in the final formation suggest that this model could even potentially have predominantly determined the prophetic transmission process in the individual writings, or even in a fixed series of writings. This model is more demanding with respect to a characteristic theology of tradition in the transmission process, but it is also more prone to discussion than the other models with respect to its indices and results. It should therefore be considered more closely in the following.

This model takes into account that the transmission does not just wish to convey actualized collections through isolated continuations. Nor does the external text material merely wish to convey combined and isolated compilational works. Rather, this model takes into account thoroughly shaped literary wholes and (a series of) books, whose entire presentation wants to carry and to convey meaning. In this case, decisive growth processes exist in the prophetic writings that intentionally profile literary entities as wholes and continue to shape these entities in the productive processes of reception. These processes presuppose not only that the individual statements in this writing remain current, but that the writing shaped as a book remains capable of bearing meaning in its entirety, when newly accentuated. That which was considered worthy of transmitting in these books would not just have been the full amount of all the individual statements. Rather, it consisted of statements in the frame of a whole that should be conveyed as a literarily and materially formed unit. In this case, the productive processes of reception would be comparable to our phenomenon of the expansion and revision of books in later editions. Naturally, this book-specific model differs in that the process lasted over a longer time, so that it was no longer the author himself who changed the book. Also, it differs especially in that the older text remains authoritatively integrated in the new form, as it corresponds to the status of divinely received prophetic transmission. As mentioned, the idea that this book-forming process occurred just for an initial redaction (while all subsequent material merely constituted isolated expansions without the horizon of the entire book)[101] is a presupposition that cannot be favored as the only possible explanation until one eliminates the alternatives. The text-finding must show whether or not several redactional processes across the whole book also encountered this expanded literary entity as a whole and allowed the book to grow as a book even to the final shaping.

One must certainly emphasize that the concrete examination of this particular book-specific redactional model may not be limited to the usual isolation and profiling of the characteristic formulations of these redactional layers. The question of redaction in general, and here in particular, correctly extends to each part, and by no means just to the new portions of this process. Rather, the approach combines that which is received, or edited, and that which is newly created and newly edited as the connection to a higher unity. Redaction history is thus reception history! One must thus ponder the new intended reading, which is potentially even multiple new readings. One must ponder the new reading of the edited literary entity as a whole in order to discern a redactional process of reception and its noteworthy intended meanings that convey the enriched prophetic writing (or series of writings).[102] The task of the historical synchronic reading in the sense of the coherent reading of the given material is thus repeated on the levels of the prior literary stages of the books. Here one should also trace an intended higher material unity in the entire state of the assertions in a specific phase of literary reception. In this manner one constantly asks the question, How does the book-redactional revision read the processed material? The characteristic redactional formulations related to the edited material certainly form a materially conceptual context among themselves.[103] They do not, however, form their own extractable, independent literary source, because they constantly relate to a given literary entity that was and is qualified to provide meaning. They also process the productive adaptation of that literary entity. Instead of inquiring about the narrow horizon of original individual logia or inquiring only about the redactional formulations for the isolated entity, one must inquire about the respective layers. How do they provide meaning in the larger literary contexts? What is the redactional manner of reading the flow of the edited literary whole (whether an individual book or a series of books)?

It is self-evident with this model that one must also meaning-fully present the individual material within the larger framework of the whole, even for the broad reception and concentration on the alignment of those statements considered essential. Also, the shape in which the book is presented has essential significance, because these statements expressly record the continuations, overlappings, accentuations, expansions, and limitations of statements in the book's flow. In this model, several elements play an impressive role as components of a higher material unity. One should follow the structure of the ascertained literary entity, the flow of reading, the literary signals, and the material signals. Last but not least, one should perceive clues about the complexity of the structure and the statements. One may now detect indices in the developmental layers of this whole that already created discussion for the historical synchronic reading of the final formation. One must exclude the fact that this flow is nothing more than an accident or a loose compilation. If this model produces a positive finding, one must plausibly show that this text flow of a conveyed, older literary entity is intentionally reached despite the connection to the existing literary material. One must show that this text flow is consciously reached and consciously oriented to the wording and position of the statements so that it conveys a material concern for the literary whole. As the probing phase can show, book specific redaction is particularly served by compositional measures and newer, prominent insertions that are generally consciously placed for this purpose. These insertions served the formation of older "books" before the prophetic book as we now have it.

To begin with, observations based upon two foundational questions aid one when examining this model:

(1) How does one delimit the diachronic book layers that were preliminarily ascertained? This question is particularly important because the beginning and end could include essential reading clues. In the final formation, the delimitations are given. How does one find the beginning and the purpose of the flow of reading in the background of these older books? The respective literary end of these redactional entities frequently can be recognized by competing designs of the completion of salvation at the end, together with preparatory redactional references at positions in the writing (or series) that point to what follows. These preparatory references appear at earlier positions all the way to the beginning. In Jeremiah, these designs particularly lack clarification in the positioning of Jeremiah 30–33, while elsewhere they are displayed especially at the end of the whole (Isa 60:1–63:6; Isa 65 and following; Ezek 33–39 [40–48]; Zech 9–14 and Mal). From that point, one must discover questions about framing inclusions, questions about the presupposed condition of the text, and clues to the beginning of the literary entity.

(2) What should be presupposed and what should be scrutinized as the practical intention of this occasional book-redactional presentation at the hand of the reception by a professional readership perceiving these signals? This question is directed to nothing

other than considering the given entity, as was done with the historical synchronic reading. If the book-redactional model should prove successful, the readership should be guided by the flow of reading the whole against any cross-sectioning and overlapping. These elements are unavoidable when a transmitted work preserves an older state of the text. Also from these books, the readership of earlier literary stages of the final formation should especially recognize the series of metahistorical stations of the intention and reaction of YHWH on his path with Israel and the nations, especially from the Assyrian period into the future completion of salvation. These stations maintain the people of God at the time of redaction and the time of reception. The readership achieves this knowledge and this confirmation of the position based upon the authoritative revelatory source of prophetic tradition. The readership concentrates and makes essential the history of experience and the history of the hope of God's people in light of the true underlying cause and the leadership of YHWH's prophetically proclaimed activity. It should also perceive the particular orientation for Israel as the intended effect in the course of time.[104] Literarily delimitable entities express a specific, redactionally established, coherent metahistorical concept, even behind the final text. This fact is the most important material sign for the existence and coherence of redactions that form books and are capable of bestowing meaning.

As we have already discussed beginning on page 17, the image of these concepts presented by book redactions and offered for reception is an image metahistorically envisioned and concentrated. It is self-evidently not the same image that historical reconstructions of the history of Israel would develop, especially those reconstructions limited to the history of events. Rather, the image treats an essential concentration of historical realities. It treats "history" as seen when accompanied by tradition. It treats history as it can be experienced now, by looking backward and by looking forward to that which one can hope. Directed experiences (!) of events, but also fears and hopes, are the essential communicative subjects of the explanatory perspectives that are divinely and prophetically initiated!

One can see this picture in Isaiah and the XII in the adoption of the experiences and fears with respect to the powers of the Diadochoi. As mentioned, we have accepted the rereading of Isaiah in the Hellenistic period. Thus, when seen from the perspective of God, one can follow the line of the nations in world history that accompanies the expounded Judah-Jerusalem theme in Isaiah. "Assyria" and "Egypt" remain as powers threatening Israel from the neo-Assyrian period until the Diadochoi period, a lengthy unit of divine objects of activity and Israelite experience. In contrast to the Babylonian exile, which dominates Deutero-Isaiah, the fact that "Assyria" and "Egypt" can be thus explained as the originating point of the diaspora in 11:11–16, 27:12–13, and 52:4,[105] as well as indirectly in Isaiah 34–35, is not just a later addition that now considers the Assyrian deportations and the Egyptian refugees of the Babylonian time. All of these statements relate to the context in the current phase of the still impending universal judgment. In fact, only deliverance from "Assyria" and "Egypt" is mentioned, while in spite of the great Babylonian exile, no mention is made of deliverance from Babylon. This fact must reflect the power constellation of the Seleucids and Ptolemies as Zechariah 10[106] confirms, and concerns "Assyria" as the reception of Isaiah in Daniel shows.[107] Certainly, when seen from the perspective of God in that late period of the Isaiah transmission, God's people also remain in the metahistorical situation of the Persian period according to the flow of Isaiah. The Persian period immediately transcends into universal judgment (on the Greek power). The people remain metahistorically in the Persian period because the intention of YHWH for this situation is revealed for the period of Cyrus (Isa 41 and following), which they had already begun to experience as realized (for example, the downfall of the Babylonian empire) and which would come to fruition in the completion of salvation as the connections of Isaiah 56–66 to statements in Isaiah 40 and following show. Other factors are also combined with this background perspective of YHWH. Potentially corresponding experiences were seen after the fact as a continuation of the events of 587 B.C.E. (Isa 63:7–64:11).[108] The current offenses of the late period were seen as similar to that of the preexilic period (Isa 56–59), and the judgment against Babylon (Isa 13) and Edom (Isa 34; 63:1–6) was seen as a beginning that would be completed in the future universal judgment according to the intention of YHWH. Thus, simultaneous periodic elements of chronologically comprehensive decisions of YHWH made known to the prophet should be deduced, starting with an initial historical realization (Assyria and Egypt in the eighth century, judgment on Babylon and Edom after the sixth century), then making their way through time until the completion of salvation. These elements should be deduced from the large flow of the book of Isaiah (together with Jeremiah and Ezekiel, and corresponding to the sequence of books in the Twelve) as H. Barth already demonstrated for a portion of the book with what he named as the "Assyria Redaction."[109] A similar case could potentially exist in the prior literary stages of Isaiah from the Hellenistic and the Persian periods, or even earlier.[110]

The recipients should correlate and explain their concrete experiential history and their perspectives with the threads of this chronologically lengthy, periodically realized execution of YHWH's plan, as Isaiah proclaims them in his book and its prior stages. This way of reading prophetic books was apparently intended for themselves. All chronological formulas ("on that day," "in the coming days," "at the end of the days," and so forth)[111] should self-evidently be taken metahistorically very precisely as differentiating references to the same final situation. The late, five-part literary division of the Psalter may have been intended to be read very similarly.[112] On the other hand, the final form of Isaiah appears demonstrably to have related the royal ideas in Isaiah 9, 11, and 32 to positive figures of the past (preexilic?) time. Hezekiah and Josiah come under special consideration.[113] The concluding chapters recognize no messianic king in the completion of salvation or, except Cyrus, in the reading flow since Isaiah 41. Instead, the final chapters royally qualify the servant of God, and Zion.

This redaction-historical possibility of the book's genesis, in a sense that encompasses the book, is directed toward the prophetic book as a book and its notable comprehensive shaping. This approach has been bypassed for too long, even though it should be foundational. More than any other approach, it begins with the shaping of the literarily existing whole. It believes that one should scrutinize this whole and its prior stages for the conveying of material perspectives that shaped the book. It primarily strives for explanations in this respect. Only concrete work can show whether the book-specific redactional possibility and its layers of origin can be proven on the prophetic text of the book, or whether it falters when it meets the text. This task, however, is unavoidable and, in the present situation of the discipline, urgently required. The potentially formative influence of these measures on the transmission cannot remain unconsidered. The fact that this work must currently concentrate entirely upon the elementary explanation should not discourage one from this task of asking which text phenomena can be seen as redactional measures in general and how existing material and adapting material relate to one another in the growth of prophetic tradition.

How does one summarize the essential indices to which one must pay attention? Reference points can be deduced for this book-specific redaction-historical model that can plausibly limit the various possibilities of a book's genesis. These reference points can be deduced in the given text of the final formation as well as in the preliminary diachronic sorting. One should explain this sorting in this ongoing procedural phase. Perhaps one may use the following questions which were already used in preceding discussion for the final form and for the probing of its diachronic nature.

(1) Guiding lines of thought. Do recognizable indicators exist in the flow of reading that were carefully created for the recipients of that time (!) and compete with presumed prior stages as well as the existing literary whole? Do these indicators generally present this flow as an intentionally structured entity? Do they point to meta-historical intentions of meaning for the respective whole that are expressed by the flow of this whole, perhaps by superscriptions, by designated organizations and breaks, by thematic or chronological-epochal blocks, by networks of formulas, or by elements of a material inclination?[114]

(2) Bridges and blocks. Are there macrostructural compositional phenomena[115] as well as narrower or wider material frameworks, or elements that structure the text flow that were created for older writings? Did these elements exist before the final formation and their intended meaning in light of the whole? The text material can potentially be of older origin. For example, instead of a flood of inclusions of individual words that are not capable of strong statements, could one find macro-inclusions in Isaiah that form the book's structure and materially lead the reading (for example between Isa 13 and following and Isa 24–27, or 34) or between the beginning and the different metahistorical concluding texts at the end of the book?[116]

(3) Beacons. As already ascertained with the fluid observations about the diachronic nature, does a prophetic writing and its presumed prior stages also contain newly written, redactional formulations that have a wider literary horizon whose receptions should also serve the whole? Here, the character of programmatic valence for specific texts plays an essential role. Do larger or smaller

texts, or even prolonged text-fields, exist that were not formulated independently and are not understandable in their own right, including images and metaphors that, from the outset, are related to and fed by the context? Do these texts thus have an older comprehensive horizon of a writing in view, or even an older series of writings?[117] Do these texts serve and process this older context? By their positioning within the whole, do they at least wish to shape the subsequent literary material for this whole as a literary and metahistorical flow of reading by its placement inside the book? Do these texts potentially even wish to shape a material structure transcending the entirety with material inclination that then appears as the goal of the whole in the text's concluding position? Do texts exist that, at least in the transmitted form, are not explained solely as the recording of older individual material? Instead, do these texts mutually presuppose and relate to one another? Also, are these texts not just focused upon the immediate context and the close context, or are they instead focused upon the larger literary whole and its intended structural parts, especially in the linguistic shaping, in the positioning inside the text-flow of the book, and in the exegetically profiled, theological function?

The investigation of texts inside their current literary context is the absolutely urgent task with respect to the text's genesis, the material profile, the intended flow of reading of this context, and its possible conveying of meaning. This urgent task must recognize these beacons in the landscape of the book within the framework of the procedural step addressed here. The prejudices of current scholarly hypotheses must yield to this task. If the evaluation of different possibilities in the realm of the texts in question proves that these markers constitute such statements, then one must reckon with book texts in the complete sense of the word.[118] One must thus reckon with redactional texts for the book as characteristic formulations for the redaction of the entire book that were essentially created in and for a literary whole. One must also reckon with texts that were always determined expressly by the well-placed position and formulation across the entire book that was context-receptive and referential. These texts continued to write literary entities as such in order to present books as meaningful wholes. Nothing about these texts forces one to go behind them. They never existed apart from a literary context of the book or even books. These texts constitute redactional texts in the strict functional sense of a book. They only serve the productive reception and communication of a whole prophetic book. They represent specially formulated elements of comprehensive literary layers of processing. If these book-texts are differentiated as conceptually incompatible, they form competing literary-structural bridges in their literary surroundings. One thus has cause for inquiring into various redactional book shapings and to investigate their character and their relationship to one another. For all book-texts of this type one can say that their literary horizon is the entire book at the time, or even a series of books. Their function as a whole is the material profiling, accentuation, and alignment of a continuum that is metahistorically oriented toward a reading context. The chief criterion for determining these texts is that, in their received form, their original relationship to the book and their function in the book (the framework from which they can be understood at all) is suggested as the most plausible explanation. The constitutive contextual networking, instructional nature, dependence, and material functionality of these texts and these redactional layers for a greater whole therefore play an essential role.

In addition to the genetic text analysis, the following are especially important as certifying questions in order to encounter these specific formulations of a redactional process. How does a redactional layer, and its particular measures, stand in the flow of the reading of a larger whole? Does this redactional layer have its own task that is compositionally comprehensive, or does it refer backward or forward? Does it convey material coherence, successive context, or material inclination for the whole in this flow of reading? Does it arrange the flight path for this whole? Are the empty spaces and their periodic incomprehensibility (even at that time) explained by this context? Do the different conceptional aspects of the purpose provide meaning in the context of these comprehensive, diachronically diverse literary wholes? Can the respective commonalities of the redactional layers in a whole be conceived as consciously intended, redactional interrelationships? Are these interrelationships significantly indicated linguistically or by the material adoption of the reference contexts? Can one recognize content-oriented references backward in these literary interrelationships that want to form balancing statements, limiting modifications, or continuing specifications for another metahistorical station or phase? And it is important to ask for the result of sequential multistaged redactional measures: Do diversely accentuated measures exist that were originally mutually exclusive for these text revisions across the entire book?

If these book-redactional measures and specific formulations do exist, then the readership is thus instructed to consider the literary whole as a material context that conveys meaning and ultimately is directed toward a purpose. Constitutive elements and rules for this phenomenon cannot be fixed in advance as prior decisions for paths of investigation.[119] Rather, one must derive these elements from work on concrete texts. From this background, the constitutive elements and rules are summarized and systematized in this essay.

Recognizing Book-Redactional Text Material

In prophetic research, book-redactional texts, their networking inside a literary whole, and their revised grasp of the edited material are new and still unfamiliar phenomena. Therefore, in the following, we turn more specifically to the question of their recognizability on the basis of our specific investigations of Isaiah.

Certain texts come under consideration as potential book-texts whose character now requires a clearer explanation. Their book-redactional character is not determined from the outset. Rather, various possibilities must be discussed. However, this book-redactional character always concerns texts that demonstrate notable commonalities with other texts in the same writing (or series of writings). In so doing, these texts proceed beyond coincidences or general similarities of the tradition that influenced religious language and topics of the time. They also proceed beyond the character of an individual prophet's specific assertions. Commonalities of a receptional nature characterize these texts, and careful exegetical text comparison can plausibly show these references are not just potential, but conscious and intentional references.

These references can be of different sorts. They can be directed toward statements in the same literary entity that are of the same literary type, material profile, and functionality within the book (book-redactional texts of the same literary layer). These references, however, can also draw upon statements that already exist literarily, and that must be older than the referencing text because of the material and formal differences in the reception. However, these older texts must be receptionally integrated in this way (dependency of so-called disciple texts upon the [literary] transmission material of the master, as one often explains Trito-Isaiah; dependency of small continuations upon the existing literary entity; or book-redactional texts related to the newly revised literary entity as a whole). The heuristic signs of these referentially dependent texts are also often mentioned in the discipline.[120] Even the catalogue of criteria from literary science concerning the phenomenon of "intertextuality" can sharpen one's awareness of references, but not for their rationale, because they cannot be not used timelessly.[121] Rather, the references must be considered based upon the character of the historical subject of prophetic books of ancient Israel. Thus, one must especially call to mind several things: the referring texts have a pre-canonically authoritative character. These referring texts are even located in the reading context of the same writing (or series of writings) of this level. The referring tradents are not oriented to a public reading audience to which the references would be directed, but toward their own professional reception culture. To the extent a reference should remain recognizable to precise reception, these tradents are independent and self-productive.

In the concrete work, as mentioned, one should first ascertain that references are not commonalities of another type between texts (see the earlier text, p. 34). Since designated quotes are not expected anywhere for the specific recognition of later literary references,[122] the most important elements are the reinterpreting adoption, or materially changing adoption, of characteristic, or even exclusive, word associations and word ensembles, supported by materially plausible, continuing, or contrary corresponding contexts. In so doing, several more referential texts come under discussion from various findings. Once one has ascertained the receptional character of a referring text to older literary texts, then with a plausible correspondence of context one must also take into account the commonalities in expounded individual words,[123] stylistic manifestations, structural parallelism, and the parallelism of flow. One must even take account of conscious adoption in material lines of thought in the case of booktexts (reading a book's assertions forms the very next framework of reception!). One must confirm dependent commonalities of the formulation as intentional references especially so that the direction of the reference can be explained and thereby a material intention be offered for the adoption. Doing so enables a judgment as to whether the donating text derives from the receiver (specific formulations on the same level) or whether the donating text is older and serves as the basis for a reaction. Thus, even a silent material reference can play an important role for the context already offered to the donating passage or offered later in the same literary entity. Conversely, the material that was de facto adopted, over against that which was not incorporated, can show what required particularly receptive explication from the donating text. Atypically recurring vocabulary between donating statements and receiving statements have no significance as such. However, with further ascertained reference, this recurring vocabulary can show that the receiving statements are also connected to the linguistic world of the donating text, potentially even intentionally imitating it, since these statements actually allow the transmitted prophets to speak further.

Various possibilities should be discussed for the origin of these receptional texts. The fact that one encounters redactional book-texts is actually only one of several cases that come into question.

One can encounter oral or written individual texts that owe their formulation to reliance upon older logia or literary entities. Such is the traditional model of Trito-Isaiah as a product of logia from a disciple of Deutero-Isaiah. Donner and Lau form a modified suggestion reckoning with scribal prophetic texts.[124]

One can also encounter receptional texts in favor of a writing that solely served the compilation of existing literary material, or that limits itself to isolated expansion oriented toward the immediate context. One can also consider glosses in the realm of the formative development of the book.

However, if these receptional texts constitute redactional book-texts directed toward the whole, then additional criteria must be fulfilled in addition to the criteria already mentioned. These texts are literarily and materially functional within the book (position, composition, inclusion, structuring the flow of reading for the whole). They depend upon the context (in that they are not understandable by themselves but explained by the flow of the book or context). Or these texts correspond homogeneously to other book-functional measures and texts (referential character, reference to the structure of the whole). These texts can be newly accentuated later than the older formative manifestations of the book of a literary and material nature. Or they can mark intentional lines of reading through a writing or series of writings (accentuating, completing, limiting, expanding). These texts thus refer to texts across the book within the same literary entity. They explicate the book's concept if the donated and received text materials are specific formulations of the same redaction. They function as continuations when they react to older preexisting material of the book by limiting contrasting or complementary sayings to another metahistorical phase (for example, judgment/salvation), or by completing and actualizing the same phase (for example, the corresponding salvation of the return, Zion, and life in the land of salvation). They explicitly overlap purpose

statements that older text layers considered sufficient and limit them
to steps toward the completion of salvation (for example, the homage of the nations before Zion in Isaiah, or the exclusivity of salvation for the [first] Babylonian exile in Jeremiah). These texts exist
completely in the book-context of the literary whole in which they
stand. They potentially consider the literary position of the donating text in the flow of the book. They are really only understandable in their own position and in statements within this framework
because they essentially constitute this framework as a materially
structured whole. The empty spots (*Leerstellen*) are even filled by
this book-context and are thus not explainable as "a small unit."
Together with similar coherent texts in this entity, they have a specific function. They structure and reaccentuate the flow of reading
for the whole, over against the older state of the text. The references
often show this function across the entire book. They also often combine the character and the alignment of the parts of the whole or of
the whole itself and thus provide the authoritatively intended reading instruction for that which follows or precedes in the framework
of the whole. The presupposition of the book and the functionality
within the book for these references also exclude the fact that someone separately formulated these references solely in the knowledge
of the statements of the book. Moreover, it insures from the outset
that the references are formulated in and for the book.

If redactional book-texts become plausible in a literary entity
according to these criteria that revise the context of a book and a
text, only then can additional observations appear. One must mainly
inquire about signs that show whether the formulation of these book-texts reflects and wants to bring to mind not just concrete references,
but also the entirety or parts of the presupposed flow of reading
with its word ensembles, explicated individual concepts, and even
its content where a formulation is not adopted (in Isa 66, for example, the כבוד or נחם concepts of the preceding part of the book).
Do these book-texts revise by accentuation or clarify the book's flow
of reading in anticipatory references or in references backward?
References of this type are seen as implausible by themselves. They
only become plausible when the layer of book-redactional measures
can be assured.

With their narrowly confined objections, Lau and Aejmelaeus
have not considered the level of inquiry in the realm of Trito-Isaiah
in general that is concerned with the shaping and reception of books
as text-flows capable of bearing meaning, to say nothing of their
sparse criteria. There has still been far too little discussion in prophetic

research dedicated to Trito-Isaiah about the fact that referencing texts could be primarily book-redactional in nature within the flow of reading of a writing (or series of writings). There has been too little discussion concerning these texts. Or when they are discussed, the discussion does not adequately take the necessary historical and diachronic precision into account.[125] Our examination suggests that, at least with respect to the latter stages of transmission, a whole series of texts in Isaiah 1–55[126] and in Isaiah 56–66[127] most likely constitute book-texts that owe their existence to the redactional growth of the book. In addition to other texts in the Twelve, one should include Zechariah 9–14 and Malachi with their characteristic position at the end of literary whole.[128] One can also find signs of parallel book-shapings in the exilic and early postexilic period in *Isaiah and the *Twelve.[129] One can find signs of successive book-shapings and their structurings in Jeremiah,[130] and signs of a multiplicity of originally mutually exclusive references in Ezekiel[131] that evidently structure the book but overlap one another. In these groundbreaking investigations, numerous examples of the methodological delimitation of book-texts are found that adapt older literary wholes and create newer continuations of literary wholes while structuring a book literarily and receiving the book materially.

Only one who places tenacious prejudices from the outset against these newly required inquiries can judge the potentially larger extent of these book-texts as a counterargument in comparison to the compilational measures and the isolated expansions of the immediate context. For the reasons already mentioned, if specific text-fields as a whole should be classified as redactional book-texts, then simultaneously the originality, creativity, and innovative nature of these texts cannot be deemed as an indicator to the contrary. Rather, one must reexamine the negative, preexisting understandings about the productive development of the book in the writings of the Hebrew Bible. Corresponding qualities certainly show themselves repeatedly in the external reception of scripture within the intertestamental sources, such as *Jubilees* 1,[132] *1 Enoch,* and Qumran. Corresponding measures could have been and must already have been possible for the internal reception processes of the Old Testament in the redactions. We have suggested that Isaiah 35 arose from the start as a redaction text with a book function.[133] To the extent that this suggestion has withstood scrutiny, one can see from this chapter how creatively and originally these tradents worked who were revising the book.[134]

However, one must once again stress that even the book-specific model of redaction is not a starting point for deciding in advance about the classification of the interrelationships of formulations. Rather, this model represents only one of several possibilities that result from text observations if it offers the most plausible explanation of the text's genesis. This possibility suggests itself when one repeatedly finds these redactional passages on the same literary layer of a writing. These passages have been prepared for the book and point to the book's context. This possibility is suggested when these passages show the condition and extent of the redactional entities by structuring and processing the context. It is suggested when they establish large and partial inclusions and when they establish composite sections that serve the entire writing of which it is a part. This possibility suggests itself when these passages furnish the flow of reading for the whole with a transcending profile and material inclinations for the reception of older text material. Thus, these passages display a way of reading that forces itself upon the continued reading from the beginning of the book, across redactional, programmatic texts, to the end of the book. In so doing, that reading potentially clarifies suspected isolated additions as book-redactional measures. If this possibility is suggested with judicious, explanatory power, in comparison with other models of origin, then on the whole one has a reliable foundation for inquiring into the intended redactional profile.

Characterizing the Book-Specific Redactional Model

The question of the redactional profile of the meaningful shape of the book of prophetic transmission asks about the intended theological and metahistorical assertion productively conveyed by a literary whole that grows from the old and the new. This question asks about potentially intended entities of meaning for the writings (or series of writings). In response, one must determine that the desires of these statements literarily and materially constitute a higher unity of older, revised material and the contemporary, revising material in the presentation and arrangement of the whole (!) text flow. One can only accentuate again and again that redactions exist not only from layers of their own new formulations, but they exist in a new reading of the revised whole!

Since these redactions process and actualize literarily preexisting material, the linguistic evidence offers an ambiguous sign, other than perhaps in characteristic formulations in the Deuteronomistic nature of Deuteronomy-Kings or the characteristic formulations of the evangelists. The coherence of a redactional layer is necessarily a material and conceptual coherence, not necessarily a linguistic coherence. The redactionally metahistorical concept can be expressed, indeed should be expressed, as necessary by borrowing upon the language of the immediate context being processed or by bundling lines of thought from widely divergent referential texts (and contexts). Moreover, this concept can be presented predominantly by compositional measures on older material. Once again, one must accentuate those elements that are decisive for characterizing the measures and formulations of a redaction: the book's functionality and the articulation of the same concept in part or in whole. The linguistic setting, by contrast, may be shaped by characteristic linguistic signs of this redaction. However, the linguistic setting is primarily determined by the formulation of existing orientational texts in the same literary entity. These existing texts are thus recognizably and referentially adopted. In addition, they are re-accented redactionally. Thus, in addition to the revised literary entity, the donating material can itself be taken from the wider literary realm of the authoritative series of writings in which this entity stands. Even this perspective is not provided by unbridled established "canonical" intertextuality. It can call upon noteworthy indicators in the current state of the prophetic books in addition to the chaining of books in the Twelve shown by Nogalski. As a result, in the Twelve, the respective state of the totality of the books is taken into account, the Twelve especially oriented toward Isaiah and this series of books plays a role in the realm of Isaiah-Jeremiah-Lamentations-Ezekiel. At the same time, or in close proximity, synonymous redactions of the series of prophetic books thus become the subject of their own investigation.[135] Since the late Persian period, an authoritative series of books existed that included Joshua-Kings and the preceding Torah. This series stood before the prophetic books.[136] The references of the growing prophetic books to this group of texts should be incorporated into the inquiry of the redactional shaping of the large literary complex, especially in the Torah.[137] Relationships that Bosshard-Nepustil and Schmid have demonstrated in their dissertations about Isaiah, Jeremiah, and the Twelve, especially relationships to the Joseph story, Exodus, Deuteronomy, and Joshua-Kings, invite one to consider further these orientations to a precanonical, authoritative series of books.

We should conclude with two warnings not to confuse the discipline's traditional observational method with the receptional view of that time. It is self-evident that, on the level of redactional reception, one should not inquire about the historically mediated original meaning of the older referential material that we mean today. Rather, one should inquire into its receptive meaning appropriated as authoritatively valid at the time of the redaction. We already indicated as much beginning on page 17. At the same time, our historically-genetic perspective, with its traditionally controlling interest in the original logia, should not erroneously lead one to conclude that only original logia continued to be explicated in the later processes of reception. The developing prophetic writings perceive the prophets as prophets transmitted in a book, and they received the given literary entity in this way. These developing writings encountered the prophets in these books and only in these books. Today's theological consideration of the reception process in the prophetic books is directed beyond the self-presentation of the books to the historical course of the literary development. For this reason, one naturally focuses interest upon the movement from the original meaning of the older material to its receptive meaning in the productive redactions of the subsequent period.

Seen as a whole, the book-specific redaction model evaluates and processes text material under the impression that prophetic books have potentially developed in multiple processes of rereadings and multiple provisions of meaning as books. In so doing, a tradition process of preservation and adaptation takes place that concerns the continuing validity of prophetic transmission over time. This tradition process does not subsequently introduce new prophets. Rather, the prophet providing the name remains presumed as the meaning of his traditions unfolds for later periods.[138] One can most readily imagine these expanding revisions that comprise entire writings in the course of the regularly required retranscription of the whole scroll(s) as the standard copy.[139] In the pre-synagogal time, these scrolls were still entirely in the hands of professional tradents. These tradents primarily continued to assure the tradition, as shown by the remarkably detailed knowledge of the wording of the entire text behind the redactional processes.[140]

The book-redactional model is currently in the phase of examination. In the foreground stands a basic question: What measures and which portions of the text of prophetic books are best explained by this model? Extended questions continue: How should a prophetic writing be read as a whole and in the details of its concrete statements? What about the redactionally accentuated material flows when reading the respective state of the entire text of a prophetic writing (or series of prophetic writings)? One asks the no less instructive question about the type and means of internal self-exegesis that a writing intends. And one asks about the character of the reception process in redactional references inside a book. These questions have only begun. To us it appears that after the Isaiah studies in the recent period, the insights of Jeremias, Nogalski, and Bosshard-Nepustil (among others) into networks in the Twelve and the insights of Schmid for Jeremiah offer promising beginnings that try a certain kind of investigation in prophetic books and their prior stages. For example, for the intended reading flow in the book of Job and its internal references that are indicated but simultaneously held open, this kind of investigation has been considered self-evident for a long time.[141]

Examining the Counterarguments of the Results and Chronological Reconstruction of the Genesis of the Prophetic Book

Material Assurances and Historical, Synthetic Counterexaminations

Ideally, after playing with various diachronic possibilities, one can process a clear image of the literary development of a prophetic writing (or series of writings). Ancient Near Eastern analogies and concrete material[142] must be incorporated into this image, especially the vivid scroll production[143] from Qumran.[144] This image should be capable of consensus to a high degree, in contrast to the multiple suggestions of research to this point because it best accounts for the concrete text realities. We must once again reiterate that these mediated phases must by no means always treat comprehensive productive book redactions in the complete sense. Even literarily and materially less articulated phases like collections, compilations, compositions of preexisting material already formulated, as well as isolated marginal expansions, can all be considered in the text-finding during the developmental phases. The decision depends upon the text-finding as one sifts through the most appropriate possibilities.

We attempt to show that this processed image of the literary development of a prophetic writing (or series of writings) is constructed as the return trip from the given material into the beginnings. However, this image, as tiresome as it is to process, must also expose itself to self-critical suspicion: Is the most plausible reconstruction of a literary-historical process just the consequence of the particular dynamic of an exegetical approach? It therefore appears to us that one cannot avoid the historical, synthetic counter-examination when processing the text-findings in a suggested model to explain the lengthy diachronic transmission impulses. Examination must now flow in the opposite direction once again, from the mediated initial phases of the book's transmission to the final form. In our opinion that image attains stability and the power to convince only when it is once again subsequently cross-checked from the opposite direction. If necessary, the image should be modified or corrected by asking whether the process of growth one has developed is also illuminating as a movement of transmission from the literary beginnings to the formation of the final form. Also, can the image be supported by parallel manifestations in the prophetic corpus through historical indicators and indicators from the history of theology through the receptional effects of the phases in other writings (especially Psalms, Wisdom, and the Chronicler's history)? Last but not least, exploring the preliterary stages as the impetus of the book's transmission should be included with special consideration in this counterexamination so that the thoroughly investigated *traditio* does not lose sight of the *traditum* with which everything began.[145] The question is also asked for redactional layers. Does a literary *traditum* suffice for their origin? Was that *traditum* read in light of new challenges and consequently reedited and supplemented? Or at the time of reception does a particular prophetic activity stand in the background that is condensed in redactional processes? Clear indications and criteria for material preceding the redaction would of course be indispensable to answer these questions. They depend closely upon others regarding how one concretely imagines the process of tradition in the prophetic transmission. After inquiring into the prophetic transmission inside the Old Testament as a productive process of reception, one must ask about the higher material unity and the intended agreement beyond the individual book. This question should be asked for the series of prophetic books in their growth and finally for the larger corpus and the Nebiim in connection to the Torah in the second century B.C.E.[146]

From Relative Dating to Absolute Dating of the Book's Genetic Stages

Dating the developmental stages of the prophetic books is an unpleasant problem. To this point, the precise suggestions we have made regarding Trito-Isaiah and the final formations of Isaiah and the Twelve[147] have been received rather skeptically[148] by the discipline. However, the suggestions are not frivolous. They have been reached in a methodically considered procedure.

The investigated literary layers in the development of a prophetic writing (or series of writings) can of course first only be brought into a relative chronological order, having been cross-checked with possible historical text indicators and text indicators from the history of theology. We must evaluate this order against the received process of reception of the literary layers. Only on this basis are precise absolute chronological datings finally possible, or even possible to discuss.[149] They represent the attempt to understand the literary finding and its profile in connection with concrete historical challenges. The formulations of the texts seldom offer unambiguous historical criteria for determining their time of origin, and one cannot recognize a satisfactorily concrete image for dating from the internal circumstances of Israel, based upon the attitude of the sources, especially in the time after Cyrus.[150] For these reasons, one must especially examine whether or not the relative literary sequence of layers can be plausibly linked with external challenges and experiential constellations in this respect.

For example, four considerations guided our suggestions for dating the late phases in the development of Isaiah and the XII.[151] (1) Not least important by any means, the literary phases show themselves in the perspectival changes toward the nations in the metahistorical final events. In this respect, Isaiah and the XII show very noteworthy agreements in the succeeding steps regarding attitudes toward God's people in the metahistorical final phase. Because of Zechariah 9, these steps begin in the Alexandrian period.[152] (2) In particular, coming after Zechariah 9, Zechariah 10:9–11 points toward the Diadochan period with its mention of the diaspora from "Assyria" and "Egypt." This layer can be correlated with a corresponding literary layer in Isaiah. This layer already provided a date in the same period based upon internal indicators of this perspective.[153] (3) The broader step from summary judgment against the nations in a series of oracles against foreign nations to total universal judgment with cosmic dimensions is, at the earliest, a reaction to the threatening breakup of the experience of world order in the Persian period that continued into the Alexandrian period.[154] (4) For the surmised experiential reactions in the late prophetic gradation of tradition, one can specify external challenges worthy of discussion, partially even characterized in individual references.[155]

Naturally, the text formulations of prophetic transmission do not freely provide precise references to their time of origin.[156] This situation differs from Daniel 11. The later formulations lack these references. Especially for the question of dating, one must follow graduated indexes. However, even these precise conclusions appear quite possible to us for the phases of the growth of prophetic books in light of existing or nonexisting networks.[157]

Inquiry into the Preliterary Orally Transmitted Material in the Prophetic Book

Naturally even today, investigation of the origin of prophetic books has not been exhausted with the clarification of the diachronic processes for the written layers. We have attempted to pave the way for this clarification in the preceding discussion. One may credit the prophetic transmission process as much as one wishes and attribute as much as one must to this process. However, the original initiating impulse toward prophetic transmission did not begin with the transmission of the comprehensive process of tradition of scribal prophecy. Rather, it began with prophecy. Often, prophetic work apparently resulted from oral communication, either in response to inquiry or by spontaneous initiation.[158] The images of an oral prophetic work (especially those presented in Isaiah, Jeremiah, Ezekiel, Hosea, Amos, and Micah) are essentially quite reliable, because the analysis that has been conducted, even in the sense we have suggested, points to individual texts whose origin is best understood in this framework. One can by no means exclude the possibility that this work originated from oral communication procedures. Nor can one exclude the possibility that this prophetic work, only secondarily recorded in written form, entered the growth of prophetic writings (or series of writings). Later, one should especially examine those places where, instead of redactional measures concerning the book, the diachronic investigation encounters measures relating to the collection, compilation, or composition of secondary arrangement and accentuation of old text material. The problem of the original "small units" continues to remain on the table.

However, these smallest building stones of the books do not concern every portion of the text. Rather, in contrast to older assumptions, they concern considerably less material. The continuing productive transmission, which has been overlooked for too long, once again claims its own space. Moreover, small units that have been recorded in written form, but that can be deduced as having an earlier oral form, must be proven on their own. They must fulfill clear criteria of internal structural and material coherence, sufficiency, and independence from the literary context.[159] We have already spoken about this when explaining the oldest literary layers of a prophetic book (see pp. 88–89). In principle, every prophetic text should be examined to see whether it owes its origin to the impetus of transmission or to the productive process of continuing transmission. One must also remember that the productive tradents maintain the style of the existing literary material. They can mold their own formulations into the shape by revelatory formula of arranged sections that function like individual logia. They can form or expand inclusions that look like original material![160] If, after reasoned exclusion of alternative genetic models, one advances to a condition of recorded words that were, however, originally expressed orally, then this condition can actually lead to an original, personal profile of the prophet providing the name or, if necessary, even to anonymous prophets integrated into the book. One does so by evaluating homogeneous agreements between those texts stylistically, tradition-receptively, and conceptually. Doing so can also allow one to reconstruct an image of the prophetic activity itself within the prescribed limits. This work may even include the initial record by the prophet himself. One should carefully consider whether the oldest attainable layer of the initial transcriptions of an individual saying is the written consolidation of a no-longer-reconstructible oral pattern of formulation, or whether the oldest layer is the codification of a still attainable orally delivered version.

With a text from a prophetic book that we must consider, one should always ask the question: Should one see the foundation as an older prophetic speech, a separate report, or a formerly anonymous prophetic saying? Or, is one dealing with a text that wishes to extend literarily existing material in the sense of a specific continuation? Or, is one dealing with a book redaction text that wishes to serve a larger literary whole? We would plead the case that, for an open result, we can only decide by connecting the analysis of a specific text and a clarified image of the development of the literary whole. Today, everything else stands as a premature prior decision that is no longer justified in light of the indices from the given material.

The question of the book's transmission stands in the foreground in our essay for reasons of the current situation of the research.

Despite this source-stipulated, effective dominance, the question of the original state of prophetic statements still has exciting significance. This question concerns the core and the impetus of the transmission. It asks about the character of the peculiar phenomenon that the prophetic figures of ancient Israel represent in working out the written, prophetic entities of transmission.[161] Relationships and agreements between these texts derived from prophetic logia then do not originate from receptive redactional processes. Rather, they should be plausibly explained as specific characteristics of a prophetic figure himself. Simultaneously, the gaps (*Leerstellen*) of the statements that existed for the understanding of that time are not explainable by the literary context in this case. Rather, these gaps were silently filled in their time by knowledge of the character of this prophet and/or the tradition that shaped them. Also, images, metaphors, and the relatively frequent artistic shaping of the text then stem not from the literary orientation of productive tradents, but from the prophet and his formative influences. Originality no longer provides a convincing criterion to the question of original prophetic logia for the present state of the discipline. Tradents also formulated with originality in their free explication of the existing text. One must thus distinguish between the originality of prophetic initiative over against the tradition and the originality of prophetic reception in light of the continuation of the literary tradition.

Prospects

O. Keel campaigned for "the right of the images to be seen" (OBO 122, 1992). It is no different for the right of the prophetic books to be read as books. Our essay should be understood as a contemporary defense of prophetic (book) research that proceeds strictly from historical literary realities. From this foundation, this research follows methodologically controlled paths to older stages of existing material back to the prophetic figure. As a result of this research, historically responsible knowledge about these figures may decrease while knowledge grows about the productively adapted tradition that these figures effected. Recently, Jeremias has soberly and appropriately affirmed something for Amos that is valid for all prophetic books: "Every step backward into the earlier layers of the book, not to mention the oral speech of Amos, is necessarily burdened with varying degrees of uncertainty."[162] However, it should not be difficult to leave behind the idea of the prophetic books as great original texts from lofty individual figures that have been combined and transmitted by small, untrained hands into entire books. We are potentially only departing from that which we have vainly sought for too long. In its place, a process of tradition becomes visible, a process of continuing adaptation and affirmation of the transmitted material. This process expresses the virile liveliness of the God who was proclaimed in words by prophetic figures and who was further explained through the ages in literary adaptations. The affirmed prophet continues to be affirmed. This prophet is encountered from the referenced books by reading and careful consideration. In so doing, theology, church praxis, and the cultural public will no longer merely receive specific, isolated, and noteworthy prophetic texts. No one will achieve a revived Amos thundering through the present time, when his time has long since passed. Rather, one will achieve texts with a particular profile, encompassed by a literary whole that is no less profiled. The profiled parts receive their transmitted meaning only from the whole. In this framework, they are ready for adaptation for all later recipients. The growing prophetic transmission manifests this whole, and in this whole the individual is placed in the movement from the oldest individual speeches onward. In so doing, tradition is not fixed into rigid channels. Rather, tradition is full of life that places new challenges with material certainty. The second part of this volume will address this aspect more closely.

We can thus summarize this first part. If we wish to understand the shape of the prophetic books and comprehend their statements, then we must again learn to read in the way that prophetic books would have been read in their formative period. We must especially relearn the perspectives in which the books would have been read in that time. We must relearn the guiding outlook of God, who effectively goes through time, explains positions, and instructs about the meaning of the future. And we must relearn the searching outlook of his proclamation by the prophets in their books that encompass God's purpose with his people and that illuminate Israel's history of experience and hope over a lengthy time period. Concerning transmission in the prophetic books, our questions are not simply the questions that encounter the development of these books. Our questions evaluating and adapting sources come into play meaningfully, but not before one has made the effort to approach the prophetic books and their original, formative perception.

Part 2

Prophetic Exegesis of
the Prophets

3

Prophetic Exegesis before and after the Boundaries of the "Canon" as a Starting Point for the Inquiry

Tradition and Exegesis in the Prophetic Books

In the first part of this volume, we pointed to indications from the recent discussion in the research that necessitate taking Old Testament prophetic books seriously as books. These indications require that one make prophetic books into a subject of investigation in their own right and with their own weight not only for reasons of their history of origins, but for theological reasons. Specifically, the impression is by no means unfounded that the ancients wished to convey instructional insights not just in these books, but with these books as whole entities. In most cases, this shape of the prophetic books, however, grew over time in phases to the complete version that now appears before us, no matter what future explanations will look like that can find consensus. In a prophetic book, older books lie behind the final version. Earlier final versions lie behind the final version. How do these versions relate to one another inside the prophetic writings? What impulses from the one motivated the other? And how are these versions understood in light of the prophetic figure in whose name they were transmitted and from whom, in the vast majority of cases, they received the initial impetus that then gave rise to a lengthy transmission event? The answer that we would like to study more closely in this essay can be indicated in two catchwords. The first catchword is "tradition" and the second is "exegesis."

No matter how one analyzes it, a tradition process of preservation and adaptation flows in the growth of the prophetic books. This process concerns the question of the continuing validation of prophetic texts over the course of time, even before the "canon" boundary. Tradents who continued this process thus shaped books and repeatedly worked at expanding and reshaping. They did not, of course, write under their own names. Rather, explicitly for the given text, they apparently still regarded the productive, continuing growth of tradition as the disclosure of the prophet who provided the name. This growth of tradition is considered as the explicitly recorded formulation of the meaning. The transmitted prophetic works also contain this meaning when conveyed in an entire book for a much later time. Prophecy continues to transmit itself, so to speak, even using written means to do so. Thus, tradition stands inside the prophetic books, not alongside or after prophecy. Rather, the adapting tradition intends to derive from prophecy and always remain prophecy. We must ask about prophecy as tradition, about the prophetic office and the tradents. We must ask how the conveying and applying of prophetic transmission continues as a prophetic process.

In this process of tradition, which the prophetic books incorporate in their growth, older formulated material continues to be carried forward. At the same time, however, this older material is productively confirmed and adapted for the challenges and the constellations of a later period. Thus, in a certain sense, an exegetical relationship exists between the transmitted material and the (continued) transmission, between the *traditum* and *traditio.* We must consider this relationship more closely. Seen from the perspective of their development, prophetic books are exegesis of the prophets. In fact, if one adds elaboration to prophecy as tradition, then prophetic books are prophetic exegesis of the prophets, in a sense requiring even more precision.[1]

> Today, we are not immediately accustomed to the aspects that one can expect in this process of the tradition of developing prophetic books. They can, however, be explained with the analogy of the sermon, if taken with a grain of salt. The truth and validity of a sermon are also not the opinions of the preacher, rather the speaking of God, for whom the preacher makes way and does not stand in the way. God speaks to people from a much later time on the written basis of Isaiah, Luke, or Paul, just as in the prophetic

books. Why does one preach instead of just reading the scripture? Because the existing message that is transmitted, even including the language, requires the unfolding of its meaning and its continuing validity in the contemporary, changed, experiential world of later people, where God continues to be present, just as in the transmitting of prophetic books.

If an Old Testament text is preached from a Christian perspective, that text also receives theological modifications. The same God was perceived differently before the birth of Christ than afterward. One must preach the Old Testament text in a new arena of truth, just as in the constantly changing development of prophetic books. The predictions of judgment of preexilic prophecy have a different meaning in the books than they did after judgment appears. They have a meaning modified by a salvific outlook.

And what about the contemporary experience of later persons, who read and hear the received message? It is this experience that necessitates renewed affirmations of a position, changed concrete references, and explanations of the message. But how can that which is contemporary be contained in the old transmitted material? Does one account for this adaptation of earlier cultural material by anthropological, existential, or psychological constants? Or does one point to historical contexts that are causal or effective in nature? Or does everything depend upon how one "comes to terms" with the present? Anyone who preaches would rather say: It is because holy scripture exposes a meaningful arrangement of time of a higher type, a depth-dimension of time and experience that also holds true for those of later periods. Holy scripture exposes that which we have earlier called "metahistory" (see above, p. 17) as the deep, divine meaning of all experiential history, by which an older text and the actualization of a later, present time are incorporated simultaneously. Constellations of time and the flow of time, which are quite different historically, require new preaching. These elements were comprehended and bridged by divine dispositions of meaning that bonded together, remained constant, and stayed valid. These positions form the higher material identity of preaching in various time periods. No matter whether one thinks of the year 403, or 1215, or 1995, the time between the resurrection of Christ and the return substantially remains the same epoch of meaning metahistorically and theologically despite the experiential constellations of each. It remains the time of Christ in the world, the time of life in God's creation and in the cross of Christ, the time of Pentecost, the time of love as one's current responsibility, the time of waiting upon God's great change, even if these qualifications constantly seek a particular, contemporary form of truth, and even if these qualifications constitute the concrete preaching in this relationship. The same is true for prophetic tradition or our altar books, as we will see. The nonconcrete, noncontemporary stereotype of the daily prayer, the collect prayer, or the creed is particularly an expression of metahistorical sameness in the manner of Christ for every Christian congregation. When it is concretized, in the sermon, in special orations, or in the communal prayers of the church alongside the nonconcrete, then it remains in this framework of a metahistorical allocation of meaning or provision of meaning.

All of these elements represent aspects of heuristic analogies, but analogies that are not materially far apart. They are initially found in the process of making explicit the continuing validity of the prophetic message, completely or in part, or only in hindsight, by means of adaptive continuation (*Fortschreibung*) of the transmitted material. From the time of Qumran one can readily demonstrate this process in separate texts alongside holy scripture. However, in the prophetic books before the time of Qumran one can show that this process took place inside the writings themselves.

Early Patterns of Exegesis outside the Prophetic "Canon"

We will discuss prophetic exegesis of the prophets within the prophetic books.[2] A brief look beyond the boundaries of the "canon" helps one perceive the way in which the process previously flowed when still within the prophetic books. We will begin by looking beyond the boundary when the prophetic books as such did not continue to be written. The second and first centuries before Christ provide findings regarding the phenomenon of earlier prophetic exegesis.

Sirach

Take the example of the book of Sirach, written around 190 B.C.E. In this book, we encounter a portrayal of the scribal sage (38:34c–39:11). The sage's activity also includes concern for prophecy (προφητείαις) from the Spirit that God furnished for insight (39:1).[3] This reference means the collection of completed books of the prophetic canon, comparable to the Torah.[4] One sees the purpose of these efforts in the hymn to the fathers in the same book. With the help of these prophetic books, Sirach wants to produce for the people of his time an image of history that runs from the beginnings of the distant past to a future salvific change toward which people can orient themselves.

The exegetical process is more clearly demonstrated for prophets in the form of prophetic writings of this time using two other examples.

Daniel 1–12

The Hebrew book of Daniel (Dan 1–12) was completed in the middle of the second century.[5] It also provides an orientation. Specifically, the book seeks the divine plan of history that ruled from the Babylonian period to the salvific change for God's people. Also, it indicates the standpoint for the understanding and hope of Israel during the contemporary time of the Seleucid rule. The continuing unveiling of this plan is, of course, not achieved by scriptural exegesis. Rather, Daniel experiences this plan more directly by visions and explanations from the mouth of the angel that the book records. Nevertheless, as we will see, transmitted written prophecy is continually brought into play. Specifically, Daniel examines the perspectives of this plan received from the angel against the seventy years of destruction of Jerusalem (9:2) that appear in Jeremiah and elsewhere.[6] In so doing, however, he stumbles upon a difference between the prophetic word of YHWH in the writing on the one hand, which only speaks of seventy years, and the received word from the angel on the other hand. The latter situates the salvific change in a "distant time" (8:26), a change which is entirely plausible from the experience of the present Seleucid period. Thus, the writing that Daniel understood literally evokes a theological problem, because it contradicts the angel's revelation as well as the historical experience of time in the present. The resolution of this problem follows in Daniel by a special revelation from the angel (9:23) that even turns specifically to the exegesis of the written statement. The revelation thus provides understanding to Daniel. The angel explains that the seventy years of this text have seventy weeks of years in mind (9:24), or 490 years, and the events indicated by the angel in the time span (9:25–27) affirm this exegesis by experience and simultaneously affirm the angel's perspective of the salvific change that will first appear in a time which is distant for Daniel, but very close to the time of the author of Daniel in the second century.[7]

As Koch has also recently shown, a whole series of significant references reveal themselves in the exegetical process in Daniel 9.[8]

(1) This process stands in the framework of a specific interest. This interest is not simply to understand a word of Jeremiah received in written form as we would understand the original intention of the author historically. This interest turns its attention much more broadly, and more fundamentally, to the task of perceiving the deep dimension of the present, experienced in the context of the ages. This dimension implies the qualitative arrangement of meaning that reigns in God's history with God's people and God's city. This arrangement will separate a continuous period of sin and judgment once and for all from the salvific change.

(2) By itself, Israel cannot know this meaningful, divine ordering of time that appears so completely unattainable to Qohelet, even though it has the prophetic writings! Israel does not understand that the meaning of the prophetic writings is comprehensive and thus up-to-date. It does not combine text and experience.

(3) Uncovering this order thus relies upon a special revelation correlated with concrete historical experience in addition to the writing. The vision and the angel in the Hebrew book of Daniel certify this revelation. In the written insertions in Daniel 2 and 7, and especially in the appending of Daniel 8–12, this special revelation is not given as a suprahuman exegesis, perhaps of the Torah or the Nebiim as authoritative sources of revelation. Rather, it presents itself as specific revelation that has occurred to Daniel.

(4) However, this special revelation does not contradict scripture. The revelation stems from God, but God also speaks no less significantly in the written transmission of the prophets. God speaks from the same perspective, as the angel's exegesis of Jeremiah ultimately shows. As the special revelation teaches one to understand, both places speak of God's ordering of time that has been sought for Israel.

(5) This understanding should also be recognized for the written transmission of the prophets. However, it is hindered by the literal understanding of the passage because it is a time-bound understanding and cannot integrate contemporary experience. Instead, taking up the comprehensive meaning also requires the exegesis of an additional revelation that uncovers the true meaning of the passage. Or as Koch has said: "The historicizing, literal understanding of prophetic predictions does not manifestly exhaust the meaning that God intended for them. For the initiated, a *sensus plenior* is uncovered

behind prophetic sayings as the secret hidden in them..."⁹ In simple terms, God revealed this perspective two or three times in the same sense. God is revealed once in the recorded prophecy whose comprehensive and contemporary meaning remains in the dark with a literal understanding. Then, God gives a second revelation to Daniel that primarily forms the hermeneutical key for observing the divine identity of the writing's meaning and the revealed order of the meaning of time. This revelation is finally clarified by an additional explanatory revelation.

At the time of the Hebrew book of Daniel, the Nebiim canon, corresponding to the Torah, already existed. Its authority was highly valued in Daniel. Although the Nebiim existed, the background of a deep crisis has already become visible in the position of Daniel 9. A higher ranking for a comprehensive, contemporary orientation and uncertainty about that understanding stand over against one another in the deposited material of the prophetic canon. They can only be brought into harmony by an additional "decoding experience" (Koch). As Koch has shown, this experience has a de facto higher ranking than the literal understanding or misunderstanding of the writing.¹⁰

(6) Into which areas does the deeper exegesis of scripture reach that the angel gives to the "canonical" wording? Three perspectives are important: (a) Over against the literal meaning, the angel lengthens the time. The word of Jeremiah is valid comprehensively, thus including the contemporary experience to the end of the ages. (b) The angel expands the list of those affected by the word. In addition to Jerusalem (9:2), God's people are now included as well. (c) The angel concretizes the deep meaning of the word under the influence of the comprehensive and contemporary experience of time, thus covering the wording and divine ordering of time by applying them to the present.

Is Daniel 9 thus an example of prophetic exegesis of the prophets? One can answer affirmatively, although neither Daniel nor the angel are characterized as prophets. However, identity exists qualitatively. The same God makes himself known in both places, and it is the same deep meaning provided in both places, even though the prophetic wording first requires decoding. What about the truth of this exegesis? The truth is evident in the Hebrew book of Daniel in God's identity in both sources of revelation. The truth is also evident from the coherence of the fundamental conviction that in the ancient prophetic word (as God's word), God simultaneously speaks for all subsequent ages in an all-encompassing and contemporary fashion. God speaks with historical experience as the angel's contemporary revelation teaches one to understand it.

The Pesharim of Qumran

The *pesharim* from the caves of the Dead Sea offer a third, even later, example from the late period of ancient Israel whose particular hermeneutic has often been investigated.[11] In these caves, one finds actual commentaries on the meaning of biblical books in great number from the sectarian community of Qumran.[12] These scrolls offer both biblical passages and exegesis one after the other. The commentary on the prophet Habakkuk from cave one is the most well known. Two passages from this commentary are especially important in our context: 1QpHab I,17–II,10 and VII,1–8.

For reasons of space, we cannot examine this significant Qumran phenomenon extensively here. Nevertheless, it should be accentuated that the image corresponds in many respects to the image attained from Daniel 9. The pesharim also show fundamental interest in the comprehensive and contemporary concern to know everything that will happen to (God's) people (and land), especially the last generation, the end time. More one-sided than Daniel, this *pesher* presupposes that God provided this knowledge specifically in the prophetic books. Habakkuk should write it down! In addition, this pesher presupposes that the wording and literal meaning of the prophetic texts by themselves do not allow one to recognize this knowledge. It was not even given to the prophets themselves. God did not (yet) make known the completion of time to Habakkuk. The prophets themselves did not see that far chronologically (VII, 1–2, 7–8). At the same time, even here, the words of the prophets have this deep meaning that is both comprehensive and contemporary for the end time. This meaning first comes to light in the Habakkuk text by an additional decoding revelation. This meaning is now recorded in the commentary. Unlike Daniel, this second revelation presupposed by the exegesis does not come from God through an angel. Rather, it comes from God through a person, specifically the priest (possibly the Teacher of Righteousness) as the authoritative leader of the Qumran community. God has given the teacher to the community so that he can explain the deep meaning of the prophetic text. God provided him directly with that which was withheld from Habakkuk, the announcement of all the secrets of the words of the prophets! What are these secrets? The Habakkuk *pesher* sees them with respect to the exegetical perspective corresponding to Daniel 9, although now they are quite contemporarily related to the situation of the Qumran community. The final time is elongated. The lengthening of the chronological perspective is necessary over against the literal meaning. Over against the literal meaning with respect to the past, present, and future, the confusing elements must be explained by positive and negative figures and proceedings in the immediate history of the community. Thus, even here, the literal meaning is concretized chronologically as well as historically and contemporaneously regarding the confusing elements in the deep meaning.

For Qumran, we maintain that the wording of the prophetic books, not the prophetic knowledge of the author, contains it all: knowledge of the end time that is contemporary and comprehensive. However, only additional revelation can bring it out. This revelation then launches its own recording and transmission of the exegesis which knows more than even the prophet himself knew. This exegesis accomplishes the orientation that hides in the prophetic texts.

A Preliminary Glance at the Finding within the Prophetic "Canon"

It would be fascinating to compare once again this late Israelite exegetical hermeneutic with the finding in Luke 4:16–30 (Jesus' initial sermon in Nazareth in Luke), with the reflective quotes in Matthew, and with the prophetic exegesis in the New Testament epistles.[13] However, that cannot happen here. For prophetic exegesis of the prophets, we must go back further, behind the late period of ancient Israel into the realm before the boundary of the "canon." We must go back to earlier biblical phenomena that have been problematized and continued in our later examples.

In this older period, the reception of prophetic texts looked completely different. The wording of the prophetic books was not yet finished and had not come to a halt. Rather, this wording continued to grow. What is meant by this difference?

Like numerous other manifestations of prophetic reception and exegesis from the late Israelite period,[14] our three examples already presuppose that "prophets" take the form of an authoritative, well-defined sequence of biblical books, even though variant versions still exist alongside one another and small actualizations are still possible in the text (Qumran and Septuagint along with their *Vorlagen*). The corpus itself can no longer grow. One may grope, at least historically,[15] for the intended assertion of the collection when it concludes. This intention would be manifold under the experiences of the immediately subsequent period, as one can readily imagine with the complex abundance of statements between Joshua and Malachi. As we saw in the examples, from that point forward, maintaining the enduring authority of this collection means exegesis. It now means exegesis by their own proceedings and even by their own writings alongside this collection. We encounter a foundational constellation for exegesis that continues to this day (including Protestant exegesis of the gospels). The authoritative, completed biblical text (which at the time, alongside the Torah, meant the prophets in the form of the completed collection of the Nebiim) and the exegesis of these texts stand apart, as do the books of Sirach, Daniel, and the *pesher* commentaries from Qumran, both over against and along with the Nebiim as a separate text.

If we go behind the quasi-canonical, concluded collections of the Old Testament prophetic books at the close of the third century B.C.E., then this literarily concrete differentiation between the prophetic text and the specialized exegesis, or reception of a text within the prophetic transmission, is not yet a given. Instead, on our trip back, we come upon a very different constellation. The literary historical period encompasses half a millennium, from the eighth century to the middle of the third century B.C.E. It was in this time period that the size and order of written prophetic transmission eventually grew to the form that was definitive at the end of the third century with respect to the comprehensive scope as well as essential structure and wording. When we say "eventually grew," we mean later components and new prophetic writings were subsequently added to an older component of prophetic books. This growth again forms the literarily existing material for later, productively expanding adaptations and book shapings that are still within the books. An immense and lengthy process of reception was underway, a process that those responsible for conveying the books apparently intended for themselves.[16] To illuminate this process is the particular task and the new frontier of prophetic research today. In the following, we will make a preliminary attempt to consider the relationship between later and earlier texts inside this internal reception process of the "prophetic books." We will attempt to follow our theme of "prophetic exegesis of the prophets" into this new field in which scribal prophecy develops.

4

Prophetic Exegesis of the Prophets in the Growth of the Prophetic Books

Orientation into the History of Research

Older Research

Very briefly, we should first recall the perspective of the research that the earlier portion of this volume explained. One has long known that the prophets from Amos to Zechariah were not solely authors of revelation. Consequently, they did not simply write the books that bore their names in their entirety. Also, no matter how one evaluates the details, based upon linguistic, stylistic, material, or chronological criteria, a considerable portion of the text material in these books does not stem from the prophet providing the name. Rather, it was added later. One can hardly change this fact, not even by running away from it too quickly as with today's fashionable leap into the so-called final text reading, a reading copied from the literary sciences. One cannot deny this fact if one is to preserve and to understand the high degree of material complexity of the existing prophetic texts. Even though researchers like Stade and Hertzberg long ago warned against ignoring the later parts of the prophetic books, for decades the trend of the research proceeded in a one-sided manner in the opposite direction.[1] This one-sided research was encouraged by the form-critical method. Its conclusions were presumably allowed by the "life setting" of the genre being utilized to provide vividness to prophetic activity. Specifically, the form-critical method tried to draw conclusions about the oldest, original logia that the prophetic personalities themselves spoke. It presumably went back to their kerygma, to which biblically oriented preaching should be similar. By contrast, the leftover, secondary material served as the object of dissension regarding the extent that it contained the *ipsissima verba* of the prophets. Otherwise, this secondary material served as undistinguished additions that commentaries to prophetic books were compelled to address, albeit resentfully and half-heartedly. Little interest was shown with respect to where the later material arose, or when, why, and how it grew onto the original material. Little interest was shown in recordings, initial collections, initial compositions, incorporations by otherwise anonymous prophets, and especially in the numerous isolated additions to specific texts in these corpora. Since the time of Zimmerli's pioneering discoveries[2] in Ezekiel, these secondary elements have become apparent as continuations (*Fortschreibungen*) of specific texts.[3] These additions, however, were often proclaimed as vague phases of the development of prophetic books.[4] Even when one spoke of "redactions" of the books, the concept was scarcely covered by the accentuated finding. Even where continuous layers were recognized, they were generally processed as isolated entities. Although inquiry into the prophet himself and the original form of his utterances still has validity, at present the trend has changed.

Changes in the Current State of Research

Today, we think that the text-finding in prophetic books requires a changed perspective. What are the main points of this change?

(1) Even in the core of a prophetic book, the prophet himself (as one may generally accept), we cannot directly reach the formerly oral work of the prophet, which is explicitly kerygmatic. We already encounter the concentrated, reduced linguistic form of the recording that includes the effect of this speech. This recording continues the transmission and validity beyond the personal appearance of the prophet. The research of J. Jeremias in the last several years into Hosea and Amos has provided groundbreaking work.[5]

(2) The originally recorded material was multiplied literarily by additional collected material, whether original or non-original. However, the original material is soon expanded by receptive passages that applied this oldest recorded material by taking up its formulations for a later period. In this case, these receptive passages are not

integrated, anonymous prophecies and not isolated additions to individual texts (although isolated additions certainly exist here and there as glosses).[6] Rather, these receptive passages are a quantitative lengthening of the initially recorded material by means of text material that has been newly formulated and adapted in an immediate literary connection to expand the same writing. These receptive passages are thus not independent. They are understandable generally only by the sequence and reading context of the entire writing in connection with the originally recorded material. One must again refer to the new insights from Jeremias with regard to Hosea and Amos. The compositions of the early versions of the prophetic writings appear to arise without necessarily having to provide completely the characteristic markers of structured book redactions. The boundaries are naturally fluid and are measured by the extent of the intended literary structuring for a literary whole. However, the reception process does not remain like this. Rather, it expands on these early, developing writings.

(3) Therefore, in order to keep open various models of origin as illustrative,[7] in one or more of the prophetic writings and their precursors, book-specific redactions of these writings occur in the subsequent period. Thus, productively-receptive reshapings and expansions of the prophetic books as books occur! In the prophetic books, texts of the same profile and origin stand out from the diverse developmental layers that follow upon one another. These texts are directed to the prophetic writings as a whole in its scope at that time. They seek to adapt the entirety (!) once again through new accents. Texts are apparently created from the outset for the larger context of an entire transmitted writing. These texts differ from the recorded, original, individual logia, but they also differ from isolated additions in their markers of literary references, cross-references, their position in the whole, macrostructural inclusions, and placement (especially at the beginning and end of the book respectively). These texts function as directions for the reader and provide perspective in this whole. They want the reader to see the entire condition of the statements in the writing with different eyes, as the writing has been conveyed. These texts are constitutively dependent upon the context. They have no function and are not understandable when seen in isolation. Rather, these texts are formulated for a book and in a book (or series of books). They are full of linguistic and material cross-references to already existing statements in the writing, and they are thoughtfully placed in the

comprehensive structure of the new edition of a prophetic book.[8] Thus, redactional book texts demonstrate their intention and function only for their perspective of this type of comprehensive writing, productively conveyed in their respective extent. These texts withhold their meaning from the exegete who remains imprisoned by filtering exegesis of specific texts that are delimited by single pericopes.[9] Or texts withhold their meaning from the exegete who even more dubiously determines that original logia exist without referring to the text and without considering a wider literary horizon for the inquiry and origin. This wider horizon potentially makes that material understandable that is not understandable when read in isolation by taking into account the framework of the created flow of reading of the whole.[10] If the discovery of redactional texts in the prophetic books related specifically to the book is correct, then the consequences are clear. The growth of one or more prophetic books is not some unplanned expansion of foundational material around numerous isolated additions that later hands continually implanted into the text. No, prophetic books grow as writings that are quantitatively expanded and reshaped as wholes by redactional processes. They grow qualitatively by the comprehensiveness of the statements, newly adapted, newly read, and newly understood. The redactional development of prophetic books from the initial recording of the original logia to the final form as we have it really does reflect the character of a reception process inside a book.[11] One process of reception of this type, as represented by a prophetic book, can be profiled historically and theologically. Its material contour, its intention, its causes, and its time period can be investigated. One can also investigate the integration and new understanding of the given literary material and the revised material. If a literarily existing prophetic writing is constantly received and interpreted productively by these redactions, then we already encounter prophetic exegesis in the literary growth of the prophetic books themselves. The received material and the receiving material both remain a valid material unity in the redactional work.[12]

In the realm of many endeavors concerning the literary development of prophetic books, the Hamburg dissertation from H. Barth in 1974 continues to point the way with respect to methodology. This dissertation exposed a productive, new interpretation of the Isaiah transmission in Proto-Isaiah during the Josiah period.[13] Others have worked further by illuminating the redaction history of the development of prophetic books. Those of us in Zürich have worked on this aspect especially in the development of the Isaiah corpus and the Book of the Twelve. In the meantime, as mentioned in the first study, more comprehensive investigations have either been completed or are in process. This leads to a final point.

(4) Specifically in Zürich, the efforts concerning redaction texts in the prophetic books have also yielded the insight that the later one finds the processes of reception inside the book, the more apparent it is that the redactions do not remain focused on the material horizon of the individual book. Rather, the material was received and revised, potentially even from the transmission phase or the preexilic period (Bosshard), in light of the smaller series first, then larger ones in which the individual books were already seen at the time.[14] A connecting horizon becomes visible. This horizon is literary as well as material and transcends the growing entities of the collection of books until it finally results in the literary and complex material unity of the amalgamation of the books of the prophetic writings in the Nebiim. A diagram ("Chart for the History of Research with Respect to the Development of the Prophetic Books," see next page) can summarize the path of the research at a glance.

Summation

Today, material is coming to light concerning the inner-prophetic reception process and for the internal exegesis within the prophetic books. Simultaneously, a modest self-assessment of the current state of research does not allow one to use this material as a sure basis upon which the evaluations can be easily anticipated for our topic. We are not yet to that point. Rather, in every respect we are still in field research. We are in the midst of an initial discussion, but one which is becoming broader. Which prophetic texts in general can be confirmed as later redaction texts for a book? Which of these texts belong to the same layer? How should they be arranged diachronically? And how are more broadly accepted redactional processes made plausible in the material profile and in dating? Above all, one must make a fundamental distinction clear in the difficult comprehension of the phenomenon. If one wishes to consider the process at all, one cannot avoid a historical diachronic perspective of the prophetic and literary process of tradition. However, the perspective of the same tradition process among the tradents, in their time, offers another perspective. In that which follows, one must speak about both perspectives, even if the perspective mentioned first takes center stage because of the historical inquiry in our

Chart for the History of Research with Respect to the Development of the Prophetic Books

Typical Representation of the Stages of Research

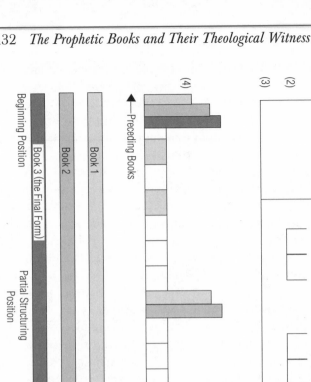
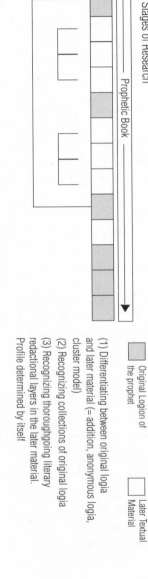

◼ Original Logion of the prophet ☐ Later Textual Material

◀—— Prophetic Book ——▶

(1)
(2)
(3)
(4)

▲ —Preceding Books

Subsequent Books—▼

Book 1

Book 2

Book 3 (the Final Form)

Beginning Position

Partial Structuring Position

Concluding Position

(1) Differentiating between original logia and later material (= addition, anonymous logia, cluster model)

(2) Recognizing collections of original logia

(3) Recognizing thoroughgoing literary redactional layers in the later material. Profile determined by itself

(4) The book as book:

In later material there are redactional texts that
— adapt/structure the entirely/transmitted material (position)
— have the entire book or series of books as their literary horizon
— establish a continuous metahistorical reading context
— establish the redaction as a reception of the whole

characterization of the tradition process. This perspective incorporates the distinct self-presentation of the prophetic books as a historical phenomenon.

At the same time, if we now survey the field and attempt to contribute to our topic in the inner prophetic realm, then it can only happen with two provisos. (1) As elsewhere in this volume, we generally support our position primarily with observations from the partial perspective of our own work.[15] These observations concern redactional processes in Deutero-Isaiah, Trito-Isaiah, and the entire Isaiah corpus from the Persian period and the Hellenistic period. They concern redactional processes at the end of the Book of the Twelve and the concluding formation of the great collection of prophetic books at the end of the process. And we also primarily relate the insights into this same group of texts, along with other texts, that have been or will be achieved by my earlier and current colleagues: Reinhard Kratz, Erich Bosshard-Nepustil, Konrad Schmid, Peter Schwagmeier,[16] and James D. Nogalski. Other starting points, approaches, and insights into the prophetic books as books were brought into the conversation in the first part of this volume that was processed later. (2) We limit ourselves to the characterization of particular fundamental aspects of inner-biblical prophetic exegesis, aspects that confront us in our current understanding of the material. For reasons of time, a comprehensive evaluation is not yet possible concerning achievement and presentation. One additional limitation should be noted as well. The text-findings themselves cannot really be introduced here with detailed rationale. The combined viewing of large numbers of texts that is necessary for redaction history, together with detailed individual investigation of the statements, would greatly exceed the bounds of this essay. The aforementioned publications must be consulted for the details. Now, on to the task.

The Basic Presupposition in the Growth of the Prophetic Books

We cannot turn to the relationships of the reception in the growth of the prophetic books without first posing preliminary questions of the foundations of this phenomenon. The preliminary questions are: Why were prophetic logia recorded at all? Then, why was this foundational literary corpus productively expanded in ever new waves of interpretation? Why was the corpus continued and revised in new adaptations up to the final form? Attempting answers requires that we mention four aspects.

Prophetic Work as the Declaration of YHWH

God, not a person, speaks out of the prophets. A fundamental conviction is authoritative for this lengthy process. This conviction already derives from the activity of the prophetic figures themselves. Their statements form the literary core of the prophetic corpus. However, this conviction drives the prophetic tradents in precisely the same manner. It is directed toward the divine word, effectively evoking events freely realizable by YHWH. This word is expressed in written prophecy.

At its heart, one finds a seemingly trivial conviction, but in reality a fundamental conviction, that the messages that come through the prophets are directly or indirectly YHWH's messages.[17] These messages were first expressed orally, but they are contemporary messages from God. Even in the preexilic period, these messages overhaul traditional expectations about God in the customary transmissions. From the mouth of the prophet, these messages declare the specific type of YHWH's activity with which one is now expressly concerned.[18] The preexilic figures of the writing prophets declare YHWH is present as the one who introduces Israel's guilt, wasted chances, judgment, and downfall. YHWH is the one with whom one must now reckon. From this time, YHWH has thus declared himself prophetically only to the prophets and their adherents. YHWH no longer addresses Israel graciously in the customary sense. This prophetically accessible perspective on YHWH remains all too valid, and requires preservation because it displays for Israel that which remains in effect, what stands before Israel, and why!

Prophetic Word and Event

The prophetic word is not just spoken, it elicits events. According to this fundamental conviction one will only hear how YHWH is currently operating. For prophets and their adherents, this conviction includes the fact that these received messages of YHWH are undeniably the *effective* word of God. These messages explain past experience. They concentrate and facilitate current experience. They qualitatively confirm and cause the resulting events of the forthcoming period in advance. From this perspective, every event related to the meaning for God's people in the realm of the nations is primarily the realization of YHWH's judgments and intentions as declared by this word. This powerful, prophetic word of God reveals and effects. The same word can find multiple historical concretions, as becomes quite clear, for example, with Isaiah in Isaiah 9:7–20.[19] The same holds true for changing, diversely concretized exhibitions of guilt for the present or the past. Primarily, these exhibitions of guilt could have once allowed the chance of a change for the guilty.[20]

Chronological Perspective of the Prophetic Activity

The prophet proclaiming God's activity speaks in his time, but does not speak only to his time. In light of the prophetic tradition, the perspective of coming events that the prophets have laid open since the eighth century B.C.E. should interest us, even if tradents from a later time could already look back on its fulfillment. Simultaneously, we want to consider the tension between the announced word of God and the experience into which this perspective undeniably leads. Prophet and tradents see their own time, with the formulations and expectations of the message in their ears. However, history can also flow differently. The prophetic formulations in advance of the subsequent events effectively announced by YHWH are directed primarily toward God's people. However, these formulations are also directed toward other peoples of the time. In reality, they explicitly or implicitly manifest the historical-political dimension that is accessible to experiential evaluation. They have in mind their own governmental state, the condition of the people, freedom, and life-potential in their own land. However, what happens if the current political-historical experiential evaluation of the prophetically shown expectations fails?

A peculiar finding provides the answer in the particular way by which the coming events are linguistically shaped. Prophetic predictions about what will happen to Israel are generally not so pointedly and concretely formulated that their statements could eventually only be verified in a single, precisely fixed event in the prophet's lifetime. Otherwise, one would have to speak of non-fulfillment. No. That which stands before Israel is in fact related to a specific time, as are the prophets expressing it. That which stands before Israel is envisioned for the Assyrian and Babylonian eras. Later it was envisioned for the Persian era and, at the end, even for the Hellenistic era. However, that which stands before Israel was qualitatively formulated in an abundance of ideas, many metaphorical. These ideas express YHWH's freedom with respect to time. YHWH has the freedom to fulfill the word in the course of Israel's journey, to execute the word in terms of historical concretization, at a later point or even several points. For example, Assyrian texts from the eighth and seventh centuries B.C.E. are read as relating to the Seleucids of the third and second centuries (Daniel). Only then are these texts confirmed as experientially evident. YHWH is the one putting forth the prophetic word, and YHWH will make its fulfillment known unambiguously. Because of this aforementioned fundamental conviction, contradictory experiences within the word concerning the things to come do not create doubts about the truth of the word in the prophets' time or their tradents. Even if, for our historical knowledge, the prophet himself understood the word more closely related to that time, doubt is not created. Instead, these experiences provide the words with evidence of facts or bring to light the untruth of popular salvation prophecies of that day, whether in the sometimes partial fulfillments (like Judah's vassal status under the Assyrians and Babylonians, or the downfall of the northern state of Israel) or even ultimately in completed fulfillments (like Judah's downfall in 587). Initially contradictory experiences of the time were, in other words, non-fulfillments contrary to expectations.[21] These experiences gave cause for prophets, and their tradents, to wait even more intensively for YHWH's historical confirmation of the promised events. The authoritative reason for the transcription and the recording of written prophetic transmission is to preserve the received messages for their affirmations in God's historical action that are still ahead of Israel, how and when God intends.[22] The two notices to record something in the core transmission of Isaiah, 8:16–18 and 30:8–17, show this reason with absolute clarity.[23]

In so doing, a theocentric interest dominated, not minute legal jumblings. The prophets and the tradents did not intend to record evidentiary material so that the prophet would at some point be proven correct. Rather, they intended to lay the foundation for recognizing when the event began. It is YHWH who acts as he is proclaimed and explained. YHWH's word and will now operate and bring forth the event! Instructions for future experience with YHWH in time (even the subsequent period, far beyond the prophet's lifetime) dominated the transmission event of written Israelite prophecy by means of the predicted and predicting prophetic word. These instructions dominate, even though one can occasionally find the commissional prophets' God-problem and life conditions of interest in a particular transmission. The prophetic narratives and confessions in the book of Jeremiah in particular demonstrate these elements. In the words of J. Jeremias in his new Amos commentary, the message "was not transmitted for the sake of a historical interest in a time that has long since passed. Rather, the message was transcribed and at the same time continually actualized based upon its meaning for a different time."[24]

Prophetic Work as the Deduction of a Far-Reaching History of Meaning

The prophet is presented in temporal historical experience. However, the tradents arrange this experience in the transcending framework of far-reaching divine history of meaning. Only on the basis of this comprehensive divine perspective do the synonymous prophetic transmissions and the continuing validity become visible. If one considers this fundamental presupposition for the formation of the written transmission more closely, then a more difficult aspect that has scarcely received any treatment to this point comes to the forefront.[25] The course of events in the world of Israel were observed from this perspective in a very characteristic fashion! Since the eighth century, the writing prophets and their tradents held the dominant conviction that (with reference to Koch[26]), only the transmitted prophetic words explain the "metahistorical," qualitatively compressed dimensions of depth and meaning for Israel in that time and in the future. In so doing, they included the expectation that the meaningful, divinely accomplished condition of Israel would undeniably follow its course, according to prophetic transmission. This conviction has consequences for the ways and means that one can see historical knowledge, diffuse and manifold experiences of time, and expectations. These experiences and expectations concentrate specifically upon that which was displayed prophetically! Based upon this perspective, the conglomeration of the history of events and experience was condensed, selected, and evaluated against the measuring rod of Israel's divine history. The conglomeration of the history of events and experience was also condensed, selected, and evaluated against the stations and phases belonging to that history, as prophetic transmission sees them in process. A variety of flowing procedures, and those that surpass one another, thus concentrate upon that which we reflectively call "metahistory" as the reason, the material depth, and the purpose of the history of events that have been experienced and that are to come. However, from the outset, the prophets and their tradents see this "metahistory" as Israel's essential path of meaning, upon which the experienced history of events had concentrated and would concentrate according to prophetic perspective. That which the Habakkuk *pesher* brings to the concept in its own way in the late period actually functions in this respect for prophetic transmission from the beginning. God announced everything that would happen to his people and [his land] through the prophets (1QpHab II, 9–10).

With this prophetically predetermined, metahistorical path of meaning for Israel, an image of history is initiated as a result. It concentrates upon the essential stages of meaning, but this image is constantly related to time and experience. This image begins with the historical appearance of the writing prophets in the eighth century and from there mentions by name everything of significance that stands before God's people in the realm of the nations. It includes recollections of Israel's past, even from the time of its founding and from the creation of the world. This image of history explains, selects, and concentrates the variety of experiences from the past, but also from the current time, especially for that which is essentially coming. Also, in the eyes of the tradents, the longer this image of history continues, the more it shapes the particular substance of the entire transmission of the writing prophets by displaying divine activity in that time and in the future. Since the eighth century, the downfall of the people overwhelmingly dominates reports about that which is to come, according to this divine, written prophetic image of history. Amos announced this downfall. Hosea, Isaiah, and Micah expected its completion by the Assyrians. Jeremiah and Ezekiel experienced this downfall through the Babylonians. They also experienced the comprehensive truth of this image of history. The rationales for guilt were perceived differently according to the standpoint of the time, even by one and the same prophet (both Isaiah and Jeremiah). However, after the exilic period, the perspective of this image of history is expanded into an even greater breadth. Prophets appear. They speak God's messages that exhibit an additional station of meaning for Israel of that time, the Israel that continued to live in the aftermath of the downfall of 722 and 587. There was a new purpose beyond the downfall. Specifically, the purpose of judgment changes into comprehensive salvation. This purpose is also confirmed in experience because partial realizations can be documented. These partial realizations include the rise of Cyrus, the downfall of the Babylonian kingdom, the favor of Darius, the return of the exiles, and the reconstruction of the temple.

After the original prophet, the prophetic transmission remains directed toward realizing this prophetically expounded image of history as that which is to come, especially for Israel. This image of history in the prophetic word is a written word. It continues to grow increasingly by later expansions, by new prophetic figures and their own developing, written transmission, and by synoptic presentation and connection of the transmissions.[27] As a result of this image of history, the textual foundation arises in the developing prophetic transmission. This textual foundation constitutes a very complex, far-reaching, written prophetic unity of sayings with a higher order that is unified by YHWH and his meaningful preliminary sketch of the entire history of God's people. Preliminary stages and changing relationships between prophetic bodies of transmission demonstrate this higher order. In the end, the collections of the books of the prophetic corpus and the Nebiim demonstrate their intended material unity as well.[28] The growth of the prophetic transmission cannot be understood without a passionate interest in the realization of God's meaning in history. This interest has been prophetically incorporated in the particular book, but also in neighboring prophetic books. The growth of the prophetic transmission cannot be understood apart from a passionate interest in the question of whether and how time and experiential history correspond in the transmission. Prophetic text and current experience can be related within the framework of the same station of meaning on the basis of this predicted, metahistorical image of Israel's history! Based upon this image of history, transmitted prophetic texts treating the same metahistorical situation became identical for the tradents in a higher sense, despite diverse formulation!

Upon what are the tradents oriented in the search for the answer? For them, the prophetic wording from the time of the transmitted prophets is authoritative in the form of the literary transmission. The wording becomes the bearer of a metahistorical meaning that will be realized. The stations of meaning perceive the divine image of history in a multiplicity of ways in prophetic writings. One should not understand the divine freedom in the when and how of the resolution as a contradiction. Rather, one should understand this freedom as different threads of expectation for the same meta-historical process that YHWH will clarify with the realization. This orientation has very concrete implications for the path of transmission. With a metahistorically oriented, watchful eye toward experiential history, the tradents recorded their prophetic texts. Further, the tradents considered prophetic transmission in light of current experience for their own time. They considered the message of God irremovable, as absolutely valid. Therefore, the transmission should not be impugned as it continues, even those parts later stricken. Prophetically seen, the tradents considered whether fulfillments of prophetic tradition manifested themselves in this transmission. Observable experience of the time, led by prophets, is here projected upon this divinely anticipated image of history in the prophetic transmission. The experience of chronological history during the continuing transmission is thus admitted, but, at the same time, it is filtered. The prophetic word and its image of history determine the perception and lead to the point that this essay finds most interesting: the continued recording or the productive transmission of written prophetic material.

Very different constellations come into view when simplified into a prototypical pattern:

(1) The current experience of time offers nothing that is metahistorically essential for prophetically directed eyes. In this case, one must conclude from the finding that the transmission was simply recorded without productive rereading. One must conclude that the remainder continues to wait for signs that YHWH has somehow brought the pronounced stages of meaning to pass.

(2) The experience of the current time offers an overwhelming contrasting experience that is surprising based upon the transmitted expectation. In this case, the tradents make explicit the divine starting point of a new reading by new formulations in the transmitted word. Statements to the contrary are then chronologically limited or suspended. Examples include: Proto-Isaiah in the time of Josiah that was dominated by an "Assyrian Redaction," imparting a salvific perspective (as H. Barth has shown); or the imminent hopes for Darius in a Cyrus rereading (which Kratz indicated as a redaction of Deutero-Isaiah[29]); or negatively, the contradiction of highest sounding expectations of salvation that the capture of Jerusalem by Ptolemy I signified and that, for a time, caused this book to conclude with an appended lament and petition text (63:7–64:11).[30]

(3) The constellation was considered different still when the tradents recorded and read their transmission material at the beginning of the sixth century. These tradents had the horrific experience of experiencing the confirmation of every preexilic prophecy of destruction concerning God's people. The proof was made explicit in new insertions, new recensions of the transmission material,[31] and/or it was brought to expression in the fixed sequence of prophetic books.[32]

(4) After the exilic period, the perspective of the salvific change also widely entered the metahistorical image of history in prophetic transmission. The view of the tradents with this purposeful perspective toward the concrete experience of time yielded manifold constellations that lead to productive, continued transmission of this prophetic and literary view, flowing into a positive outlook. Changed messages from God of this type are documented by new prophets and texts like Deutero-Isaiah (and its foundational layer) or Haggai and Zechariah (and their records). They are also potentially documented by Ezekiel himself. Also, early salvific expectations in existing writings like the expectation of Isaiah 33 in Proto-Isaiah point in that direction.[33] These changed messages demonstrate that the judgment perspective of the given transmission to that point was broken and fundamentally altered by chronological indices, by the reflection of the tradents about YHWH as the God of Israel who would not turn his back forever, and by new prophecies announcing salvation from this new purposeful perspective.

A permanent problem results in these tradent circles from the delay of the promised salvific change or from the exclusion of the complete, comprehensive realization, despite the partial realizations that have been experienced.[34] The prophetic messages transmitted in this manner remain valid. However, the certainty and nearness of the salvific change are underscored in view of the contradictory experience of the time. The preformulated salvation is further concretized in view of current deficits and deficiencies. This change happens, for example, in the Zion continuations,[35] in the Cyrus redaction in Deutero-Isaiah, and exhaustively with the instability of Persian domination by the Ebed-Israel redaction explicated by Kratz, to which we would add the continuation (*Fortschreibung*) in Isaiah *60–62.[36] One can also see corresponding elements in the development of Proto-Zechariah. In conjunction with existing sayings related to the preexilic period, new demonstrations of Israel's guilt in the postexilic period can also be incorporated as the reason for the delay of the change and as warnings. Those heeding these warnings will participate in the onset of impending change.[37] One sees just how precisely and sensitively current processes are noted with the perspective of meaning and time held ready by prophetic transmission. One sees this sensitive precision when considering grand political constellations for God's people and in differentiations that are adopted in the current period with respect to God's people themselves. The consideration is demonstrated in constantly changing actualization and changed references of meaning in the wording of the existing, irreplaceably valid prophetic text through renewed measures of rereading. In the Ebed-YHWH texts, the servant of God, for example, was originally the prophet himself, but can be seen in the Persian king and the salvific place of Zion. Later, the servant of God can only be seen in Zion and God's people. Later still, the servant can be seen in the prophet of the book and in the narrow circle of the true pious ones.[38] Or take the example of the nations. In the exilic period, the guilty among the nations would be punished like Israel, while during the orderly experience of the Persian period, the nations as a whole are included in Israel's salvation. After the breakup of the world order of the Persian and Alexandrian empires, the judgment sayings about the nations and the power of the nations that existed in the transmission are ultimately expanded into a universal judgment that is yet to come, complementing Israel's salvation[39] as a new aspect of the image of history.[40] If we have seen correctly, then processes of rereading tumble over one another toward the conclusion of the transmission of the prophetic book in the highly charged period at the end of the fourth and third centuries. They do so in order to correlate the historical political experiences with the transmitted prophetic material in an intense expectation of change corresponding to universal political disaster and in order to formulate this correlation.

(5) Finally, material problems also continue to drive the transmission. These problems are provided from the apparent contradiction that appears inside the transmission material in the eyes of the tradents as it grows. For example, the entire diaspora of Israel should return in the process of a new conquest in the sense of the displayed expectation at the end. But how can this happen when YHWH's universal judgment rages in Edom in the concluding passage about the return path? We have suggested that the redaction of the return, which takes place in the Diadochan period, attempts in

part to solve this problem with the insertion of Isaiah 35.[41] How extensive is the universal judgment if foreigners have already attached themselves to God's people, and if more distant peoples survive this judgment? The final redaction of the book of Isaiah and in the Book of the Twelve make the solution of this problem explicit.[42]

Summary

All in all, the fundamental presupposition in the origin and growth of the prophetic books and collections of prophetic books includes the fact that the individual book, as well as the series of books, should be read as the recording of a great, divine, predictive event by the tradents. The diversity of text statements in its image of history should thus be read as materially unified. Accordingly, YHWH's word has sought and will seek its fulfillment in this event. The eminent complexity of the individual sayings in the developing prophetic corpus concentrate and condense in an almost credo-like manner. This prophetic, materially unified, predictive event in the books ultimately encompasses the following primary metahistorical stages: from the preexilic period to the guilt and guilt status of the people in the exile, the judgment and judgment status of the people in the exile, the behavioral status of Israel after the exile, Israel's salvific change in the world of the nations, and in many respects the realization of that salvation. The predictive event also encompasses the entire time regarding the history of events that had been experienced. In the eyes of the tradents, this predictive event, recorded in written form, proceeds from the prophet's providing the name to their own time as the truth that arrives for that time. From the perspective of historical inquiry, the predictive event ultimately extends, literarily, across developing stages. It extends from the book of Isaiah to the book of Malachi. As a whole, it points to a path of stages of the meaning of Israel's history to the completion of salvation to come. This path of stages should coordinate the unswerving linguistic validity with the transpired and expected experiential history of the subsequent period. It should hold fast to the eschatological excess in the transmission. This transmission is not accomplished slavishly through pure repetition. Rather, it is conscious of the time and open to the world because experiential history brings movement in the productive process of transmission when observed with eyes that are directed by the prophets in their apparent metahistorical indices. One essential motivation for the respective rereading is clear.

Now is the time toward which the transmitted material aims. A great, divine predictive event from books begins in the eighth century and ends with Zechariah and Malachi in the Persian period, according to the self-presentation (although according to historical inquiry, it ends de facto in the Diadochan period), and it remains valid and undiminished for all subsequent time. However, not everything that is recorded is equally relevant for the respective later generation in the tradent's time. From the perspective of the tradents, much of the material has already been fulfilled. It lies in the past and has ceased to have any effect.[43] For example, this material includes the work of Cyrus. Prior to Cyrus, it especially included the onset of the destruction of Israel and Judah, but also YHWH's return to Zion with the temple reconstruction. Other material relates directly to the respective current generation of tradents because in the prophetic book it is addressed to them, to their time, and to the future. By borrowing from the received material, the current validity is now expressly formulated. It instructs the present and continues to be refined along with the unfulfilled salvation from the older material. It is the declaration of that which stands meaningfully ahead of Israel. It comes from God as the breakthrough or, at any rate, as the completion of salvation that is supposed to follow the judgment.

The Growth of the Prophetic Books as Prophetic Exegesis

Concerning the Concept "Exegesis"

These processes of rereading show traces of adapting the historical actuality of the tradition between the eighth and the third century whether they arise from isolated insertions or comprehensive book redactions. Should one perceive these processes as "exegesis" over against the respective older, literarily existing material? These processes should not be perceived as exegesis in the sense of Daniel and Qumran that we have previously encountered. As already stated, a specific contrast between text and exegesis does not yet exist. From the text, one cannot recognize a need for the legitimization of an independent interpreter. One lacks special revelations that provide authority to an exegesis over against the current ambiguous text. Still, the rereadings of these passages are clearly formulated upon existing text material in the same book, as well as other prophetic books, using literary references related to the wording, the material, and the context. They are so clearly formulated upon these texts that one must speak of an exegetical relationship. Exegesis of a linguistic type in a later text orients itself toward another existing text in the same corpus. In the realm of the prophetic transmission, the received texts are divine messages and thus authoritative texts. The reception of these texts for a subsequent period proceeds beyond mere transcription. This reception necessarily becomes exegesis when it guards the continuing validity and bridges the distance between a text and its changing time. Thus, the phenomenon presents itself to historical inquiry in the following manner. The finding shows that the tradents live in their own time, but they observe and believe their time using their book and their books. The tradents explicate the validity of the written material in those books for the experiential realms of their present time. This exegesis can also produce innovative references that transcend and essentially continue the existing transmission. One can readily demonstrate in those passages where the received judgment perspective remains valid and continues to operate in the tradents' time, but where that perspective is expanded by a new purpose–salvific change and the completion of salvation. Of course, once it arises, this salvific perspective itself becomes the subject of exegetical text reception. However, by no means do text and exegesis always stand one right after another within the book. The received text is not seen as deficient for understanding. In this kind of exegesis, references to several texts standing in various positions flow together toward a single purpose like guiding lines in certain instances. To be sure, one does not yet find a commentary on the meaning that proceeds word by word, and an exhaustive interpretation of a text is not yet the purpose that conveys the text's statements into a whole. In short, the text material to which the tradents refer does not require explanations, but it needs explication by literary supplements and reformations of the existing material. One must apparently perceive this exegetical event more openly and more broadly.

Two Examples

Initially, we should examine at least two examples from the realm of Isaiah 40–66. The first text is Isaiah 40:1–11 and its exegetical adaptation in Isaiah 62:10–12, a solemn, concluding passage of a book of Isaiah in the shape of the so-called return redaction (*Heimkehrredaktion*) at the end of the fourth century. Isaiah 62:10–12 is completely unintelligible by itself. In the flow of the Isaiah book, the tradents read Isaiah 40:1–11 as the metahistorical view of the issuing of orders for the return of YHWH and YHWH's people at the salvific change. The tradents read the subsequent text in Isaiah 40 and following as further references to this return of Israel. However, in their own time, these tradents have added a demand more closely related to the completion of salvation for the Jerusalemites who already existed in the city, based upon statements in Isaiah 49:14–26; 52:7–10; and 60. The Jerusalemites are challenged to receive these returnees who are saved by the judgment upon the nations, a demand that explains the completion of salvation for Zion and God's people in the mind of these later ones as the conclusion of the book and the conclusion of the metahistorical perspective of expectation. With considerable freedom and independence, the tradents have accomplished this demand by referring to Isaiah 40:1–11 using its wording, style, structure, and position. In addition, they have referred to additional texts in their book of Isaiah, thereby creating Isaiah 62:10–12 as the concluding passage of their book. Since Isaiah 40 and the newly formed statement are identical, they are only two sides of the same salvific event: divinely punctuated proclamation and historically phased realization over a lengthy period.[44] YHWH's own return is thus not taken up again. At the time, YHWH's return was already a present experience in the temple, an experience that was read as fulfilled in the prophecy 52:7–10.

The second example appears in the third song of the servant of God. Originally, this song referred to the prophetic servant of God himself. However, a comprehensive book of Isaiah later used the applicable, existing wording differently. For a long time, the broader textual context supplied the idea that one must relate the servant to Zion, her suffering and her salvation, as a literary context shows (such as Isa 50:1–3; 51:12–15, 17–23, and so on). The return redaction inserted 51:1–3,* 4 and following, 6–8, 10b. However, it interpreted the wording of 50:4–9 in a materially expanded manner. As the new composition in Isaiah 51:1–8 makes explicit, the deliverance statements are now related to the returning people of God. Also, statements about the downfall of the opponent are related to the universal judgment.[45] References back to this text in its literary context are even more extensive in the potentially later rereading of 54:11–17. The same metahistorical event is conducted in an expanded and more precise manner. The truth of the wording in the divine servant sayings is now seen in the majesty and unassailable nature of Zion and her children. They are seen as the true pious ones, who participate in salvation and as YHWH's disciples.[46] In contrast to the rereading of Isaiah 51:1–8, Isaiah 54:11–17 consciously limits the meaning of the reference by a virulent distinction between the empirical Israel and the true Israel.

Concerning the Character of the Exegesis in the Productive Prophetic Tradition

Now we will attempt to understand this exegesis more closely in the productive prophetic tradition as a whole. If one surveys the material in broad strokes, then the following shows itself in the exegetical process.

If formulations in the rereading refer back to existing statements in the transmission as already recorded, then this rereading allows one to recognize a connection. In this matter, the conscious identification with the contents of the existing word means that the continuation (*Fortschreibung*) also speaks about the same metahistorical aspect and the same message as in the existing material as the references make clear. From the perspective of undiminished validity, the rereading essentially says nothing that was not already present. Therefore, the rereading can forego any self-legitimation.[47] Through historical inquiry, we recognize later material and altered or new statements as coming from the tradents. For the tradents themselves, this material that we recognize is not a different word or a new word over against the received transmission as such. In the same book, this material blends with the received material into a whole that continues to be valid. This whole is seen as a unity lacking any aspects of growth. It is seen as a metahistorically oriented reading context of an entire book, or even a whole series of books, in which the position of the later insertion ignites the redactional beacon for the whole.

But then why do the tradents continue to write with references to existing material? They do so because in subsequent times, the given material requires the unfolding of its validity and absolute validation. It requires this validation in light of changed experiences of observable history that are perceived prophetically, and/or in light of theologically necessary clarifications of the existing literary material. Thus, exegesis should be more precisely characterized as the material explication of the continuation of truth claims of the existing, formulated, and transmitted material. Received written material seeks its continuing truth-form for the time, and the tradents, with their rereading, are concerned with the unfolding of the implicit material already contained therein. This explication can also chronologically limit the valid transmission and include its essential continuation toward a new perspectival goal. This adoption of salvific perspectives into the metahistorical image demonstrates this fact.

For what purpose do the tradents reread and continue to write? Stated pointedly, they do not explicate the wording of the older text, or even reformulate it, as though it indicated a deficiency. Glosses or isolated insertions do that. Rather, with respect to orientation and expectation that is offered in this wording, the metahistorical aspect of the prophetically opened image of Israel correlates with changed historical experience. In the redactional processes of rereading, this aspect compels the continuing unfolding, precision, expansion, broadening, and limitation of this metahistorical aspect in conjunction with the existing writing in its wording. The wording continues to be transmitted and is essentially unaffected. The transmitted wording offers the metahistorical material, just not yet in a form that is fully explicated or currently concretized. Therefore, the continuation (*Fortschreibung*) borrows from this wording. The writing grows, the received material now stands in another context. In other words, the wording is not exegetically explicated. Rather, the material addressed therein is unfolded. God's lengthy chronological intention with God's people is correlated with the respective experience. However, this explication of the material, seen from the entire book, leads to a continuation (*Fortschreibung*) of the transmitted wording. The fact that the exegesis works so freely with the referenced texts coheres precisely with the material rationale of the exegetical perspective. God institutes the higher unity of the textual relationships!

From this point, a series of manifestations can be explained. The referential material is never taken up as a whole in the rereading. It is not necessary and thus should not be expected. The referential statements already exist. They are understandable in themselves, and as such, they are valid for the time provided by God. In contrast to exegesis today, that which the referential statements intend in their comprehensive wording in a changed constellation is not of concern for the tradents. Instead, the tradents are concerned with how, in a changed experiential situation, the material should now be explicated, expanded, and made more precise. They are even concerned with how it should be limited chronologically and materially, with respect to the continuing validation by the formulation of delimiting statements to the contrary.[48] Corrections, or even annulment of the existing material, are never the intention of the tradents, despite our impression from an exegetically historical comparison. Partial "citations," decisive adoption of individual word connections, and words from the reference text form the entry point for observing the rereading's statements. For our exegetical knowledge, these elements, like other characteristics of references,[49] serve as connections to that which was already said. For the tradents, as with the reader of the redacted prophetic book, these elements have a referential function in the reading flow of the recorded predictive whole. These elements signify a challenge to be moved while reading the book and a challenge to observe the explanatory expansion or precisioning of the references inside the material flow of the text in the writing.

Characteristically, redactional statements have the literary whole in view and possess very precise knowledge of the entire book in the flow of reading as a stipulation for understanding. These statements are indicated by references to the entire referential text in its context, along with additional referential texts in their contexts in the book. The statements are often presumed as having been read and adopted without being stated. The statements of the rereading are not yet formed as *Florilegia* ("garlands of blossoms") or mosaics already existing from statements.[50] Rather, as in the examples already noted, they are formed in great freedom and independence.[51] Even if the formulational references backward are only partial, the process of reception should not be characterized as "atomistic exegesis," because something essential would be overlooked in so doing. The process of reception does not shatter a historically elicited, original meaning that the tradents did not recognize or intend. Rather, the transmitted word essentially offers stations of meaning for the metahistorical image of history that are prophetically anticipated in the book.[52] These stations of meaning are made recognizable by the referential relationships and made explicit in the rereading of the whole book. In this sense, it is not exegesis in our traditional sense that dominates in the growth of the prophetic books.[53] Instead, prophetic exegesis in a broader sense dominates as the exegesis directed toward Israel's stages of meaning as forecast by YHWH.[54] The intention of this exegesis, as already mentioned, appears to be best encountered with the concept "explication."[55] In the opinion of the tradents, this exegesis makes explicit that which the existing referential text implicitly forecasts, including the transcending continuations. They do so in the fundamental conviction that the transmitted text, as information about God, contains more in its book than it states. The transmitted text includes a potential metahistorical meaning that transcends explicit formulations.[56] This transcended material is now discussed in the continuation (*Fortschreibung*).

In this explicative exegesis of the tradents, for example, Isaiah *60 and 61 later draw upon prominent texts in Second Isaiah, like Isaiah 49, Isaiah 40, or the servant song texts. These later texts unfold details about the existing linguistic material. They show how the present phenomena of deficiency will be overcome. They also show when the salvific event of return and restitution in the land will be completed. One reads the starting point of this event in the divine proclamation of Isaiah 40 and 49.[57] They did not read with the eyes of the historical exegete who extracts the originally sufficient meaning from the Deutero-Isaiah text, but with the eyes of the people of that time, who only concentrate and look upon the wording of the transmitted material, as they now understand it, concerning the metahistorical orientation of Israel. They see what is required for the continuing unfolding inside the comprehensive flow in order that the final stage of the leading image of the history of the completion of salvation be correctly read, explicitly in light of their own concrete experiences. It also appears in the book of Isaiah that we find an abundance of signs that show why the rereading drew upon those passages, together with their context in the existing material out of chronological or theological necessity. These passages were mostly highlighted because of their literary position or content. Consider the example of the clarity of these measures up to the point of the attempted reader-reception of the newly reread whole. Trito-Isaiah texts are quite typically rereadings that continually draw upon pivotal and materially decisive texts like Isaiah 1, 40, and 55.[58] However, they also draw upon a massive text about the nations like Isaiah 30:27–33.[59] They draw upon statements profiling the mediator of salvation like the servant songs,[60] and upon sayings from the immediate context. The presupposed identity and the unity of the prophetic word are open to multiple validations. These validations show that concerns about guilt, warning, and predictions of the later time are subsequently oriented toward sayings that prophetic books attribute to the image of history of the past, preexilic period.[61] This orientation occurs in formulations and also in catchword references in the prophetic corpus. Naturally, it follows that the exegesis by no means intends to replace the text material in the book that furnishes that material. Rather, the exegesis must continually be seen with it.[62] The older material maintains its validity in its literary and metahistorical place. It is the source of the rereading. The literary flow of the rereading can be possibly limited to a partial validity for an earlier period. Rereadings preserve older predictions of salvific procedures in particular. However, the full validity continues as that which already exists even when, for the same event, the rereadings require continuing explication or, if need be, the limitation of their complete duration of validity.[63]

How is the redactional exegesis represented as such? According to everything that has been said, redactional exegesis is not presented as a word-for-word exegesis. The transmitted word, which already exists, is clear by itself and continues to be evident. Rather, the redactional exegesis is presented as it corresponds to the demand for material limitation and the demand for preserving identity for the reader. Redactional exegesis is exegesis for the sake of a more or less decisive new reading of the flow of the entire book, or at least parts of it. Thus, redactional exegesis is presented more as thematic explication of text and context by adopting the style and significant expressions, at times even quoting, although the references are never introduced as quotes. Redactional exegesis is also presented by adopting those linguistic and material elements that catch the eye of the tradent for chronological or theological reasons.

Exegetical explication can lengthen the chronological extent of the text, as we observed in Daniel and in Qumran. Even the current time period can be explicitly considered as in Isaiah *56–59, over against Isaiah 55:6 and following. Or, the explication can be lengthened, as in the return redaction as a whole, in view of the salvific event of Israel's return over against Isaiah 40. Also, seen from the perspective of historical exegesis, explication can see the circle of those affected by a speech as currently expanded, narrowed, chronologically differentiated, or changed. However, in the mind of the tradents the circle of those affected is made more precise over against the received text, as for example, the reception of the servant texts inside Isaiah or the rereading of Isaiah 65 and following show. Finally, exegetical explication can concretize the deep meaning of a message that now includes comprehensive and current chronological experience, as one may deduce from redactional texts of Isaiah 60 and following as well as Zechariah 9–14.[64]

One can ask whether hermeneutical rules come into play in this explanatory exegesis, rules like those we find preserved in later rabbinic transmission.[65] One can apparently find starting points, and a redaction historically explained image of the prophetic transmission incorporates foundations for renewed inquiry. However, it should be clear from all that has been discussed that the exegesis does not yet result in decisions from rules. A particular heremeneutical horizon dominates in a system of texts, a horizon that is still in flux at the onset of the second century B.C.E.

Literary Exegesis of the Prophets as Prophetic Exegesis

Innovation in the Productive Prophetic Tradition

Is this explicatory rereading of the prophets itself prophetic in the development of the prophetic books? One must answer this question yes for two reasons.[66]

Historical exegetical inquiry demonstrates that material for the rereading in the books is full of innovative new ideas without harming its exegetical character. These ideas are by no means only provided from the wording of the transmission material being considered, either for the reception of the chronological period, or for the time of the image of history in the certainty that the turning point, toward which the explanation is aimed, is now very close, or with respect to the concretions around which the existing material is expanded. Also, one must speak about these new theological concepts of the whole that the rereadings and redactions put forth.[67] The tradents are convinced that they are offering the ultimate proclamation of YHWH in prophetic transmission. If one so desires, one finds inspiration at work among these tradents concerning the quantity and quality of their statements, despite all the references back to existing material. Instead, one also finds an innovative aptitude for wording. One finds innovation and not just a creative exegetical method that runs parallel to existing material.[68] This innovation now operates over against the reception of the word of the original prophets in the powerful explication of the existing prophetic material. This innovation was oriented toward a writing and becomes a writing

from the outset because for a long time prophecy was also constituted as written prophetic transmission, nothing else. After Zechariah,
prophecy was exclusively constituted as written prophetic transmission. Last but not least, this innovation is certain that the constellations of its own time period belong to the turning point that the
book proclaims, which is now very close. Innovation makes certain
that the time of rereading is the last time period presupposed. Later,
Daniel, the Qumran texts, the animal apocalypse of *1 Enoch*, and
other writings know the divine plan of time by special revelation. I
have therefore used the term "tradent prophecy" to describe this
phenomenon.[69]

With the formation of the statements, the view of YHWH is also
prophetically announced in his presence to the current time period
of the tradents. Thus, the view of that time and experience is also
prophetic for the purpose of transmitting metahistorically current
knowledge of YHWH to Israel. They attempted to preserve as valid,
and to strengthen by explication, the transmission of the derived
truth of YHWH and Israel's meaningful time in the face of the subsequent challenges. This endeavor corresponds to the character of
Israelite prophecy as the prophets described it at the beginning of
the transmission. Tradent prophecy also concerns prophecy in the
certainty of time and in the material proceedings. Naturally, this
prophecy occurs in the medium of written transmission and the orientation toward the written transmission. Thus, innovation belongs
to the character of these tradents, even though it is not accentuated
as their own inspiration, but was seen as the continually effective
material of the prophet who provided the name. Their activity is
prophetic to the degree that they explain received prophecy!

However, these tradent prophets do not appear as specific prophets alongside the transmission, and they say virtually nothing about
their special exegetical inspiration in contrast to Sirach, Daniel, and
Qumran. We (still) do not know who the tradents are.[70] The high
cultures of reading and learning presupposed by the continuation
process (*Fortschreibungsprozesse*) in the prophetic books point toward
particular, professional, school-like circles. These circles have apparently learned from the way in which wisdom was transmitted
and potentially from legal transmissions.[71] However, it is still too
early to surmise every historical concretion of this lengthy phenomenon of prophetic tradition. For example, it is pure conjecture to
accept an Isaiah school that blossomed for centuries. One may think

first about groups of students and disciples of the prophets themselves such as we have transmitted about Elijah, Elisha, Isaiah, and Jeremiah. In the postexilic period one may also potentially think about groups of temple singers whose care of tradition was still separate from, though closely related to, that of the priests and wisdom teachers. The confirming perceptions of these temple singers are closely associated with late rereadings of texts. At any rate, it is clear for the late period that these prophetic rereadings that dominate the large mass of texts with respect to memory and intellect are not concerned with processes directly in a congregation or for a congregation (whatever this Protestant exegetical construct might have meant in that time period). Rather, these prophetic rereadings dominate with respect to the standpoint of Israel on God's path of history. These rereadings concern a theological and professional event of confirmation of the prophetic books. They treat the books as theological confirmation literature among specialists to whom are presented the problems of the connection between concrete experience of time and Israel's divine transmission. In this line, one may see the later works as interpreters of the prophets: in Sirach, the angel and the wise Daniel, and the priests of Qumran. These specialists, trained insiders who trained themselves, were professional groups of authors and readers in one. They knew their writings in the most precise details in the sequence and statements in the service of fluid rereadings. Only after canonization, as the river of productive rereadings had come to a standstill, did this situation change. Only then could exegetically isolated usage give way to atomistic exegesis. Before that point, however, specialists tended whole books and the series of books. However, it is also clear that knowledge tended in this manner, the insight achieved internally with respect to the standpoint of Israel in God's prophetic meaning of history, was no end in itself. This knowledge must also serve the general public of God's people, as can be clearly recognized, for example, in Isaiah 35:3 and following with respect to the spiritual care oriented toward hope, or in Isaiah 58 and following with respect to the hope-filled teaching about the suitable attitude toward YHWH. This general public must also be sought at that time.[72] Experiences from these communications can also influence the shaping and contents of the continuations, even if we do not yet have a really adequate historical representation of the manner in which this external contact took place. Only at the very end can one think of synagogues or their precursors.

If one wishes to procure an unguarded perspective of the tradition process among these prophetic tradents, then one should perhaps consider the following aspects by inferring the result that lies in the books.[73]

Later tradents adopt a fundamental conviction from the original prophet and the first tradents. Namely, the divine words, prophetically spoken and recorded in written form, assert the past, present, and future conduct and condition of God's people among the nations until the downfall of God's people. Or later, divine words assert what happens from the downfall to the completion of salvation as YHWH's meaningful activity. The activity will come to fruition in accordance with YHWH's effective word. This fundamental conviction resulted in the permanent alignment of the tradents toward the concretely experienced path of historical events in Israel's world. This pathway was viewed from the perspective of received prophetic transmission. Confirmations already experienced have the greatest weight, but they are not a prerequisite. Rather, the fundamental conviction persists. In so doing, the interest lies in interpreting the material correlation and the correspondence between the concrete history of events of the respective time of the tradents and the state of the divine history for Israel drawn from prophetic tradition. This tradition continues to be read and learned.

For this process, one must think of professional "school" discussions in the groups of tradents. These discussions dealt with new political constellations, new phenomena of guilt, and new concretions of judgment in light of the transmission material. However, they also dealt with further concretions of salvation based upon deficiencies of experience and/or theological consequences. The discussions continually asked about the reasons for the delay of salvation in the current experiential period. The transmitted wording of the prophetic texts in the book or series of books is authoritative for these discussions. Later, the Torah and texts from the former prophets also became authoritative. Of course, among the tradents, the question was not directed toward the original meaning of the wording for the prophet, as in historical exegesis. The tradents did not know this question. They knew that the prophet providing the name received the transmitted wording in his time, but that he spoke not just to his time. Far more material is fixed within this wording. Specifically, one may deduce the meaning anticipated by YHWH for Israel's entire path. For later generations, this meaning has already occurred in part, or has happened again, according to the

divine truth of YHWH's prophetic word, which is not bound chronologically. The question of text material received from prophets
was thus directed by the tradents in light of the authoritative transmission toward the extent to which current problems of the particular contemporary experience that are discussed in this wording of
the received material have a metahistorical starting point for a solution or potentially demand a delimiting understanding of the
tradition.

This process of recognition that generally surmounts exegesis in
the narrow sense comes to a close when statements of the transmitted material show themselves in the discussion as the foundation
required for the current solution. Then one can seek formulations
that explain this foundation afresh in cross-references. These formulations process their foundation so that their actualized,
metahistorical meaning now anticipates YHWH's judgment and
activity for Israel. The meaning extends to the experience and the
divine future perspective of the tradents' time. This meaning can be
perceived in the words, in fact in a new reading, a new structuring,
and a redaction of the entire prophetic transmission, no matter the
size. Instead of their own, new, current oracle, the meaning becomes
the metahistorical matter hidden in the wording of the transmitted
material. This material should be preserved by continuation
(*Fortschreibung*) and redaction of the transmitted material. It expli-
cates transmitted prophecy in view of the entire intention of YHWH,
as YHWH is present in the current time—no more and no less! Therefore, the explication is even qualitatively the word of YHWH like
the material now explained. The explication is itself prophetic, surpassing all intellectual creativity in the adaptation of the transmission. The explication itself becomes the spirit of the spirit of the
prophet and is not literarily distinguished as the growing part of the
written transmission material.

Thus, these tradent prophets as such disappear in their tradition, but their anonymity has meaning and is materially determined.

Productive Tradent Prophecy as the Statement of the Prophet

The previous observations show the second condition that we
must consider under the aspect of the prophetic element of this prophetic exegesis in the growth of the books. This condition takes
account of the self-presentation of the transmission in the prophetic

books. While the formulations of the rereading are neither accented nor introduced on their own merit, they appear simultaneously on a par with statements of the prophet providing the name! Even the later insertions and redactions are a part of the prophetic writing and are not distinguished as later material.[74] In other words: For these tradents, YHWH also continues to speak in their later formulations, through the prophet Isaiah from the eighth century, for example. Isaiah speaks out of the tradents in his own time, beyond his own Assyrian period, even to the changed experiential constellations of the Babylonian, Persian, and even Hellenistic periods. Zechariah spoke in the Darius period in the sixth century and continues to speak in Zechariah 9–14 to the conditions of the Alexandrian and the Diadochan periods. For these tradents, the elements are qualitatively all the same: reception and allowances, exegesis and text, continuation (*Fortschreibung*) and existing text. The books of Isaiah and Zechariah, like all the other prophetic books, are materially nothing more than different messages of the prophets themselves.[75] Our historical-analytical perspective is one perspective, and the self-understanding of the tradents in their time is another perspective. For example, for them, YHWH speaks the book of Isaiah through Isaiah in its entirety. For them, Isaiah is not contradictory. He only continues to speak with respect to different times and aspects. For them, the entire developing book is a single, continuous self-explication and self-actualization of Isaiah, or more precisely, a *self-actualization of YHWH* through Isaiah. With respect to the salvific change, the tradents add new elements (seen historically) to the received material that was dominated by the (encountered) judgment of YHWH, but they add that material as the message of the same prophet. Even this material is understandable in this aspect. YHWH's transformation enters in connection with and in reference to the received message of the prophet. This self-explication of YHWH as time continues thus belongs materially in the mouth of this prophet who is proclaiming YHWH. For the tradents, the rereading and exegesis are therefore prophetic because they also stem from the prophet as God's message.

Seen historically, this direct personal allocation is misguided, but it corresponds to a material reason for the tradents of that time. We have already learned this reason with respect to the qualitative self-assessment of the rereading processes. Under the aspect of the author, the contents of the rereading express that which was already valid for the statements. They do not want to be derivative concerning the received prophetic transmission. Rather, they want to explain YHWH who expressed himself in the valid message of the prophet(s) during the continuing, comprehensive divine journey with Israel, as can be observed from the respective standpoint of reception. To this extent, the rereading processes are necessarily understood as the message of the prophet himself.[76] Potentially, one also finds a critical accent of its own time in the prophetic material of this prophetic exegesis, as with the Protestant, incarnationally grounded material of the exegesis of the gospel.[77] One has to reckon with an adequate reception for the prophetic material with an eschatological perspective over against the currently freely appearing prophets (Zech 13:2–6) and over against theocratic takeovers of prophetic transmission in other circles of postexilic Israel.[78]

Seen historically, can one perceive the lengthy growth of tradition of the prophetic books as the history of the effect of the message of the original prophet who provided the name to the book? And are the terms "history of effect" (*Wirkungsgeschichte*) and "reception history" even interchangeable for characterizing the growth of the tradition?[79] In many instances, this growth of tradition suggests that the impulses from the original core of transmission and from the original prophetic figure certainly continue to work in a receptive version. At the same time we prefer,[80] with Koch, to connect the phenomenon of the prophetic transmission of the book with the term "reception history" rather than the "history of effect" (*Wirkungsgeschichte*). We do so in order to maintain the noteworthy, active, innovative, and creative-prophetic material. If one desired, one could even maintain the inspired prophetic material of this related (!) adaptation and continuation of the received material. The process of prophetic tradition in the growth of books thus satisfies the precise term "reception history." As a result, not every manner of adoption of existing material satisfies this term. Rather, the responsible adoption of authoritative text material is in view. This adoption wants to keep alive and affirm the validity and spirit of this transmission material in subsequent historical constellations.

In order to clarify the question we have raised concerning the relationship between the book and the message, one must distinguish between that which actually occurred in this literary process of tradition and the manner in which the tradents could have seen their inserted adaptations of the prophetic material and the assignment of these adaptations among the prophets. For the first aspect, one should observe that continuations (*Fortschreibungen*) and reshapings of a prophetic book are by no means supplied only from the oldest material of the book. According to our inquiry, the original message of the prophet is not the dominant perspective of the prophet at that time. Rather, the prophet is only confronted in his transmitted form. Above all, one may affirm orientations toward the later transmission form of the prophet of the book as we have it. And also, one may affirm orientations toward transmission material of other prophets (and prophetic books). Last but not least, one may affirm that creative new assertions are sometimes sketched in the contours of salvation. Thematically, these assertions can be associated with the received material of the prophet, and thus be arranged as the metahistorical explication of the prophet's transmission. However, they are not simply derived from this material.

One should therefore accept a second aspect. This process is founded upon the understanding that it is God who speaks through the prophets as time advances. God founds the higher material unity of the entire formation of the written prophetic transmission. God expresses himself for the self-perception of the tradents in the processes of productive rereading. This constitutive interim consideration appears to drive the connection between the material already transmitted and the continuation (*Fortschreibung*). It leads to the assigning of the continuation's statements to the prophet transmitted with the book. It does so because these statements materially explain that which God continues to say and do beyond the previously recorded transmission of the prophet yet in material connection to that transmission (and therefore bound with revelations to the prophets themselves). The process thereby proceeds far beyond the effect of the original message as the core of the transmission. Instead, the confirmed history of the validity of the entire divine-prophetic message conveys this process. With this presupposition, one can also understand that the prediction of peace in Isaiah 2 and Micah 4 can be bound with Isaiah and Micah, that one will find text repetitions between Jeremiah 49 and Obadiah, and that toward the end of the growth of the prophetic transmission, in our opinion, 2 Isaiah could be taken from Jeremiah and connected with Isaiah.

There is a late rereading text in Isaiah that recognizes this position of the prophets for Israel. In the case of Isaiah, it also recognizes Isaiah as the first book in the developing series of prophetic books and even its paramount position. In so doing, it even for a moment illuminates the self-understanding of the tradents and their role in the transmission. As an important concluding passage for the time before the coming completion of salvation discussed after Isaiah 60, Isaiah 59:21 offers a divine speech:[81]

> *But I—this is my covenant "with them" says YHWH: My spirit which is upon you and my words which I have placed in your mouth will not depart from your mouth or the mouth of your offspring, or your offspring's offspring, says YHWH now and forever.*

A chart of the translation of the text provides an overview of the external textual influences (see next page).

In this late text, YHWH defines his covenant with "them," with the (true) people of God, by a precisioning of covenant sayings that already appear literarily in the book.[82] In so doing, the people are not themselves addressed. Rather, the "you" in this paragraph is the prophet, as in the opening in 58:1. Which prophet? The character of Isaiah *56–59 as a redactional composition for a large book of Isaiah in the Ptolemaic period in general and the orientation backward to Isaiah 8:16–18 in particular, shows that the "you" intends no one other than the prophet Isaiah from the eighth century, the prophet of the book. One can say that Isaiah also received this message in his time, and that it encompasses the direct and indirect effect for the entire subsequent period. Thus, the message de facto encompasses the period up to the tradents' time in the Hellenistic period. Beyond that, the prophet includes this message as the covenant of YHWH with the people. The individual expressions and the parallel statements in Isaiah 51:16 show that the Isaiah of the book receives cumulative characteristics of the servant of God (42:1; 49:2) and of Zion (61:1). In addition, he receives characteristics of Jeremiah and Ezekiel from texts about the prophetic office in the attached books; one even recalls Deuteronomy 18:18, with the promise of a continual presence of a prophet like Moses, and the image of the successor Joshua (Josh 1:8, which leads to the singular agreement in 59:21aβ, bα). Thus, one can say that the Isaiah of this book was perceived as the prominent, initial one and the beginning of a literary series of prophetic books. With his equipment and teaching the words of YHWH, Isaiah constitutes the irrevocable covenant of YHWH with the people. The people are directed toward the prophetic transmission for their salvation and for the expression of the

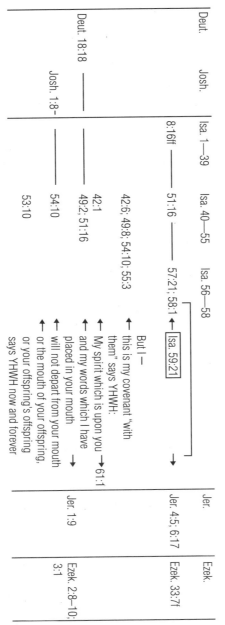

Isaiah 59:21 as the Bundling of Literary References in a Sequence of Writings

nearness of YHWH. Israel can endure by this prophetic, literary instruction for the sake of the participation in salvation throughout the time period in which YHWH would otherwise not have been made known (58:1 and following). Isaiah was first, but not alone, as the prophetic, literary servant of God whom the other prophets resemble with their books in divine inspiration.

Just like 53:10, 59:21 also speaks of the offspring of the servant of God. In reference to the correspondingly understood saying in Isaiah 8:6–18, God's people should also hold fast to the distant offspring of the prophet Isaiah, from whom the words of YHWH do not deviate. The offspring of Isaiah was endowed with God's words. We do not hesitate to see Isaiah's tradent posterity herein, potentially even the tending of tradition in a specific scribal milieu in which YHWH's spirit, loaned to Isaiah, continues to operate. The tradent offspring of the prophet kept continual watch over, and maintained as authoritative, the prophet's message of YHWH through the subsequent period. Our essay has attempted to probe tradent prophecy with its prophetic exegesis of the prophets.

Theological Impulses from the Process of the Transmission of a Prophetic Book

We stand at the end of our initial approach to a scarcely treated topic. What does a review show? Anyone who turns to the prophetic books of the Hebrew Bible in scientific inquiry must distinguish two perspectives.

The first perspective is directed toward the manner in which these books present themselves according to the understanding of their tradents. As a result of this understanding, each prophetic writing documents how these persons successively made God known in particular disclosures directed toward the various stages along Israel's way. They also document how God determined the activity, or occasionally even the effect, of the respective prophet while alive. The individual prophets of each book, and ultimately the cumulative witness of their books, thereby effectively reveal far-reaching perspectives. These perspectives are thoroughly perceived in their diversity and stand on their own. However, for the tradents, these perspectives do not express confusion and contradictions. Rather, they express comprehensive material unity, and the validity of this unity is gradually disclosed. They are YHWH's truth for the ages expressed in characteristically prophetic speech. All of these manifold proclamations of YHWH in the inventory of the prophetic books were seen by the tradents as the fluid self-explication of the divine intention for Israel in the realm of the nations. The process that these writings convey is the process of the self-proclamation of YHWH by partial acts of different disclosures to different persons over the course of different time periods. From this process, the comprehensive intention of God for the condition of Israel can be seen as a higher unity of transmission in the individual sayings' relevant reference to particular stages along Israel's way. Stated more specifically, one must deduce the comprehensive intention of YHWH. It can be continually processed in the subsequent period, even if the characteristic work of the tradents in the prophetic books does not appear specifically. For material reasons, the time of recorded divine proclamation is limited to the framework of the lifetime of the writing prophet. In this respect, the shape of the prophetic books is thus determined by concepts with respect to the revelation and prophecy of ancient Israel.

Scientific inquiry demands another perspective. Scientific inquiry is trained differently than the ancient tradents and inquires into the historical processes of origin in the prophetic books. That which the books present as a process during the lifetimes of the prophets actually shows itself more as a lengthy process of tradition that often extends over centuries. That which the books connect with the prophetic figure appears as a productively adaptive process of reception in which a tradent group is active long after the prophet. As we saw, the reception process was full of connection and simultaneously full of flexibility. This reception process wants to perceive YHWH's freedom for the historical realization in the realm of the subsequent period. For our historically trained eyes, this process is full of change, differentiation, complexity, and contradictions. The process requires that one consider, even chronologically, more or less prolonged growth of the prophetic books and series of books. One should, however, not overlook the signals that the tradents have incorporated. These signals indicate a sense of the sayings' higher unity and comprehensive agreement. Also, under the recent historical approach, one can acknowledge that the prophetic books want to convey a perspective from the outside, that they mean God when they say God,[83] and that their sayings provide a clarification of meaning that may be investigated historically and theologically in the respective chronological environment of the transmission.[84] If so, then in the development of the written prophetic transmission it appears that the tradents themselves have presented the prophets biographically. The development expresses the perception of YHWH in the long subsequent periods. This perception is bound to tradition, but it is also creative. The development also appears in the tradents' meandering, comprehensive horizons of purpose as insight into the continuing work of the completely valid message of YHWH in the realm of new experience. When seen in this manner, the material movement of this tradition is carried by the message and continuing experience when seen and considered together. The result is recorded as the inherent aspect of the message itself. According to historical inquiry, the tracks of the evidence of this authoritative, but at the same time extended knowledge of God in the experiences and hopes of the subsequent period became the object of the tradents' search. These traces were found by the tradents with certainty and materially attributed to the prophets of the books, even if the limitation remained that the complete demonstration of truth still lies in the future because of the freedom of divine realization of the word. Future constellations of experience in the life of God's people could show further aspects of meaning in the message of the prophetic book. Also the completion of Israel's time more or less lies in the future for the reception processes.

Both perspectives, the ancient (as the prophetic books present themselves) and the recent (as suggested by historical inquiry), relate to one another. Both share the same subject, God, who is prophetically made known in these books concerning the time frame of God's people in the world of the nations. Both share the existing contents of this proclamation and the effects that are described therein. That which changes from a historical perspective is the insight into the historical conditionality and the character of the means of conveying this proclamation in the books. One now sees changing experiences and challenges over a lengthy time, well beyond the original prophetic figure. These changes shape the formulations, contents, and horizon of prophetic perception of YHWH. They lead to changes. Tradents consider moving toward experiential constellations of their own time in conjunction with the prophets transmitted to them. They also continue to write the received material in order to go further. The connection of time, even the arrest of time, comes to expression in the process of the growth of the prophetic books. One also finds therein the conviction that God and experiential life should remain in connection to one another. The God conveyed prophetically also remains a dynamically present God in the subsequent period and in reference to his character. One should speak about God in the respective present time in connection with the transmission and under the influence of changing perspectives. The fluidity of the growing prophetic tradition and the fluidity of the dynamic God who turns to every generation are connected. As the prophetic reception of late Israel and the reception of emerging Christianity demonstrate, this process by no means stops with the close of the inventory of the prophetic books. The transmission now becomes foundational and, as such, is no longer changeable. However, question and answer continue in view of the metahistorically chronological realm and the realm of validity. They add precision to the transmitted sayings that were affected. They lead to changes of the foundational transmission in the meaning, in the material expanse, limitation, and formulation. They also admit the entry of new experiences and challenges as intertestamental texts, Qumran, and the New Testament show.

If this review has perceived something essential in the transmission process of the prophetic books, then the phenomenon as such is worthy of consideration. We will now conclude the next two sections of our contribution with thoughts about a question: What theological impulses could still lie in this phenomenon today?

The Temporal Nature of Tradition in the Growth of the Prophetic Books

The process of "tradition" is especially significant with its essential temporal nature. If we have seen correctly, this process confronts historical inquiry from the Bible. It can include impulses beyond the ancient finding that could still benefit theology today.[85]

The development of prophetic books signifies a particular type of notification that a problem exists, specifically the relationship of the scripture and tradition. Much has been considered about scripture and tradition, but far too little about scripture as tradition. This type of writing was a reception process instigated from outside, over lengthy time periods. This process contains more than just intelligible content in an environment of life and experience that demands attention.[86] Are the reasons for the problems of understanding between exegesis and dogmatics not such that one distinguishes "holy scripture" in the outlook of the phenomenon while hardly presenting its own character of tradition? "Holy scripture" as a collection of sentences that are true for all time constantly stands over against "holy scripture" as a dynamic process of the transmission of developing truth in time. In a particular respect, it is certainly correct. To the extent that the event of Jesus Christ, with the comprehensive temporal perspectives disclosed in it, was perceived as the conclusion and purpose of divine self-proclamation, it should thus be distinguished from the developing truth of prior prophetic transmission.

However, one has not yet settled the following question not only in view of the New Testament that has developed similarly: Must "holy scripture" be transformed by this essentially new hermeneutical situation into sentences that are true for all time? Or, does the process of biblical tradition contain lines of thought that point beyond itself, that are also characteristic and worthy of consideration? Insights into the temporally oriented development of prophetic books like those that we have treated could, of course, only be disturbing. Scripture preserves its validity only in the blurring of its historical origins and growth processes, only where the writing is understood as the foundation of doctrinal reflection about particular sayings that have proven true and are valid in themselves, when taken from their time and placed in very different intellectual realms. By contrast, the prophetic books show a manner of speaking about God that does not perceive the everlasting validity of God in temporally neutral sentences that remain valid for all times, and that one need only continuously explain and utilize. As historical perspective recognizes, the received prophetic transmission in these books also remains completely time-bound according to origin and saying. Its affirmation in later periods requires not only interpretation, but also the literary and material continuation of the transmitted material. The message continues only as this historical process unfolds, as the tradition moves. It is not just these transmitted texts that remain moving in the continuing flow of time. No. More is reflected there. God himself is also moving in the perception of the developing books. This movement remains foundational for the lines of meaning noted in the developing books when the books reach their developed final form. Even then, the final form does not become an arsenal of timelessly valid sentences for an authoritative text. It is itself a historical entity and materially incorporates a process of tradition over a lengthy period.

We attempt to preserve this tradition process as such, as it shows itself today, without the necessarily new accentuations of Christian hermeneutics. From this tradition process, one can also recognize God from the transmitted material as time advances for Israel, but God surpasses this transmitted material. God is thus not present in general determinations or just in the original meaning at the beginning of the transmission. God moves in the course of time with the transmission, personally encountering and acting. According to prophetic proclamation, God remains identical with himself in this way and no other in the experiential realm of Israel's entire time in the world.

Therefore, transmission about God in the realm of written prophetic tradition must be an active process that observes the dynamic nature of God in time. As a result, even the contents of this transmission arise as a literarily developing affirmation of God's initiation in the course of time. Prophetic theology is of necessity a living tradition with wide-open horizon in its orientation toward God in transmission and the suitably examined change of time. Prophetic theology is not always merely the actualization of the prototypical genius of poetic, kerygmatic, and social reforming material with its overtly pointed sayings that are deemed valid for all time and that must be maintained in every time with equal fervor. This tradition accompanies the living God, led by received transmission, on God's way through the time of transmission. This tradition is essentially temporal for the sake of God's initiative in Israel's time.

Hasty actualization is not the way of this tradition in the growth of the prophetic books. As we saw, their temporal connection was not only directed toward the punctilliar, nor isolated in the present time of the recipients. It was also directed toward the entire realm of time that Israel could recall and that they could expect, even up to the point of the completion desired since the late Israelite transmission phases. This realm was condensed, ordered, and clarified as a process of God's favorable inclination that was granted, denied, and hidden. After universal judgment and the disempowering of every opposing force, this favorable inclination would finally be completed without hindrance. In this broad material and comprehensive framework of the growth of tradition within the prophets, one should ask the question about the transmission's realm of validity! Because this comprehensive framework is set, the formulated transmission points well beyond itself to the task of its respective current adaptation. Theology in the transmission process is therefore the thoughtful conveying of the received material as a whole, because it perceives the entire realm of time for specific divine knowledge. At the same time, theology again perceives its current confirmation as time-bound because the experiential constellations change, meaning the question of the God who is now present also changes. Theological confirmation of truth in the development of the prophetic books is and remains an advancing tradition that is open to life and experience. It remains a tradition directed toward broad fields of experience and validity that proceed beyond a single generation. Also, as this development comes to a halt and authoritative tradition and exegesis appear alongside one another, this character continues to operate, even if other concepts of the path of God's people are made serviceable alongside prophetic sayings in isolation (compare the Chronicler's History, the Psalter, Wisdom, *Jubilees*, Qumran texts like 4QMidrEschat, CD, New Testament). The purpose of the tradition process in the development of the books is the orientation based upon the current lengthy temporal perspective of Israel and encouragement in the constitutive framework of historical experiential reality as the realm of the perception of the sympathetic God. The task that continually dominates this tradent prophecy in ongoing and literarily productive reflection is not the reflection upon truth that only continues to be valid spiritually, and that is proscribed in assertions that are valid for all time. Rather, the task is perceiving the continuing protection of the received proclamation of God through the experiential world in the entire time-frame of God's people.

The Process of Prophetic Tradition as Stimulation

As today's historical investigation suggests, the prophetic books do not stand alone in the Old Testament transmission with this particular perspective of a theology woven together in the ongoing progression of time. One finds a similar type in the growing transmission of Moses up to and including the final texts of the Torah.

Certainly, assertions about God exist that separate God from the concrete flow of time. They speak of the eternally enduring character of God. However, these assertions are far less common and have another place. The Hebrew Bible does not speak about the eternal, ever valid character of God at the beginning of every theological effort as with opening statements as the starting point of conclusions. Rather, it speaks only after extensive and intensive consideration of God in the realm of time and experience in the entire historical framework of Israel's reality that the historical and prophetic books offer. Thus, the Hebrew Bible speaks only at the end as the summation of experience and trust in the linguistic world of praise and liturgy as the psalms show. In the Hebrew Bible, these final assertions offering proclamations are the place to speak of the essence and characteristics of the eternal, the place to speak of the God who endures from the most distant time into the farthest reaches of time. Or the final assertions speak about this lengthy time in the wisdom reflection from its experiential crisis in the limited human life, as Job and Qohelet consider it, at least in factual critique of the prophetic view that more openly considers meaningfulness in the lengthy chronological period.

By contrast, theological thinking in the process of prophetic transmission, but also historical and legal transmission, does not concentrate on the comprehensive validity of God in these kinds of assertions. They maintain this validity just as strongly. This prophetic tradition does not become a broad, colorful, and multidimensional stream capriciously. Rather, because this tradition limits and observes connecting transmission in the freedom of God, how God turns to Israel and the world over time, therefore the observation of God is even exposed for the concrete flow of time. In so doing, this transmission continually attains its intimacy from the immediate life reference of the whole, and does not fear the time-bound limits and the surpassable nature that belong to the received formulations. This view of theology as a process of tradition in the development of prophetic books is shaped de facto by its own temporal nature in the reception of tradition. It is constitutively related to the current constellations of life, even when it limits the temporal nature of God's sympathy in the proclamation to the lifetime of the prophet. These books did not have in mind a theology that perceives itself sufficient in a manner that is essentially neutral toward time and life as a proper system of thought. A kind of theology that overlooks the fact that it must affirm the relative and dynamic shape of the transmitted truth as historically related to its current (entire) situation would not fit these books. Nor did they have in mind theological exegesis of texts and the formations of a system that, in their use of scripture, connects philology to the historical aspect and philosophy to the essential questions. Theology in the process of tradition for the prophetic books gives itself to the changing relationship between the transmitted material and the present time. It does so, not by abstractly preserving traditions of thought, but by intellectually integrating life's breadth and history's depth. This integration is characteristic of a tradition responsible for the transmitted material and a tradition that simultaneously perceives and develops that material. One perceives the eternal validation of the truth of the biblical word that is related to different times of immediate validation. It is enriched by present experiences and silently limited by new experiential constellations of the future that no one yet knows but that will later force persons to additional continuations and interpretations. In the prophetic books, the coordinated nature of life in the entire realm of time for Israel thus replaces the coordinated nature of the system on fundamental grounds and not just temporally stipulated grounds in the perception of God. The truth and validity of the transmission should only be considered for God's sake so that they can be experienced and expected in this realm, explained by the prophets, and continually clarified for every epoch by a newly explained realm.

Concurrent, considered, and reflective affirmation has its own special task in the form of intellectual clarification that certainly came into operation in the process of the productive conveying of the prophetic transmission. However, it is a partial task that has its limits in the challenges and puzzles of a multidimensional life. In the view of this tradition, the living God operates in this broader realm of life that takes in experience. It is God who, in his presence and turning to historical life, urges the continuing formation of tradition.

This finding has consequences if the continuing validity of the biblical basis is to be affirmed in later times. Specifically, this process must accept that the prophetic transmission recorded the perception of God within the limits of a set time frame. It must accept that the texts not only speak a different language than later texts, but that they also operate in another time that has its own experiences and experiential handicap in the frame of its own world of thought and life. This entire process determines the biblical formulation whose own imprisonment to time cannot be separated from it. Stated positively: later movement of the transmission of the foundational tradent material also opens changing experiential constellations, and places changing references on the tradent material. It continues to ponder and to formulate this material without giving it up as a valid basis from an earlier time. The prophetic process of transmission even allows us to recognize that, in light of experiential change, one can essentially say the same thing, only in the framework of received material that is preserved and simultaneously expanded.

The effective discovery of these potentially parallel threads may even be constitutive for conveying the old transmitted material. The discovery of these potentially parallel threads between the tradition process of ancient prophetic theology and the traditional task of today's theology must naturally look beyond the essential limits placed between the coming of Christ and the canon. It must also look beyond differences that are connected to the manner of transmission. Time-related theology in the prophetic transmission could also still move in a homogenous realm of reception within the lengthy time of the growth of the prophetic transmission. In the subsequent period, time-related theology could therefore read the transmitted material itself in a new way and directly expand that material. The escalation that the prophetic canon represents as a textual entity that is now closed results henceforth in the appearing alongside one another of the foundational prophetic transmission and its adaptation with respect to the shape of the transmission and recipients. Indeed, they drift apart from one another in growing historical difference. Likewise, the growth phase of the prophetic books, the eminent time difference, and the experiential difference lead to the fact that adaptation also includes a renewed intellectual, linguistic adaptation of the foundational transmitted material. Such is the case after the books of Chronicles, but certainly since the book of *Jubilees* and Qumran. In the subsequent period, this challenge continues to escalate. The changing shape belonged to the process of tradition when the process was not closed. The shape continued to grow when the material identity and the closeness of time had to be preserved in like manner in this process. The process of adaptation must thus also include the expansion of time-bound biblical limits of experience, thought, and language. The process must allow critique of the antiquated and dated material, as well as critiques of the potentially merged interests of legitimation of the tradent groups in the transmission material. On the other hand, all power must also remain for the opening of internal limits in later times by effective biblical perspectives.

Still, these differences do not signify a break in every respect from that which came before. Rather, as we saw, these differences continue lines that have their origin in the prophetic transmission. The prophetic transmission even brings to expression the fact that it owes its linguistically conceived perception of God to particular constellations of life and experience of the respective time. As a result, the prophetic transmission leaves the received material with a certain reshaping adaptation in changed experiential constellations within the historical perception of God. As it perceives and conveys valid material, prophetic transmission remains within the perceptual and formulational limits of its time-bound nature. It also continues to write the received material within this valid material. In so doing, the growth of the transmission demands and further incorporates the later experiential realm and the respective constellation of life. These elements are kept for the sake of the transmission's subject and for the sake of the God who grants time and life. It protects the received material, but nevertheless surpasses that material despite the restriction of the state of its text and the formulational limits. A hermeneutic of the potentiality of meaning for the same ancient wording, even into modern times would prove insufficient. It has been demonstrated that a received text included more than the original meaning only when correlating later constellations of life. The continuing life of these texts is not simply limited to the exegesis of the given material. Rather, it gives additional thought to changed experiences in the meaning of the transmitted God. It also continues to formulate the received material with an eye toward that which is new or newly conscious, in this manner comprehending the God of the transmission as the continuously living God. The transmission of the prophetic books, when historically investigated, thus presents a contrasting perspective with the result that the matter can rest with the presumed chronologically neutral validity of its intellectual coherence to a system like all biblical assertions. For the biblical texts, the transmission points more toward a tradition that continues to relate to time, meaning that it is also determined by time and limited by time. This tradition is directed toward the adaptation of the preserved basis of transmission in the breadth and innovation of the reflective nature of life. Thus, this tradition continues to consider, reformulate, and explain the foundation in light of the God who goes through time. In so doing, it unfolds a perception of God and continues to bring to life the transmitted truth in theological reflection in time.

Hermeneutical Considerations

In the previous section we devoted ourselves to those impulses that result when one sees prophetic books in light of the tradition process inherent in those books. As contemporaries, we did not search behind the process and facts of the "canonization" of the Nebiim, for this entity was the subject of our historical inquiry. However, we included the movement of tradition that for its part was already authoritative and standard and ultimately led to the final formation of the books as they entered Jewish and Christian canonical collections. We also reckoned with the lengthy historical nature of this growth of the books as the impulse of power against the ancient self-presentation, because this historically investigated aspect cannot be abandoned from our perception. We did so, because this aspect belongs to the reality of the prophetic books.

Nevertheless, can this inner-prophetic tradition process that was incorporated into the final formation of the canon simply be continued and actualized in its own sense? Can this tradition process be a direct model that today's theology and proclamation could follow without additional material? Could this innovative manner of movement also be our own, a movement with which the tradent prophecy of that time continually sought a form of truth close to experience for a valid wording? Does the late Israelite perspective of a higher unity not devalue our efforts for differentiation and diachronic awareness of the Isaiah book, for example, or even the prophetic transmission or the transmission of the Old Testament? We want to consider these questions more closely in selected aspects in the following sections.

Canon and Historical Perception

I believe that no theologian wants to jump behind the boundaries of canon. To that extent, the prophetic tradition process as such is surrounded by the absolute priority of holy scripture. On the other hand, our own traditional instruction, deliberation, and proclamation can only be derived and subordinated speech, but not less certain speech, about making God relevant. To that extent, later tradition is not the unbroken descendant of the prophetic tradents. Neither post-canonical Jewish tradition nor later Christian tradition determined by the Christ event of the New Testament can make this claim. Biblical prophetic tradition is the foundation of all further tradition and not just its starting point, which can be directly continued in the prophetic transmission process. To that extent, one must distinguish between the foundational, inner-biblical tradition concluded in the canon and all later tradition that is based upon the foundation of the canon. The latter always necessarily stands alongside the Bible, in distinction to the inner-biblical tradition process. So, can the tradition process that came to a halt in the final form of the canon be ignored from that point? An answer to this question must combine various aspects.

I believe no one would want to jump behind historical perception which alone is able to be correct for the complexity of prophetic tradition. It brings the transmission process that dominates here to the forefront and protects critically the opposite perspective of the transmitted material in the face of a diverse and often misunderstood history of effect (*Wirkungsgeschichte*). This has consequences for the theological self-certainty of the Christian faith. Consequently, the meaning appropriated today for prophetic sayings of the Hebrew Bible in the Christian church can only be found from the higher unity of the historically investigated original meaning at the beginning of the transmission, the meaning(s) preserved in the temporal nature of the tradition process in holy scripture itself, and in a connection to the Christian credo.[87] As such, the meaning must be theologically and creatively processed in a post-canonical way. It must be reformulated on its own in a responsible manner in view of the foundationally transmitted material, instead of being expressed in its own prophetic innovation.[88]

Can both leaps be avoided at the same time? The fact that both are prevented would appear to exclude this possibility because the historical perception of the processes that lie behind the formation of canon provide weight and thereby relativize the text's meaning at the time of the canon's formation. We believe that the challenge continues so that, as indicated above, one may simultaneously see the canon as an authoritative and historical entity, while keeping in mind that, the canonization of the biblical books gave a qualitative degree to a historical movement of tradition. This movement remains essential.

The biblical transmission of the word and deed of God as an essentially temporal process of tradition is the basic *extra nos* (beyond ourselves) for Christian theology. All Christian speech and activity, as well as all Christian concretions and utilizations are processes derived from this transmission. They are accountable to this foundation! Theology is the large and broad intellectual effort to preserve this biblical witness to God. The proof of its truth becomes a subject by the inclusion of everything real that should be contemplated in the limits of the current temporal nature and that should be determined in contemporary, concrete forms. The enduring theological right of Christian teaching about the Bible remains. It remains in this process of the confirmation of the fundamental divine witness of the history of the biblical perception, the simple instructional nature of Christian existence related to this witness, and the measurable lines of meaning first opened by this witness and not by later recipients. This teaching expresses that God himself may be perceived in this witness, and will convey himself to human beings. Such is the case, even if today one sees the witness in the theological adoption of historical research as the course and as that time-related perception by historically oriented persons. But these persons did not want to transmit punctilliar facts of historical accuracies. Rather, they wanted to convey history in divine perspective from outside, as the depth of meaning of lengthy experience with its events, fears, perspectives, and hopes. In other words, in material relating to God one should speak of the sufficiency of the holy scripture as the sufficiency of the fundamentally conveyed self-proclamation of God. This material relating to God may not be blurred as the subject of the transmission even in the reconstruction of historical inquiry. Rather, now as before, this material essentially comes to people from outside as unknown material through the biblical witness that lies well back in time and that continues to confront in a manner that is critically revealed. Thus, one justifies the fact that the biblical transmission as such should be kept alive through the ages and should be continually offered for knowledge and encounter.

However, this ranking does not veil the fact that the process of biblical tradition in this continuing role as a measuring rod simultaneously confronts us as an ancient book deriving from a long-distant past. One is surely correct in preserving its character. Thus, this ranking simultaneously includes the Bible's openness and lack of closure to the unfolding of the life and times and to the formulation of the message as demanded today in the continuation of the times, experience, and insight. Last but not least, the growth of the prophetic transmission shows this movability of tradition that conveys the fundamental material and simultaneously continues to adapt for the ongoing flow of time. By no means does tradition cease with the close of the written canon with respect to concretizing the perception of God in time. Tradition does not mean the canonically concluded aspect and the continuing, affirmative aspect contained therein. However, tradition means an aspect differentiated from mere continuation by responsible, perspectival adoption of the transmitted material in subsequent times. God's intention and foresight, as fundamentally formulated by the biblical transmission for its times, also prove true in the march of time, experience, and better knowledge. This fact continually requires affirmation. One must provide room for the insight that the canonical text material, even the material that makes ready the inclusion of meaning for the entire realm of time, asserts this material in the specific perception of an ancient time frame that is thus limited in every respect. If one follows the trail of the tradition process, one thing becomes clear. The adoption of the foundational earlier material is more than the continuing reaffirmation of the same enduring ancient formulations. Instead, this adoption continues to experience, think, formulate, and concretize the material of that time that was perceived as time-bound in the received, foundational transmission!

Within this framework, the question with which we began the last section should be taken up again.

The Aspect of Confirming Time in the Actualizing of the Book Prophets as a Theological Model

What weight does one give the actualization process that plays out in the growth of the books inside the prophetic transmission itself and then ceases? Does this process as such have continuing theological significance? Does it continue to play a role later where one seeks the proclamation of God in ancient, closed books in a living form closer to the current time? One could say: Let us, in our time, renounce an image of this lengthy development in the course of the long history in ancient Israel! Let us limit ourselves to the final phase, to the books and series of books in the social environment at the time of the formation of the canon. Let us in particular do so because the final measurable determination of the meaning of divine self-disclosure for Christianity should be taken only from the New Testament. One must decisively oppose this misleading reductionism with which the ongoing dissonances of Old Testament research can apparently be eluded with respect to the prior history of given text complexes. One must do so for many reasons, all of which resist limiting tradition solely to this foundational aspect and continue to ponder the largely confirmed aspect of tradition related to the progression of time.

Tradition may not become motionless for the sake of its temporal nature and for the sake of its continuing intelligibility. This statement should also be true for the canonized entities. The received formulation, the word, remains. However, its adaptation in both inner-biblical and post-biblical tradition is forced to change. For ancient prophetic transmission itself, its broad historical growth was not a subject as already acknowledged. As we see it, the transmission still perceived this growth as the multiplyiing of divine proclamation in the name of the prophet providing the name. It did so as a result of its ancient prophetic image in order to express the unity of God in the proclamation of his effective word in the unity of the authority of the founding conveyor. One did not yet differentiate between an original person as author and the growth of tradition attached to that person, as the self-presentation of the prophetic books allows one to recognize. However, our historical exploration of this growth does not stand in the way. It can clarify the origin, time reference, and meaning of this finding and can help to translate it into the framework of more recent perception of historical reality. We could not understand the constitution of the text formulation in particular without clarifying their situation of origin while still conceding its further inner-biblical and extra-biblical accretions of meaning.

The Hebrew Bible is transmission literature, meaning that it is characterized not only by the latest perceptions of God, but that it offers these perceptions in conjunction with older but also preserved transmissions. These transmissions were not just archived, but remain decisive for God to the point of their delimiting, surpassing, and even critical adoption in the subsequent tradition. Thus, it is the historical path of the perceptions of God that is decisive for recognizing God and the world! It is not the current individual oracle and not the rigid complex of canonized writings, but the transmission process that grows over time. If we take the prophetic books in their self-presentation, as with the historical inquiry according to their development as a whole, then we recognize God in the thoughts of these writings as books on the pathway to God's self-disclosure. God took this pathway through a fundamental time-flow for the ancients through the prophetic work itself, but from our perspective through lengthy, continuing, productive transmission. The relatedness to the history of the perception of God is an expression of God's dynamic nature related to this world. This insight into the character of time-nested tradition, changing, moving, and continuing, becomes just as lost when it disappears in the euphoria of the canonical final form of the text, as it does when the Bible is used as a source theologically for proof text truths for all time.

Historical inquiry also opens a very indispensable dimension of meaning in the realm of the prophetic books for the current theological perception of reality in the course of time when it maintains the divine sayings of the texts, and when it traces the clarification of meaning that the transmission material holds ready for the recipients' situation. This inquiry confronts the rigid canonical final forms of biblical books (even in the sense of text blocks taken out of time) and the dimension of the historical expanse of the disclosure and that which is disclosed. It can thus also confront the history of the perception of God that is true to life and demanded by life and that lies buried in the growing complexity of shape and formulation of these books from the beginnings to the final formations. Historical inquiry thus enables insight into the elementary relationship of time for the presence of God. It also does not close its eyes to the fact that even the canonical final forms of the books owe their character to a time that is long past for us, but that for its part is also the endpoint of a lengthy process. It is historical inquiry that holds the historically established truth in life (which is thus considered the truth of God) over against God's truth in valid determinations abstracted from time. Historical inquiry does not fear the price of the respective, time-bound nature of the form of the saying or even of the foundational canonical texts. It does not fear the ever-renewed approach of historical and theological affirmations. Such is the price that one should unquestioningly offer for achieving a personal, historically moving encounter in the devotion to God, as well as the devotion to humanity in the course of time. Thus, contemporary experience is adopted from old texts and continually arises against the will, trends, and "likenesses."

For its part, historical inquiry into the Bible as the historical awakening of the texts to life in their time of origin guards the fact that the secret of the freedom of divine presence remains protected in God's personal relationship to time. The secret continually reveals itself on the basis of old texts. Last but not least, historical inquiry preserves the character and the opening of meaning for the time of revelation as the time of fundamental biblical disclosure of God. It also enables one to contrast the biblical tradition with the manifestation of their diffuse effects and the multiple possibilities or their current adoption. Historical inquiry into the perceptions of God during the developing biblical transmissions is thus no external approach that is just possible, or that is even disturbing or destructive, for the continuing tradition event in which all later generations stand. Historical inquiry is also conscious of its own historical standpoint and is able to see the limits of those things shaping its history of research in view of its entire subject matter. As such, historical inquiry is done to convey responsibly the foundational processes and the essential presupposition of the transmission itself. The fact that the biblical formulation and its horizons and perspectives thus appear under the stipulations of its own time does not relativize their truth and validity. This validity should be preserved in explanatory form in this ongoing tradition in later periods. However, this limitation does perhaps relativize the version of this truth that from the beginning can only be expressed within the limits of time-bound perception. Ancient transmitted material, and specifically the proclamation of the biblical God, can be fundamentally assured only by the inquiry into this earlier material. All affirmations of the spirit and of life in the subsequent period must be measured against this origin. Changing images of historical investigations, as the discipline characterizes them, are the price to be born for the clarification of the dynamic vividness of ancient texts. However one can bear these changes in the confidence that God's attested disclosure also simultaneously brings itself to the forefront and to the effect despite the unavoidable detours and false paths of these efforts. The achievement of historical inquiry stands alongside its limits. It simultaneously reveals obligation and liberation by insights into the temporal nature of the foundational biblical origins of all subsequent tradition, as must be done in a close material form of life for all later historical constellations. We must now speak about the ideas of this subsequent tradition.

TRADITION AS HISTORICAL MOVEMENT

For our insight into this process, prophetic tradition conveys a unity perceived in movement according to its development and contents. The identity of the biblical God is provided by the traces of the ancient prophetic transmission process, not just from the canonical measures of the final hand, and not by a collection of individual biblical sayings, but by the gradually recognized flow of a history of perception as a whole. This history is a context of a peculiar kind in the meaning of the prophetic books, a context that wants to be preserved. This history of perception is complex in its process and contents. It expresses the freedom of God's presence including the concrete element. It even includes the limits and the surpassing of its biblically formulated message. The history of perception occurs in the historical movement of the living God to living persons in time and space. This movement is aimed at the Hebrew Bible itself and at the continuity/discontinuity of God's unsurpassable final disclosure in Christ. Biblical sayings are then only adopted materially when they can be perceived in their place on this path and in the life references in their own time. In other words, biblical sayings adopt the movement of meaning instead of the original meaning or the meaning of the final text.[89] They continue beyond the original meaning as historically ascertained. This movement found expression in the biblical transmission process, an expression that was foundational, perceived as time-bound, but nevertheless encompassed time as a whole.

The transmission process in the prophetic books themselves may not be idealized into a constant material progression. Because the perception of God in the time of Israel is the moving of this prophetic transmission in every phase, this movement does not run from step to step until the final step in an irreversible qualitative climax. The movement of the tradition follows God in life and experience. It is no linear theological process of escalation. It is the reflex of the movement of God in Israel's experience of reality in the course of time and as time changes. The material inclination of the comprehensive metahistorical image naturally remains as the prophetic books present it, for the beneficent God in the entire realm of time until the appearance of the completion. However, the perceptions in the earlier contours of the transmission can also become virulent in later experiential constellations because they remain threads of the acting God, and they disclose the God now present. For example, the following would fall under the intention of this tradition movement. Instead of again seeing the shortening of Isaiah 6 or Isaiah 53 in the formative final form of the development of the Isaiah book,[90] the cross of Christ can be seen with the unfathomable, original meaning of these texts (Isaiah 6:1–11 in the framework of Isaiah *6–8 and Isaiah 52:13–53:12 in the framework of the "songs" of God's servant). Doing so leads to a deep insight that is also not explicitly addressed in the New Testament formulations.

TRADITION AS THE CHANGING CONCRETIZATION OF LIFE

The considerations of this essay for the continuation of tradition move in the parallel framework of the theological discipline's acts of confirmation from a later period toward much earlier texts. These old texts can also come much later to direct, material effect if someone far away from scientific reflection relates these texts directly and spontaneously to their own life and experiential world in the realm of the church or outside it. This fact is not in question. By contrast, experience teaches that the effects of the intended meaning of a text can find a dynamic form in this direct adoption from a different time. These effects can more likely be neglected in the argumentative explorations of historical theological inquiry into the foundational original meaning of the text. Nevertheless, experience also teaches that inappropriate adoptions of the text also exist that misunderstand the text's direction of meaning. At any rate, one should not spare the historical-theological clarification of the historical meaning of the text in the time frame of its inner-biblical transmission as an act of confirmation. Otherwise, the impulse of the text's meaning would be different from the impulse that later persons perceive, or the fertile enriching otherness of the (ancient) text and (later) receivers remains protected. The clarifying power of the text and the adopting imagination of the receiver should move along the same material line,[91] so that the receiver in a much later time does not force his/her own provision of meaning (whether pious or impious) onto the biblical text. Rather, the receiver hears what the biblical text says in its own world. Historical-theological inquiry protects the direction of meaning that is provided for the text from the time of its biblical origin. Historical-theological inquiry watches over this direction of meaning so that it remains the leading direction of meaning in the subsequent period. Historical-theological inquiry examines the later adoption of the meaning of older texts and processes them to the extent that today they often cause silent biblical texts to speak. Historical-theological inquiry also considers the material that points further and clarifies these texts in the continuing flow of time because it recognizes the phenomenon and the task of productive transmission from the biblical transmission finding.

The character of prophetic tradition accomplished by the continuation of time, experience, and knowledge in Israel also teaches later tradition to preserve this character. We cannot quote the identity of the biblical God from the Bible for our own particular historical context. Rather, God's identity can only be considered from the formulated perceptions of the foundational biblical period and then responsibly actualized in a new, contemporary linguistic shape. The ancient prophetic transmission already established this type of movement in a precanonical situation and the more homogenous reception situation of that time. Since then, the time-tested mobility of tradition is required even more strongly. The time difference determines essentially everything for the biblical formation of statements in the distant past. The time difference can only be annulled by relinquishing the special element from the past and today. Seen in its original historical meaning, a biblical sentence is scarcely directly understandable today. Historical affirmation of the fundamental tradition event shows this original meaning. Rather, a biblical sentence requires a mediated understanding examined by a historical-theological affirmation of meaning.

Even today, ancient biblical formulations continue to work in their direct meaning only as mediated by the continuation of time and time difference. This mediated directness also concerns the linguistic form. Its hearers require accompaniment through regulated exegesis and instruction, accompaniment which responsibly considers the boundaries and power of the texts for the conditions of life for the later time. All translations are mediations of this type that must be justified. Thus, the biblical hermeneutic of "address and claim" that brackets out time is refuted as a sufficient concept of affirmation. It surpasses the historical nature of the biblical witness in the susceptibility of direct spiritual effects that are, however, primarily capable of examination. Or it surpasses the historical nature of the biblical witness by abstracting threads of existence dressed as Christian and contemporary. This hermeneutic also overlooks the phenomenon of elongated time.[92] Even with psychological means, one cannot attain direct access to ancient texts. Of course, biblical truth must be unfolded into psychic dimensions. The bridge cannot be erected with psychological neutrality of time because one cannot eradicate the historical character of biblical texts and their character as elements of a comprehensive context of meaning. With all these considerations, the deceptive narrowing is refuted, as though faith occurred only from the spirit and the letters of a biblical text. The voice of the gospel must become a vivid voice, continually using contemporary means of transmission. The meaning of the text is neither identical with its time-bound formulation nor with the temporal conditions of its origin!

Instead, the prophetic books stimulate responsible tradition that ensures foundations and relates changing challenges. This tradition continues to find its dynamic form of truth as material that is received because of a process constantly granting life and the completion of life. As we saw, this conveying does not result in the direct, general validity of individual biblical statements that are believed to be timeless and temporally neutral. As historically dependent entities, these statements could never have this validity so directly. If one allows one's self to be led by the process and contents of the transmission of the prophetic books, then the conveying results much more from the path of God through time to the present and the future. The authoritative transmission is closed in post-canonical time, and therefore no longer expanded. This path displays transmission that is to be affirmed in a connection backward from the beginning to the goal. In so doing, it also incorporates the depth of meaning of experienced and expected time. The prophetic books do not perceive validity as lifted from the realm of historical experience. They perceive it as allocated from the just and redeeming God through time.

If conveying transmission will take its current stimulation from efforts of theological affirmation, then the processing of the valid as truth in the form of comprehensive, historical movement and changing concretizations of life becomes a matter of importance. What would happen if theology, starting from a biblical impetus, again considered casting itself as a historical image of reality before God, before sacred scripture, and before history that is changing, comprehensive, and yet still conscious of its own standpoint? Historical exegesis and dogmatics could work hand in hand, as has not been the case to this point. Revelatory historical constructs from individual parts of biblical formulations would not be stimulated. Rather, newly formed perceptions would be opened without fear. These perceptions would be the comprehensive refinement of meaning over time and for the future as they reveal themselves based on the foundational biblical transmission that is nevertheless also receptive to its time. These perceptions would adopt and sift historical knowledge, differentiated insight, and later (different) experience. In their development, the prophetic books opt for a theology that remains transmission bound but still steps courageously toward the changed experiential realms of its own past and future, because it presents its own temporal nature and responds in trust before the self-proof of God. When it enters the changed experiential realms of its own time, canon-bound, post-canonical theology is not irritated by time-relative biblical formulations. However, it also preserves the boundaries of its own temporal nature and does not deviate from the incorporated power of biblical perception specifically because of its temporal life form. In precisely this way, theology's truth becomes pertinent when it maintains its historical form as a contemporary form, and when it observes the form of the biblical text from the historical past, whether the form relates to experience, life, thought, or language. Theology again seeks its truth for today in a historical form relating to experience, life, thought, and language. Therefore, theologies of the Old Testament (those that deserve this name and go beyond the description of past times), dogmatics (despite their time-appropriate contents as a whole), and the sermon (like other Christian forms of transmission) are not written for eternity. Rather, they have to be continually rewritten. In so doing, the biblical perception of meaning and the quality of meaning for the present can remain identical. These two are not directly identical (the historical difference stands in the way), but can be identical in a mediated form. A higher unity of meaning encompassing the difference of times and experiences thus becomes apparent. Changed experiential constellations demand renewed adaptation of the transmitted material that is both conscious of and limited by its standpoint. The biblical tradition itself kept this principle in motion.

This mediated, theologically assured identity of biblical truth pushes toward the general public in its dynamic, granted to persons. Even the transmission of the prophetic books does not remain in the back room of professional tradent theology. Naturally, this mediated identity of biblical truth can and will be provided again in disclosed references to its basis as the exegesis of individual biblical texts, especially in the sermon. The connection of all transmission processes to the foundational transmission is expressed therein. However, this time-proven exegesis is not the same as the primary historically-exegetical affirmation of the biblical wording in the framework of the historical development of the Bible. On this biblical foundation, exegesis now searches and unfolds that current form of truth that is time-contingent but also close to life and experience in the vessel of the ancient text in which it is received and conveyed with confidence.

THE SEARCH FOR HIGHER UNITY

The character of tradition as an essentially time-bound tradition continually seeking new concretizations of life shows that the question of the presence of God based on the foundation of the biblical transmission remains a question for every time. Taking seriously the development and growth of the prophetic books as such also safeguards the multiplicity and broad nature of the perception of God in light of the multiplicity of experience of historical life in that time. One is encouraged in the way the tradents of these books did not worry about facing new challenges. They clarified these challenges from the validly transmitted material in creative, productive explication. By contrast, one finds resistance to fixating solely on the makeable, logical, opportune, and the fatally irrevocable. An incentive exists to discover the biblical God of the prophetic books, the One who holds time in his hands and enters with the movement of time. An incentive exists to discover God in direct experience, in a time not prepared, in secret where humans remain themselves, and in the hopeful perspectives that go with us. The encounter with God and God's prophetic word continues to discover the essential elements that humans would not know by themselves from knowledge and would not even want to know without this perspective. And this encounter preserves the fact that God must not simply satisfy the challenges to the doctrine from God. Rather, God remains freely as the one announced in multiplicity and the one who surprises from the pathway of the times.

The finding that we constantly encounter in the development of the prophetic books, especially in later stages, is an essential help and measuring rod for this task that protects from one-sidedness and fantasy. The process of the book's development does not just highlight a single perception as the measuring rod. Many perceptions are highlighted (some even contradictory). The biblical transmission did not purify them or make them egalitarian. The transmission protected them and kept open possibilities for their reception. In their meaning, different partial truths relate to specific times, to epochs of meaning, and to constellations that also simultaneously limit one another. One never finds one without the other. These partial truths demand that all subsequent generations inquire into the higher unity for the question of God's presence that they are seeking. They do so, not from every individual passing Bible passage, not from options for this or that "middle of the writing," but from the whole and the inclinations of the entire perception of God that the two testaments together provide for Christians. The precanonical tradent prophecy performed this work for its time. It is not removed from all subsequent theology despite the canonical restriction. It was not performed by abstract reduction or by isolating the transmitted material. Rather, this work was provided by the exegetical, productive, continuing transmission of the authoritatively received material for the exhibition of the God who continues to be experientially close. Through this process, the perceptions of God that the canon incorporates in the subsequent period were continually reconsidered, whereby the word continually found its dynamic form.

Also, within the canon, in the final versions of the prophetic books, material that is not contemporary again becomes contemporary material in a higher sense for all later generations who wish to orient themselves toward the Bible. This change occurs even in the canon as a closed entity as it did in the course of the history of origin of the prophetic books themselves to the extent that, even in that time, prophetically transmitted material confronts later times. However, in so doing, the prophetic texts inside the biblical transmission-history do not become timeless. In the long-lasting historical realm of divine favor in which one is properly oriented, the prophets were always seen in a specific time. The foundational history of creation to Nehemiah, Daniel, and Esther remains a history of a metahistorical quality seen before God. This history contains a comprehensive perspective of expectation that includes every future meaning. It should address and lead both earlier and later experiences, as well as the experiences of subsequent times that are chronologically no longer directly adopted. In the perspectival extension that is presented for a comprehensive historical time frame, there is a specific time. Therefore, every time of the recipients can find and explain a standpoint of deepening meaning in this time frame. Temporality is specifically maintained in a foundational and, of course, an essentially selective concentration of the metahistorical perspective. As a result, the condensed, orientational image of the history of the world and Israel that conveys divine meaning comes to prominence.

We contemporary persons, with our historical view, perceive a chronological nexus from the development of the books, from the texts' direct time references, and from indirect indices in the formulations and accents. That which we perceive was also attainable for the tradents and recipients of that time in the decisively essential element. Correlating the flow and the statements of the prophetic books with the formative stations of the meaning of its history, as demonstrated by experience and transmission, results in an orientation. In this orientation, one resides in the experiences, the hopes, and in the revealed, divine favor toward God's people over time that includes temporary alienation. To this extent, it is no less appropriate in a higher sense, that an understanding of the sayings of the prophetic books oriented toward life is a historical understanding in recent time. This historical understanding invites one to transform a history of facts and events into the deepened perspective of the history of experience and meaning. In so doing, one should above all consider a concrete orientation to life. This understanding recognizes that the truth of transmitted events of that time was not grounded on punctilliar facts, but on the history of experience from that point. It concentrates the embodiment in the transmitted event. This understanding recognizes that determinations of the meaning of the truth of the transmitted material are continually reformed by contemporary challenges. In this sense, this understanding can even preserve factually irreversible turning points in the course of tradition in which the transmission as the fundamental basis and exegesis as adaptation confront one another. This understanding can also take over the canonical whole at the end of the literary processes of development as historical judgment over an entity of divine self-proclamation. Judaism and Christianity, each in its own way, also fundamentally shaped this entity as holy scripture for self-affirmation in all subsequent periods. This shaping is not affected by use as a timeless book of oracles for every period. It is affected (1) by material inclinations (for Christianity, this inclination involves discontinuity and a new starting point for the New Testament) and (2) by responsible, theological determination to differentiate and concretize that which is valid for our time from both testaments.

In this task, which falls to the theologians and preachers, the growth of the prophetic books, like the Hebrew Bible as a whole, already provides a model. Already in the formative time when these books came to be, not everything was brought to bear on every time period. Instead, much was chronologically and materially limited. Its validity was limited to earlier times in light of experience. It becomes outmoded or continues to operate only in the future. And from the other side, older texts contain even further expanses of meaning. These texts are directed toward new times and situations beyond their original meaning of the constitutive formulations for the sake of the dynamic nature of the God who discloses himself in them. This alternating extension first provides and forces renewed reshapings in light of the coming of God in Christ, and in light of new experiential constellations that the Bible did not yet know and explain at the time of its origin and formulation.

The change of perspectives and the accentuations in the course of the prophetic transmission should thus not frighten. To the contrary, these perspectives show the dynamic nature of God and realistic experience. They also restrain doctrinaire one-sidedness. They are not just encompassed by a higher material unity of divine activity in the realm of the time about which we have spoken. These perspectives are condensed in the existence of the Hebrew Bible, and in prophetic transmission in particular, even in notably recurring basic rhythms. Transmission arenas existed during the Persian Empire that captured the life-granting presence of God and that one must connect with life perspectives of active responsibility for the present in loyalty to the state. These arenas reflect the experiential times of a largely successful world that can be connected as the granting of life of our world in an engaged conquering of reformable deficits with gifts and tasks out of the first article of the credo. Here lay the impulses, orientations, and perspectives of activity, which can and must proceed into the wider public from the prophetic tradition material as cultural material. Because of the experiential situation of the time, far more frequent arenas of the transmission also exist that highlight the hope that the world would change from that present time. Transmission phases provide the pain, the social grievances, the oppression by power, the political confusion, and the inability to better the human realm. These phases are directed toward an enduring future of God in which humans are no longer delivered over to humans. Rather God acts powerfully. One should connect these constellations with the gifts and tasks of the second and third article of the credo. One can recognize that these foundational rhythms do not simply alternate. They are responsibly placed in relationship to one another by the complex state of transmission from the time of late Israel. The current qualification of the salvation of the present in the Psalter, and in characteristic form in the New Testament, stands alongside the continually revised expectation of the imminent world change in prophetic tradition and the apocalypses. Also, especially in Qohelet, later Wisdom relativizes particular eschatological perspectives.

With our approach, we have turned to the development and growth of the prophetic books in a very distant period. We have dedicated our deliberations to attempting to preserve the independence and character of these transmissions. If one were to annul the historical elements and interpret these books in a direct christological manner, then one would lose their fertile independence as a path to the New Testament and as an antecedent history of perception about the same God whose becoming human the New Testament proclaims.[93] This independence only remains preserved when we first understand the Hebrew Bible and the meaning of its assertions in its own historical setting. One understands these assertions as assertions of their time that also point toward Christ, but not directly. Only in this way do the particular challenges become visible. Only then can one determine, theologically and responsibly, that which endures from this perception of God and that which God alone transcended in the subsequent period. Therefore every theological approach, including the meaning of the prophetic transmission, should begin with the original movement of meaning in these books in the situation of their origin. Above all, exegesis should turn toward this foundational movement of meaning. This original constellation determines the linguistic form, as well as the chronological and material contour of the texts, as they are given to us from their time. However, in the movement of time, this movement of meaning continues as the mobility of the God who shows interest. The movement of meaning also teaches one to discover a God closely related to life amidst the challenges of changed experiential constellations based on the foundation of the biblical transmission. It teaches one to discover the meaning of biblical texts and relationships that the biblical formulation in its time had not yet expressed, a discovery that corresponds to the growth of the prophetic transmission and its exegetically "discovered" meanings.

Outlook

We no longer possess the immediacy of the prophetic reception of the word. We no longer possess the innovation of continuing

prophetic transmission, and we are not pointed to current proclamations of God. Rather, on this side of the canonical boundary we
affirm the foundation of holy scripture. In spite of this situation, it
would appear that even today, theology and preaching could
generally learn something essential in a specific respect from the
prophetic exegesis of prophets in the pre-canonical period , whose
characteristics we have tried to investigate. They should seek to be
more attentive to the changing times and experience and the
foundational insight that the valid word of God always requires a
temporal and linguistic form that is bound to and clarifies experience. If exegetical effort does not just trace time-bound effort, but
also traces the essential ideas of inner-biblical exegesis, then biblical
truth cannot be adapted in the philosophical and theological reflection of ancient biblical formulations. It can only be adapted in living tradition. This living tradition ventures to formulate anew and
to extend the formulation in changed realms of thought, life, and
experience. It thus protects the fact that speech about God is always
time-bound speech. To that extent, speech about God is close to
history, life, and experience. Stated pointedly, one must certainly
not steadfastly affirm ancient formulations, ancient ways of thinking, and ancient experiences in a later time. Rather, one should
expose earlier perceptual worlds perceived in ancient texts in every
subsequent period of new testing in thought and life. As Gustav
Mahler purportedly said, "Tradition is the preservation of fire, not
the worship of ashes." Every sub-discipline of theology should consider what that saying means today when taking up biblical impulses.
They should do so in order to explore the truth-form of biblical
transmission not just in thought, but also in the experiential realm
of life. In so doing, one perceives scripture as tradition and the unity
of scripture and tradition.

I close with the words that Herman Barth used to close his distinguished book on the redaction of Isaiah: "Processing the
transmitted word of God ultimately aims toward expressing God
for today. This speaking demands the courage (or should we say the
freedom of the spirit of God) to venture a really contemporary word.
In so doing, one will go beyond the genuine historical meaning of a
text for the sake of the truth of God in the present."[94]

Bibliography

Ackerman, S. *Under Every Green Tree: Popular Religion in Sixth-Century Judah*. HSM 46. Atlanta, 1992.

Ackroyd, P. R. "Isaiah I–XII: Presentation of a Prophet," *Congress Volume Göttingen 1977*. VTSup 29. 16–48. Leiden, 1978.

Adam, A. K. M. *What is Postmodern Biblical Criticism?* Minneapolis, 1995.

Aejmelaeus, A. "Der Prophet als Klageliedsänger. Zur Funktion des Psalms Jesaja 63, 7–64,11 in Tritojesaja." *ZAW* 107 (1995): 31–50.

Aitken, K. T. "Hearing and Seeing: Metamorphoses of a Motif in Isaiah 1–39." *Among the Prophets. Language, Image and Structure in the Prophetic Writings*. P. R. Davies and D. J. A. Clines, eds. JSOTSup 144. 12–41. Sheffield, 1993.

Albertz, R. "Die 'Antrittspredigt' Jesu im Lukasevangelium auf ihrem alttestamentlichen Hintergrund." *ZNW* 74 (1983): 182–206.

———. "Das Deuterojesaja-Buch als Fortschreibung der Jesaja-Prophetie." In *Festschrift R. Rendtorff*, 241–56. Neukirchen-Vluyn, 1990.

Alexander, P. S. "Jewish Aramaic Translations of Hebrew Scriptures." *Mikra. Text, Translation, Reading, and Interpretation of the Hebrew Bible in Ancient Judaism and Early Christianity*. M. J. Mulder, ed. CRINT II/1, 217–53. Assen, 1988.

Allen, L. C. *Ezekiel 1–19*. WBC 28. Dallas, 1990.

———. *Ezekiel 20–48*. WBC 29, Dallas, 1994.

Auld, A. G. "Prophets Through the Looking Glass: Between Writings and Moses." *JSOT* 27 (1983): 3–23.

Baltzer, K. *Die Biographie der Propheten*. Neukirchen-Vluyn, 1975.

Barr, J. "The Literal, the Allegorical, and Modern Biblical Scholarship." *JSOT* 44 (1989): 3–17.

Barstad, H. M. "No Prophets? Recent Developments in Biblical Prophetic Research and Ancient Near Eastern Prophecy." *JSOT* 57 (1993): 39–60.

Bartelmus, R. "Ezra 37:1–14: die Verbform w^{e}qatal und die Anfänge der Auferstehungshoffnung." *ZAW* 97 (1985): 366–89.

Barth, H. *Die Jesaja-Worte in der Josiazeit. Israel und Assur als Thema einer produktiven Neuinterpretation der Jesajaüberlieferung*. WMANT 48. Neukirchen-Vluyn, 1977.

191

Barthélemy, D. *Critique textuelle de l'Ancien Testament: 2. Isaïe, Jérémie, Lamentations*. OBO 50/2, Freiburg (Switzerland), 1986.

Barton, J. *Oracles of God. Perceptions of Ancient Prophecy in Israel after the Exile*. London, 1986.

Bassler, M., ed. *New Historicism. Literaturgeschichte als Poetik der Kultur. Mit Beiträgen von St. Greenblatt, L. Montrose u.a.* Frankfurt a.M., 1995.

Becker, J. *Isaias–der Prophet und sein Buch*. SBS 30. Stuttgart, 1968.

[Becker, U. "Jesajaforschung (Jes 1–39)." *ThR* 64 (1999): 1–37.]

[Berges, U. *Das Buch Jesaja. Komposition und Endgestalt*. Herders Biblische Studien 16. Freiburg, 1998.]

Bernstein, M. J. "Introductory Formulas for Citation and Re-Citation of Biblical Verses in the Qumran Pescharim." *DSD* 1 (1994): 30–70.

Beuken, W. A. M. "Isaiah Chapters LXV–LXVI: Trito-Isaiah and the Closure of the Book of Isaiah." *Congress Volume Leuven 1989*. VTSup 43. 204–21. Leiden, 1991.

———. "Isaiah 34: Lament in Isaianic Context." *OTES* 5 (1992): 78–102.

———. "Jesaja 33 als Spiegeltext im Jesajabuch." *EThL* 67 (1991): 5–35.

———. *Jesaja*. Deel II A, II B. *POT*. Nijkerk, 1979, 1983.

———. *Jesaja*. Deel III A, III B. *POT*. Nijkerk, 1989.

Blau, L. *Studien zum althebräischen Buchwesen und zur biblischen Literaturgeschichte*. Budapest, 1902.

Blum, E. "Jesajas prophetisches Testament. Beobachtungen zu Jesaja 1–11." Part 1: *ZAW* 108 (1996): 547–68; Part 2: *ZAW* 109 (1997): 12–29.

Bosshard-Nepustil, E. "Beobachtungen zum Zwölfprophetenbuch." *BN* 40 (1987): 30–62.

———, *Rezeptionen von Jesaja 1–39 im Zwölfprophetenbuch. Untersuchungen zur literarischen Verbindung von Prophetenbüchern in babylonischer und persischer Zeit*. OBO 154. Freiburg (Switzerland), 1997.

———, and Kratz, R. G. "Maleachi im Zwölfprophetenbuch." *BN* 52 (1990): 27–46.

Brewer, D. I. *Techniques and Assumptions in Jewish Exegesis before 70 CE*. TSAJ 30. Tübingen, 1992.

Broich, U. and M. Pfister, ed. *Intertextualität. Formen, Funktionen, anglistische Fallstudien*. Konzepte der Sprach- und Literaturwissenschaft 35. Tübingen, 1985.

Brooke, G. J. *Exegesis at Qumran. 4QFlorilegium in its Jewish Context.* JSOTSup 29, Sheffield, 1985.

———. "Ezekiel in Some Qumran and New Testament Texts." StTDJ XI, 2. 317–37. Leiden, 1992.

[———. "Isaiah in the Pesharim and Other Qumran Texts." *Writing and Reading the Scroll of Isaiah. Studies of an Interpretive Tradition.* 2 vols. C. C. Broyles and C. A. Evans, eds. VTSup 70. 609–32. Leiden, 1997.]

[Broyles, C. C. and C. A. Evans, eds. *Writing and Reading the Scroll of Isaiah. Studies of an Interpretive Tradition.* 2 vols. VTSup 70. Leiden, 1997.]

Carr, D. "Reaching for Unity in Isaiah." *JSOT* 57 (1993): 61–80.

[———. "Reading Isaiah from Beginning (Isaiah 1) to End (Isaiah 65–66): Multiple Modern Possibilities." *New Visions of Isaiah.* R. F. Melugin and M. A. Sweeney, eds. JSOTSup 214. 188–218. Sheffield, 1996.]

Carroll, R. P. "Intertextuality and the Book of Jeremiah: Animadversions on Text and Theory." *The New Literary Criticism and the Hebrew Bible.* J. Cheryl Exum and D. J. A. Clines, eds. JSOTSup 143. 55–78. Sheffield, 1993.

———. *Jeremiah. A Commentary.* OTL. London, 1986.

———. *When Prophecy Failed. Reactions and Responses to Failure in the Old Testament Prophetic Traditions.* London, 1979.

Chernik, M. "Internal Restraints on Gezerah Shawah's Application." *JQR* 80 (1990): 253–82.

[Childs, B. S. "Retrospective Reading of the Old Testament Prophets." *ZAW* 108 (1996): 362–77.]

Clements, R. E. "Patterns in the Prophetic Canon." *Canon and Authority. Essays in Old Testament Religion and Theology.* G. W. Coats and B. O. Long, eds. 42–55. Philadelphia, 1977. [(Now in *Old Testament Prophecy. From Oracles to Canon.* 191–202. Louisville, 1996.)]

———. "Prophecy as Literature: A Re-appraisal." *Festschrift J. L. Mays.* 59–76. Allison Park, 1986. [(Now in *Old Testament Prophecy. From Oracles to Canon.* 203–16. Louisville, 1996.)]

———. "The Prophet and His Editors." *The Bible in Three Dimensions. Essays in Celebration of Forty Years of Biblical Studies in the University of Sheffield.* D. J. A. Clines et al., eds. JSOTSup 87. 203–20. Sheffield, 1990. [(Now in *Old Testament Prophecy. From Oracles to Canon.* 217–29. Louisville, 1996.)]

————. "Beyond Tradition-History: Deutero-Isaianic Development of First Isaiah's Themes." *JSOT* 31 (1985): 95–113. [(Now in *Old Testament Prophecy. From Oracles to Canon.* 78–92. Louisville, 1996.)]

————. "The Unity of the Book of Isaiah." *Int* 36 (1982): 117–29. [(Now in *Old Testament Prophecy. From Oracles to Canon.* 93–104. Louisville, 1996.)]

[Coggins, R. J. "Do We Still Need Deutero-Isaiah?" *JSOT* 81 (1998): 77–92.]

————. "The Minor Prophets–One Book or Twelve?" *Festschrift M. D. Goulder.* Biblical Interpretation Series 8. 57–68. Leiden, 1994.

Collins, T. *The Mantle of Elijah. The Redaction Criticism of the Prophetical Books.* JSOTSup 20. Sheffield, 1993.

Conrad, E. W. *Reading Isaiah.* Minneapolis, 1991.

Culley, R. C. "Exploring New Directions." *The Hebrew Bible and Its Modern Interpreters.* D. A. Knight and G. M. Tucker, eds. 167–200. Philadelphia, 1985.

Dalferth, I. U. "Gott und Zeit." *Religion und Gestaltung der Zeit.* D. Georgi et al., eds. 9–34. Kampen, 1994.

Darr, K. P. *Isaiah's Vision and the Family of God.* Literary Currents in Biblical Interpretation. Louisville, 1994.

Davies, G. I. "The Destiny of the Nations in the Book of Isaiah." *The Book of Isaiah. Le livre d'Isaïe. Les oracles et leurs relectures.* J.Vermeylen, ed. 93–120. BEThL 81, Leuven, 1989.

Davies, P. R. and D. J. A. Clines, eds. *Among the Prophets. Language, Image and Structure in the Prophetic Writings.* JSOTSup 144. Sheffield, 1993.

Dicou, B. "Literary Function and Literary History of Isaiah 34." *BN* 58 (1991): 30–45.

Dohmen, C. "Rezeptionsforschung und Glaubensgeschichte. Anstöße für eine neue Annäherung von Exegese und Systematischer Theologie." *TThZ* 96 (1987): 123–34.

Donner, H. "Der Redaktor. Überlegungen zum vorkritischen Umgang mit der Heiligen Schrift." *Henoch* 2 (1980): 1–30. (Now in *Aufsätze zum Alten Testament aus vier Jahrzehnten.* BZAW 224. 259–85. Berlin, NewYork, 1994.)

————. "'Forscht in der Schrift Jahwes und lest!' Ein Beitrag zum Verständnis der israelitischen Prophetie." *ZThK* 87 (1990): 285–98. (Now in *Aufsätze zum Alten Testament aus vier Jahrzehnten.* BZAW 224. 199–212. Berlin, NewYork, 1994.)

Draisma, S., ed. *Intertextuality in Biblical Writings. Essays in Honour of Bas van Iersel.* Kampen, 1989.

Duhm, B. *Das Buch Jeremia.* KHC XI. Tübingen, 1901.

———. *Das Buch Jesaja.* HK 111/1. Göttingen, 1914.

Eagleton, T. *Einführung in die Literaturtheorie.* Stuttgart, 1994.

Ebeling, G. *Evangelische Evangelienauslegung. Eine Untersuchung zu Luthers Hermeneutik. FLGP* 10/I. Munich, 1942 (Tübingen, 1991).

Emmerson, G. I. *Isaiah 56–66.* OTG. Sheffield, 1992.

Evans, C. A. *To See and not Perceive. Isaiah 6:9–10 in Early Jewish and Christian Interpretation.* JSOTSup 64. Sheffield, 1989.

———. "On the Unity and Parallel Structure of Isaiah." *VT* 38 (1988): 129–47.

Exum, J. C., and D. J. A. Clines, eds. *The New Literary Criticism and the Hebrew Bible.* JSOTSup 143. Sheffield, 1993.

[Fabry, H.-J. "Methoden der Schriftauslegung in den Qumranschriften." *Festschrift E. Dassmann.* JAC 23. 18–33. Münster, 1996.]

[———. "Qumran." *NBL* 3 (1998): 230–60.]

———. "Schriftverständnis und Schriftauslegung der Qumran-Essener." *Festschrift Maier.* BBB 88. 87–96. Frankfurt a.M., 1993.

———, and H. Ringgren, eds. *Theologisches Wörterbuch zum Alten Testament.* Begun by G. J. Botterweck and H. Ringgren. Vols. 1–8. Stuttgart, 1973–1995.

Feist, U. *Ezechiel. Das literarische Problem des Buches forschungsgeschichtlich betrachtet.* BWANT 138. Stuttgart, 1995.

Feltes, H. *Die Gattung des Habakukkommentars von Qumran (lQpHab). Eine Studie zum frühen jüdischen Midrasch.* FZB 58. Würzburg, 1986.

Fewell, D. N., ed. *Reading Between Texts: Intertextuality and the Hebrew Bible.* Louisville, 1992.

Fischer, I. *Wo ist Jahwe? Das Volksklagelied Jes 63:7–64:11 als Ausdruck des Ringens um eine gebrochene Beziehung.* SBB 19. Stuttgart, 1989.

———. *Tora für Israel–Tora für die Völker. Das Konzept des Jesajabuches.* SBS 164. Stuttgart, 1995.

Fishbane, M. *Biblical Interpretation in Ancient Israel.* Oxford, 1985.

———. "Revelation and Tradition: Aspects of Inner-Biblical Exegesis." *JBL* 99 (1980): 343–61.

Fitzmyer, J. A. *The Dead Sea Scrolls. Major Publications and Tools for Study.* SBLRBS 20, rev. ed. Atlanta, 1990.

Flint, P. W. *The Dead Sea Psalms Scrolls and the Book of Psalms.* StTDJ 17. Leiden, 1997.

[————. "The Isaiah Scrolls from the Judean Desert." In C. C. Broyles and C. A. Evans, eds. *Writing and Reading the Scroll of Isaiah. Studies of an Interpretive Tradition.* 2 vols. VTSup 70. 481–90. Leiden, 1997.]

Fox, M. V. "The Identification of Quotations in Biblical Literature." *ZAW* 92 (1980): 416–31.

Freedman, D. N., ed. *The Anchor Bible Dictionary.* Vol. I–VI, New York, 1992. (ABD)

————. "Headings in the Books of the Eighth-Century Prophets." *AUSS* 25 (1987): 9–26.

Fuller, K. E. "The Form and Formation of the Book of the Twelve: The Evidence from the Judean Desert." *Forming Prophetic Literature. Essays on Isaiah and the Twelve in Honor of John D. W. Watts.* J. W. Watts and P. R. House, eds. JSOTSup 235. 86–101. Sheffield, 1996.

————. *The Minor Prophets Manuscripts from Qumran, Cave I.* Diss. Harvard, 1988 (UMI Dissertation Services), Ann Arbor, 1995.

Garcia Martinez, E. *The Dead Sea Scrolls Translated. The Qumran Texts in English.* Leiden, 1994.

Gese, H. "Alttestamentliche Hermeneutik und christliche Theologie." *ZThK* 9 (1995): 65–81.

Gevarjahu, H. M. I. "Biblical Colophons: A Source for the 'Biography' of Authors, Texts, and Books." *Congress Volume Edinburgh 1974.* VTSup 28. 42–59. Leiden, 1975.

Gleßmer, U. "Liste der biblischen Texte aus Qumran." *RevQ* 62 (1993): 153–92.

Gosse, B. "L'alliance d'Isaïe 59, 21." *ZAW* 101 (1989): 116–18.

————. "Deuteronome 32:1–43 et les rédactions des livres d'Ezéchiel et d'Isaïe." *ZAW* 107 (1995): 110–17.

————. "Isaïe 1 dans la rédaction du livre d'Isaïe." *ZAW* 104 (1992): 52–66.

[————. *Structuration des grands ensembles bibliques et intertextualité à l'époque perse.* BZAW 246. Berlin, 1997.]

Groß, W. "Neuer Bund oder Erneuerter Bund. Jer 31:31–34 in der jüngsten Diskussion." *Festschrift Th. Schneider.* 89–114. Mainz, 1995.

————. "Israel und die Völker. Die Krise des YHWH-Volk-Konzepts im Jesajabuch." *Der Neue Bund im Alten. Zur Bundestheologie der beiden Testamente.* E. Zenger, ed. QD 146. 149–67. Freiburg, 1993.

Harrelson, W. "Isaiah 35 in Recent Research and Translation." In *Festschrift J. Barr.* 247–60. Oxford, 1994.

Hartman, L. *Prophecy Interpreted. The Formation of Some Jewish Apocalyptic Texts and of the Eschatological Discourse Mark 13 par.* CBNT 1. Lund, 1966.

Hengel, M. "'Schriftauslegung' und 'Schriftwerdung' in der Zeit des Zweiten Tempels." *Schriftauslegung im antiken Judentum und Urchristentum.* M. Hengel and H. Löhr, eds. WUNT 73. 1–71. Tübingen, 1994.

Hermisson, H.-J. *Deuterojesaja.* BK XI, 7ff. Neukirchen-Vluyn, 1987ff.

———. "Einheit und Komplexität Deuterojesajas. Probleme der Redaktionsgeschichte von Jesaja 40–55." J. Vermeylen, ed. *The Book of Isaiah. Le livre d'Isaïe. Les oracles et leurs relectures.* BEThL 81. 287–312. Leuven, 1989. [(Now in *Studien zu Prophetie und Weisheit. Gesammelte Aufsätze.* FAT 23. 132–57. Tübingen, 1998.)]

———. "Notizen zu Hiob." *ZThK* 86 (1989): 125–39. [(Now in *Studien zu Prophetie und Weisheit. Gesammelte Aufsätze.* FAT 23. 286–99. Tübingen, 1998.)]

———. "Zeitbezug des prophetischen Wortes." *KuD* 27 (1981): 96–110.

Holladay, J. S. "Assyrian Statecraft and the Prophets of Israel." *HTR* 63 (1970): 29–51.

Hossfeld, F.-L. "Das Buch Ezechiel." *Einleitung in das Alte Testament.* E. Zenger et al., eds. Studienbücher Theologie, vol. 1/1. 3d ed. 440–57. Stuttgart, 1995.

House, P. R. *The Unity of the Twelve.* JSOTSup 97. Sheffield, 1990.

Die Interpretation der Bibel in der Kirche. Das Dokument der Päpstlichen Bibelkommission vom 23.4.1993 mit einer kommentierenden Einführung von L. Ruppert und einer Würdigung durch H.-J. Klauck. SBS 161. Stuttgart, 1995.

Japhet, S. "Composition and Chronology in the Book of Ezra-Nehemiah." *Second Temple Studies. Second Temple and Community in the Persian Period.* Tamara C. Eskenazi and K. H. Richards, eds. JSOTSup 175. 189–216. Sheffield, 1994.

Jeanrond, W. G. *Theological Hermeneutics. Development and Significance.* Basingstoke, 2d ed., 1994.

Jeremias, J. "Amos 3–6: Beobachtungen zur Entstehungsgeschichte eines Prophetenbuches." *ZAW* 100 Suppl. (1988): 123–38. [(Now in *Hosea und Amos. Studien zu den Anfängen des Dodekapropheton.* FAT 13. 142–56. Tübingen, 1996.)]

————. "Amos 3–6: From the Oral Word to the Text." *Festschrift B. S. Childs.* 217–29. Philadelphia, 1988.

————. "Am 8:4–7–ein Kommentar zu 2:6f." *Festschrift W. Richter.* 205–20. St. Ottilien, 1991. (Now in *Hosea und Amos. Studien zu den Anfängen des Dodekapropheton,* FAT 13. 231–43. Tübingen, 1996.)

————. "Die Anfänge des Dodekapropheton: Hosea und Amos." In *Congress Volume Paris 1992.* VTSup 61. 87–106. Leiden, 1995. [(Now in *Hosea und Amos. Studien zu den Anfängen des Dodekapropheton,* FAT 13. 34–54. Tübingen, 1996.)]

————. "Die Deutung der Gerichtsworte Michas in der Exilszeit." *ZAW* 83 (1971): 330–54.

[————. *Hosea und Amos. Studien zu den Anfängen des Dodekapropheton.* FAT 13. Tübingen, 1996.]

————. "'Ich bin wie ein Löwe für Efraim...'" In *'Ich will euer Gott werden'. Beispiele biblischen Redens von Gott.* SBS 100. 77–95. Stuttgart, 1981. [(Now in *Hosea und Amos. Studien zu den Anfängen des Dodekapropheton.* FAT 13. 104–21. Tübingen, 1996.)]

————. "Jakob im Amosbuch." *Festschrift J. Scharbert.* 139–54. Stuttgart, 1989. [(Now in *Hosea und Amos. Studien zu den Anfängen des Dodekapropheton.* FAT 13. 257–71. Tübingen, 1996.)]

————. *Der Prophet Amos.* ATD 24/2. Göttingen, 1995.

————. *Der Prophet Hosea.* ATD 24/1. Göttingen, 1983.

————. "Das Proprium der alttestamentlichen Prophetie." *ThLZ* 119 (1994): 483–94. [(Now in *Hosea und Amos. Studien zu den Anfängen des Dodekapropheton.* FAT 13. 20–33. Tübingen, 1996.)]

————. "Rezeptionsprozesse in der prophetischen Überlieferung– am Beispiel der Visionsberichte des Amos." *Rezeption und Auslegung im Alten Testament und in seinem Umfeld. Ein Symposion an Anlass des 60. Geburtstags von Odil Hannes Steck.* R. G. Kratz and Th. Krüger, eds. OBO 153. 29–44. Freiburg (Switzerland), 1997.

————. "Tau und Löwe (Mi 5:6f.)." *Festschrift H.W. Wolff zum 80. Geburtstag.* 221–27. Munich, 1992.

[————. "Neuere Tendenzen der Forschung an den Kleinen Propheten." *Festschrift A. S. van der Woude.* 122–36. VTSup 73. Leiden, 1998.]

————. "Tod und Leben in Am 5:1–17." *Festschrift A. Deissler.* 134–52. Freiburg, 1989. [(Now in *Hosea und Amos. Studien zu den Anfängen des Dodekapropheton.* FAT 13. 214–30. Tübingen, 1996.)]

―――. "Völkersprüche und Visionsberichte im Amosbuch." *Festschrift O. Kaiser.* BZAW 185. 82–97. Berlin, 1989. [(Now in *Hosea und Amos. Studien zu den Anfängen des Dodekapropheton.* FAT 13. 157–67. Tübingen, 1996.)]

―――. "'Zwei Jahre vor dem Erdbeben' (Am 1:1)." *Festschrift H. Graf Reventlow.* 15–31. Frankfurt, 1994. [(Now in *Hosea und Amos. Studien zu den Anfängen des Dodekapropheton.* FAT 13. 183–97. Tübingen, 1996.)]

Jones, B. A. *The Formation of the Book of the Twelve: A Study in Text and Canon.* SBLDS 149. Atlanta, 1995.

Jüngling, H.-W. "Das Buch Jesaja." *Einleitung in das Alte Testament, Studienbücher Theologie.* Vol. 1/1. 3d edition. E. Zenger et al. 381–404. Stuttgart, 1998.

―――. "'Die Eichen der Gerechtigkeit'. 'Protojesajanisches' in Jesaja 61." *Festschrift N. Lohfink.* 199–219. Freiburg, 1993.

Kaiser, O. *Grundriß der Einleitung in die kanonischen und deuterokanonischen Schriften des Alten Testaments.* Vol. 2: *Die prophetischen Werke.* Gütersloh, 1994.

―――. "Literarkritik und Tendenzkritik. Überlegungen zur Methode der Jesajaexegese." *The Book of Isaiah. Le Livre d'Isaïe. Les oracles et leurs relectures.* J. Vermeylen, ed. BEThL 81. 55–71. Leuven, 1989.

―――. *Das Buch des Propheten Jesaja. Kapitel 1–12.* ATD 17. 5th ed. Göttingen, 1981.

―――. *Der Prophet Jesaja. Kapitel 13–39.* ATD 18. Göttingen, 1973 (3d ed., 1983).

Kellermann, U. "Tritojesaja und das Geheimnis des Gottesknechts. Erwägungen zu Jesaja 59:21; 61:1–3; 66:18–24." *BN* 58 (1991): 46–82.

[Knauf, E. A. "Audiatur et altera pars. Zur Logik der Pentateuch-Redaktion." *BK* 53 (1998): 118–26.]

―――. *Die Umwelt des Alten Testaments.* NSKAT 29. Stuttgart, 1994.

Knierim, R. "Criticism of Literary Features, Form, Tradition, and Redaction." *The Hebrew Bible and Its Modern Interpreters.* D. A. Knight and G. M. Tucker, eds. 123–65. Philadelphia, 1985.

Koch, K. "Der doppelte Ausgang des Alten Testaments in Judentum und Christentum." *JBTh* 6 (1991): 215–42.

―――. "Die Bedeutung der Apokalyptik für die Interpretation der Schrift." *Mitte der Schrift?* M. Klopfenstein et al., eds. JudChr 11. 185–215. Bern, 1987.

————."Geschichte/Geschichtsschreibung Geschichtsphilosophie. II. Altes Testament." *TRE* 12, 569–86. Berlin, 1984.

————. *Die Profeten.* Vol. 1: *Assyrische Zeit.* UB 280. 3d ed. Stuttgart, 1995.

————. "Der Psalter und seine Redaktionsgeschichte." *Neue Wege der Psalmenforschung. Festschrift W. Beyerlin.* K. Seybold and E. Zenger, eds. Herders biblische Studien 1. 243–77. Freiburg, 1994.

————. *Die Reiche der Welt und der kommende Menschensohn. Studien zum Danielbuch. Gesammelte Aufsätze.* Vol. 2. Neukirchen-Vluyn, 1995.

————. "Rezeptionsgeschichte als notwendige Voraussetzung einer biblischen Theologie; oder, Protestantische Verlegenheit angesichts der Geschichtlichkeit des Kanons." *Sola Scriptura. Das reformatorische Schrift prinzip in der säkularen Welt.* H. H. Schmid and J. Mehlhausen, eds. 143–55. Gütersloh, 1991.

Koch, K., et al. *Amos. Untersucht mit den Methoden einer strukturalen Formgeschichte.* AOAT 30. Kevelaer, Neukirchen-Vluyn, 1976.

Koenen, K. *Ethik und Eschatologie im Tritojesajabuch. Eine literarkritische und redaktionsgeschichtliche Studie.* WMANT 62. Neukirchen-Vluyn, 1990.

————. *Heil den Gerechten—Unheil den Sündern! Ein Beitrag zur Theologie der Prophetenbücher.* BZAW 229. Berlin, 1994.

Koenig, J. *L'Herméneutique analogique du judaïsme antique d'après les témoins textuels d'Isaïe.* VTSup 33. Leiden, 1982.

Kooij, A. van der. *Die alten Textzeugen des Jesajabuches.* OBO 35. Freiburg (Switzerland), 1981.

[Koole, J. L. *Isaiah III.* Vol. 1: *Isaiah 40–48.* Kampen, 1997.]

Kratz, R. G. "Der Anfang des Zweiten Jesaja in Jesaja 40:1f. und seine literarischen Horizonte." *ZAW* 105 (1993): 400–19.

————. "Der Anfang des Zweiten Jesaja in Jesaja 40:1f. und das Jeremiabuch." *ZAW* 106 (1994): 243–61.

————. "Die Gnade des täglichen Brots. Späte Psalmen auf dem Weg zum Vaterunser." *ZThK* 89 (1992): 1–40.

————. *Kyros im Deuterojesaja-Buch. Redaktionsgeschichtliche Untersuchungen zu Entstehung und Theologie von Jesaja 40–55.* FAT 1. Tübingen, 1991.

[————. "Die Redaktion der Prophetenbücher." *Rezeption und Auslegung im Alten Testament und in seinem Umfeld. Ein Symposion an Anlass des 60. Geburtstags von Odil Hannes Steck.* R. G. Kratz and Th. Krüger, eds. OBO 153. 9–28. Freiburg (Switzerland), 1997.]

————. "Redaktionskritik/-geschichte." 367–78. *TRE* 28. Berlin, 1997.

————. "Die Suche nach Identität in der nachexilischen Theologiegeschichte. Zur Hermeneutik des chronistischen Geschichtswerkes und ihrer Bedeutung für das Verständnis des Alten Testaments." *Pluralismus und Identität.* J. Mehlhausen, ed. 279–303. Gütersloh, 1995.

————. *Translatio imperii. Untersuchungen zu den aramäischen Danielerzählungen und ihrem theologiegeschichtlichen Umfeld.* WMANT 63. Neukirchen-Vluyn, 1991.

Krüger, Th. "Dekonstruktion und Rekonstruktion prophetischer Eschatologie im Qohelet-Buch." *Festschrift D. Michel.* BZAW 241. Berlin New York, 1996. 107–29. [(Now in *Kritische Weisheit. Studien zur weisheitlichen Traditionskritik im Alten Testament.* 151–72. Zürich, 1997.)]

————. *Geschichtskonzepte im Ezechielbuch.* BZAW 180. Berlin, New York, 1989.

————. "Komposition und Diskussion in Proverbia 10." *ZThK* 92 (1995): 413–33. [(Now in *Kritische Weisheit. Studien zur weisheitlichen Traditionskritik im Alten Testament.* 195–214. Zürich, 1997.)]

[Kuan, J. "The Authorship and Historical Background of Isaiah 35." *Jian Dao* 6 (1996): 1–12.]

Kuhl, C. "Die 'Wiederaufnahme'– ein literarkritisches Prinzip?" *ZAW* 64 (1952): 1–11.

Laato, A. "History and Ideology in the Old Testament Prophetic Books." *SJOT* 8 (1994): 267–97.

[————. *History and Ideology in the Old Testament Prophetic Literature. A Semiotic Approach to the Reconstruction of the Proclamation of the Historical Prophets.* CBOT 41. Stockholm, 1996.]

Lau, W. *Schriftgelehrte Prophetie in Jesaja 56–66. Eine Untersuchung zu den literarischen Bezügen in den letzten elf Kapiteln des Jesajabuches.* BZAW 225. Berlin, New York, 1994.

Lescow, Th. *Das Buch Maleachi. Texttheorie - Auslegung - Kanontheorie.* AzTh 75. Stuttgart, 1993.

Levin, Chr. *Die Verheißung des neuen Bundes in ihrem theologie-geschichtlichen Zusammenhang ausgelegt.* FRLANT 137. Göttingen, 1985.

Lohfink, N. "Gab es eine deuteronomistische Bewegung?" In *Jeremia und die 'deuteronomistische Bewegung.'* W. Groß, ed. BBB 98. 313–82. Weinheim, 1995.

————, and E. Zenger. *Der Gott Israels und die Völker. Untersuchungen zum Jesajabuch und zu den Psalmen.* SBS 154. Stuttgart, 1994.

Lust, J. "Isaiah 34 and the *ḥerem.*" *The Book of Isaiah. Le livre d'Isaïe. Les oracles et leurs relectures.* J. Vermeylen, ed. BEThL 81. 275–86. Leuven, 1989.

————. "Ezekiel Manuscripts in Qumran. Preliminary Edition of 4QEz a and b." *Ezekiel and his Book. Textual and Literary Criticism and their Interrelation.* J. Lust, ed. BEThL 74. 90–100. Leuven, 1986.

McKane, W. *A Critical and Exegetical Commentary on Jeremiah.* Vol. I: *Introduction and Commentary on Jeremiah I–XXV.* ICC. Edinburgh, 1986.

McLaughlin, J. L. "Their Hearts Were Hardened: The Use of Isaiah 6:9–10 in the Book of Isaiah." *Bib* 75 (1994): 1–25.

Maier, J. *Die Qumran-Essener: Die Texte vom Toten Meer.* Vol. 1: *Die Texte der Höhlen 1–3 und 5–11.* UTB 1862. Basel, 1995.

————. *Die Qumran-Essener: Die Texte vom Toten Meer.* Vol. 2: *Die Texte der Höhle 4.* UTB 1863. Munich, Basel, 1995.

Mason, R. *The Books of Haggai, Zechariah and Malachi.* CBC. Cambridge, 1977.

————. *Preaching the Tradition. Homily and Hermeneutics after the Exile.* Cambridge, 1990.

Matheus, F. *Singt dem Herrn ein neues Lied. Die Hymnen Deuterojesajas.* SBS 141. Stuttgart, 1990.

[Mathews, C. R. "Apportioning Desolation: Contexts for Interpreting Edom's Fate and Function in Isaiah." SBLSP 34. 250–66. Atlanta, 1995.]

————. *Defending Zion. Edom's Desolation and Jacob's Restoration (Isaiah 34–35) in Context.* BZAW 236. Berlin, 1995.

Mathys, H.-P. *Dichter und Beter. Theologen aus spätalttestamentlicher Zeit.* OBO 132. Freiburg (Switzerland), 1994.

Meade, D. G. *Pseudonymity and Canon.* WUNT 39. Tübingen, 1986.

Meier, S. A. *The Messenger in the Ancient Semitic World.* HSM 45. Atlanta, 1989.

————. *Speaking of Speaking. Marking Direct Discourse in the Hebrew Bible.* VTSup 46. Leiden, 1992.

Meinhold, A. "Maleachi/Maleachibuch." *TRE* 22. 6–11. Berlin, 1992.

[Melugin, R. F., and M. A. Sweeney, eds. *New Visions of Isaiah.* JSOTSup 214. Sheffield, 1996.]

[Metso, S. *The Textual Development of the Qumran Community Rule.* StTDJ 21. Leiden, 1996.]

[Miscall, P. *Isaiah.* Sheffield, 1993.]

[————. *Isaiah 34–35. A Nightmare/A Dream.* JSOTSup 281. Sheffield, 1999.]

Motyer, J. A. *The Prophecy of Isaiah. An Introduction and Commentary.* Leicester, 1993.

Moxter, M. "Gegenwart, die sich nicht dehnt. Eine kritische Erinnerung an Bultmanns Zeitverständnis." *Religion und Gestaltung der Zeit.* D. Georgi et al., eds. 108–22. Kampen, 1994.

Neumann, P. K. D. *Hört das Wort Jahwähs. Ein Beitrag zur Komposition alttestamentlicher Schriften.* Schriften der Stiftung Europa-Kolleg 30. Hamburg, 1975.

————. "Das Wort, das geschehen ist. Zum Problem der Wortempfangsterminologie in Jer I–XXV." *VT* 23 (1973): 171–217.

Nielsen, K. "Intertextuality and Biblical Scholarship." *SJOT* 4 (1990): 89–95.

Nissinen, M. *Prophetie. Redaktion und Fortschreibung im Hoseabuch. Studien zum Werdegang eines Prophetenbuches im Lichte von Hos 4 und 11.* AOAT 231. Kevelaer, 1991.

Nogalski, J. *Literary Precursors to the Book of the Twelve.* BZAW 217. Berlin, 1993.

————. *Redactional Processes in the Book of the Twelve.* BZAW 218. Berlin, 1993.

[————. "Intertextuality in the Twelve." *Forming Prophetic Literature. Essays on Isaiah and the Twelve in Honor of John D. W. Watts.* J. W. Watts and P. R. House, eds. JSOTSup 235. 102–24. Sheffield, 1996.]

O'Connell, R. H. *Concentricity and Continuity. The Literary Structure of Isaiah.* JSOTSup 188. Sheffield, 1994.

Odashima, T. *Heilsworte im Jeremiabuch. Untersuchungen zu ihrer vordeuteronomistischen Bearbeitung.* BWANT 125. Stuttgart, 1989.

Ohnesorge, S. *Jahwe gestaltet sein Volk neu. Zur Sicht der Zukunft Israels nach Ez 11, 14–21; 20, 1–44; 36, 16–38; 37, 1–14. 15–28.* FZB 64. Würzburg, 1991.

Olley, J. W. "'Hear the Word of YHWH': The Structure of the Book of Isaiah in 1QIsaᵃ." *VT* 43 (1993): 19–49.

Oswalt, J. N. *The Book of Isaiah. Chapters 1–39.* NICOT. Grand Rapids, 1986.

Otto, E. "Techniken der Rechtssatzredaktion israelitischer Rechtsbücher in der Redaktion des Prophetenbuches Micha." *SJOT* 5 (1991): 119–50.

Patte, D. *Early Jewish Hermeneutic in Palestine*. SBLDS 22. Missoula, 1975.

Petersen, D. L. *Late Israelite Prophecy: Studies in Deutero-Prophetic Literature and in Chronicles*. SBLMS 23. Missoula, 1977.

———. *The Roles of Israel's Prophets*. JSOTSup 17. Sheffield, 1981.

Pohlmann, K.-F. "Ezechiel oder das Buch von der Zukunft der Gola und der Heimkehr der Diapora." O. Kaiser. *Grundriß der Einleitung in die kanonischen und deuterokanonischen Schriften des Alten Testaments*. Vol. 2: *Die prophetischen Werke*. 82–102. Gütersloh, 1994.

Prinsloo, W. S. "Isaiah 12: One, Two, or Three Songs." *Goldene Äpfel in silbernen Schalen. Collected Communications to the TWELVEth Congress of the International Organization for the Study of the Old Testament*. Leuven, 1989. K.-D. Schunck and M. Augustin, eds. BEAT 20. 25–33. Frankfurt, 1992.

Rabinowitz, I. *A Witness Forever: Ancient Israel's Perception of Literature and the Resultant Hebrew Bible*. Bethesda, 1993.

Rad, G. von. *Theologie des Alten Testaments*. Vol. 2: *Die Theologie der prophetischen Überlieferungen Israels*. 10th ed. Munich, 1993.

Rendtorff, R. "The Book of Isaiah: A Complex Unity. Synchronic and Diachronic Reading." SBLSP 30. 8–20 Atlanta, 1991. [(Now in *New Visions of Isaiah*. R. F. Melugin and M. A. Sweeney, eds. JSOTSup 214. 32–49. Sheffield, 1996.)]

———. "Jesaja 6 im Rahmen der Komposition des Jesajabuches." In *The Book of Isaiah. Le livre d'Isaïe. Les oracles et leurs relectures*. J. Vermeylen, ed. BEThL 81. 73–82. Leuven, 1989.

———. "Zur Komposition des Buches Jesaja." *VT* 34 (1984): 295–320.

———. *Das Alte Testament. Eine Einführung*. 4th ed. Neukirchen-Vluyn, 1983 (1992).

Robinson, J. M. Die Logienquelle: Weisheit oder Prophetie? Anfragen an Migaku Sato. Q und Prophetie. *EvTh* 53 (1993): 367–89.

[Rofé, A. *Introduction to the Prophetic Literature (1992)*. Sheffield, 1997.]

———. "The Piety of the Torah-Disciples at the Winding-up of the Hebrew Bible: Joshua 1:8; Psalm 1:2; Isaiah 59:21." *Festschrift J. Maier*. BBB 88. 78–85. Frankfurt a.M., 1993.

Römheld, K. F. D. "Von den Quellen der Kraft (Jdc 13)." *ZAW* 104 (1992): 28–52.

Ruiten, J. T. A. G. M. van. *Een begin zonder einde. De doorwerking van Jesaja 65:17 in de intertestamentaire literatuur en het Nieuwe Testament.* Sliedrecht, 1990.

Ruppert, L. "Das Heil der Völker (Heilsuniversalismus) in Deutero- und 'Trito'-Jesaja." *MThZ* 45 (1994): 137–59.

Sæbø, M. "Vom 'Zusammen-Denken' zum Kanon. Aspekte der traditionsgeschichtlichen Endstadien des Alten Testaments." *JBTh* 3. 115–33. Neukirchen-Vluyn, 1988.

Sarna, N. M. "The Order of the Books." *Festschrift I. E. Kiev.* 407–13. New York, 1971.

Sato, M. *Q und Prophetie.* WUNT II/29. Tübingen, 1988.

Savran, G. W. *Telling and Retelling. Quotation in Biblical Narrative.* ISBL. Bloomington, 1988.

[Schart, A. *Die Entstehung des Zwölfprophetenbuchs.* BZAW 260. Berlin, 1998.]

[———. "Zur Redaktionsgeschichte des Zwölfprophetenbuchs." *VF* 43 (1998): 13–33.]

Schmid, K. *Buchgestalten des Jeremiabuches. Untersuchungen zur Redaktions- und Rezeptionsgeschichte von Jeremia 30–33 im Kontext des Buches.* WMANT 72. Neukirchen-Vluyn, 1996.

Schnabel, E. J. *Law and Wisdom from Ben Sira to Paul.* WUNT II/16. Tübingen, 1985.

Schniedewind, W. M. *The Word of God in Transition. From Prophet to Exegete in the Second Temple Period.* JSOTSup 197. Sheffield, 1995.

Schottroff, W. "Jeremia 2:1–3. Erwägungen zur Methode der Prophetenexegese." *ZThK* 67 (1970): 263–94.

Schramm, B. *The Opponents of Third Isaiah. Reconstructing the Cultic History of the Restoration.* JSOTSup 193. Sheffield, 1995.

Schreiner, J. "Interpretation innerhalb der schriftlichen Überlieferung." In *Literatur und Religion des Frühjudentums. Eine Einführung.* J. Maier and J. Schreiner, eds. 19–30. Würzburg Gütersloh, 1973.

Schultz, R. L. *The Search for Quotation. Verbal Parallels in the Prophets.* JSOTSup 180. Sheffield, 1996.

Seeligmann, I. L. "Voraussetzungen der Midraschexegese." In *Congress Volume Copenhagen, 1953.* VTSup 1. 150–81. Leiden, 1953.

Seitz, Chr. R. *Isaiah 1–39.* Interpretation. Louisville, 1993.

[————. "How is the Prophet Isaiah Present in the Latter Half of the Book? The Logic of Chapters 40–66 within the Book of Isaiah." *JBL* 115 (1996): 219–40.]

————. "On the Question of Divisions Internal to the Book of Isaiah." SBLSP 32. 260–66. Atlanta, 1993.

————, ed. *Reading and Preaching the Book of Isaiah.* Philadelphia, 1988.

————. *Zion's Final Destiny. The Development of the Book of Isaiah. A Reassessment of Isaiah 36–39.* Minneapolis, 1991.

Sekine, S. *Die Tritojesajanische Sammlung (Jesaja 56–66) redaktionsgeschichtlich untersucht.* BZAW 175. Berlin, New York, 1989.

Seybold, K. *Der Prophet Jeremia. Leben und Werk.* UB 416. Stuttgart, 1993.

Sheppard, G. T. "The Book of Isaiah: Competing Structures according to a Late Modern Description of Its Shape and Scope." SBLSP 31. 549–82. Atlanta, 1992.

————. "The Book of Isaiah as a Human Witness to Revelation within the Religions of Judaism and Christianity." SBLSP 32. 274–80. Atlanta, 1993.

————. "Canonization. Hearing the Voice of the Same God through Historically Dissimilar Traditions." *Int* 36 (1982): 21–33.

————. *Wisdom as a Hermeneutical Construct. A Study in the Sapientializing of the Old Testament.* BZAW 151. Berlin, 1980.

Skehan, P. W. "Qumran IV. Littérature de Qumran. −A." *Textes bibliques. DBS* 9. 805–22. Paris, 1979.

Skehan, W., and A. A. Di Lella. *The Wisdom of Ben Sira.* AB 39. New York, 1987.

Smend, R. *Die Entstehung des Alten Testaments. ThW* 1. 4th ed. Stuttgart, 1978 (1990).

Smith, P. A. *Rhetoric and Redaction in Trito-Isaiah. The Structure. Growth and Authorship of Isaiah 56–66.* VTSup 62. Leiden, 1995.

[Sommer, B. D. "Allusions and Illusions: The Unity of the Book of Isaiah in Light of Deutero-Isaiah's Use of Prophetic Tradition." In *New Visions of Isaiah.* R. F. Melugin and M. A. Sweeney, eds. JSOTSup 214. 156–86. Sheffield, 1996.]

[————. *A Prophet Reads Scripture. Allusion in Isaiah 40–66.* Stanford, 1998.]

[————. "The Scroll of Isaiah as Jewish Scripture. Or Why Jews Don't Read Books." SBLSP 132. 225–42. Atlanta, 1996.]

Stadelmann, H. *Ben Sira als Schriftgelehrter. Eine Untersuchung zum Berufsbild des vor-makkabäischen Sofer unter Berücksichtigung seines Verhältnisses zum Priester- Propheten- und Weisheitslehrertum.* WUNT II/6. Tübingen, 1980.

Steck, O. H. "Zur Abfolge Maleachi - Jona in 4Q76 (4QXII[a])." *ZAW* 108 (1996): 249–53.

———. *Der Abschluß der Prophetie im Alten Testament. Ein Versuch zur Frage der Vorgeschichte des Kanons.* BThSt 17. Neukirchen-Vluyn, 1991.

———. *Arbeitsblätter Altes Testament für Einführungskurse.* 2d ed. Zürich, 1993.

———. "Autor und/oder Redaktor in Jesaja 56–66." *Writing and Reading the Scroll of Isaiah. Studies of an Interpretive Tradition.* C. C. Broyles and C. A. Evans, eds. 2 Vols. VTSup 70. 219–59. Leiden, 1997.

———. *Das apokryphe Baruchbuch. Studien zu Rezeption und Konzentration 'kanonischer' Überlieferung.* FRLANT 160. Göttingen, 1993.

———. "Zu Eigenart und Herkunft von Psalm 102." *ZAW* 102 (1990): 357–72.

———. *Exegese des Alten Testaments. Leitfaden der Methodik.* 13th ed. Neukirchen-Vluyn, 1993.

———. "Der Gottesknecht als 'Bund' und 'Licht'. Beobachtungen im Zweiten Jesaja." *ZThK* 90 (1993): 117–34.

———. *Gottesknecht und Zion. Gesammelte Aufsätze zu Deuterojesaja.* FAT 4. Tübingen, 1992.

———. *Bereitete Heimkehr. Jesaja 35 als redaktionelle Brücke zwischen dem Ersten und dem Zweiten Jesaja.* SBS 121. Stuttgart, 1985.

———. *Israel und das gewaltsame Geschick der Propheten. Untersuchungen zur Überlieferung des deuteronomistischen Geschichsbildes im Alten Testament, Spätjudentum und Urchristentum.* WMANT 23. Neukirchen-Vluyn, 1967.

———. "Der sich selbst aktualisierende 'Jesaja' in Jesaja 56:9–59:21." *Festschrift M. Metzger.* OBO 123. 215–30. Freiburg (Switzerland), 1993.

[———. *Die erste Jesajarolle von Qumran (1QIs[a]). Schreibweise als Leseanleitung für ein Prophetenbuch.* SBS 137/1 and 137/2. Stuttgart, 1998.]

———. "Der Kanon des hebräischen Alten Testaments." *Verbindliches Zeugnis I. Kanon-Schrift-Tradition.* W. Pannenberg and Th. Schneider, eds. *DiKi* 7, 11–33. Freiburg, 1992.

————. "'…ein kleiner Knabe kann sie leiten'. Beobachtungen zum Tierfrieden in Jesaja 11:6–8 und 65:25." *Festschrift H. D. Preuß.* 104–13. Stuttgart, 1992.

————. "Prophetische Prophetenauslegung." *Wahrheit der Schrift– Wahrheit der Auslegung. Eine Zürcher Vorlesungsreihe zu Gerhard Ebelings 80. Geburtstag am 6. Juli, 1992.* H. F. Geißer et al., eds. 198–244. Zürich, 1993.

————. "Rettung und Verstockung. Exegetische Bemerkungen zu Jesaja 7:3–9." *Wahrnehmungen Gottes im Alten Testament. Gesammelte Studien.* ThB 70. 171–86. Munich 1882.

————. "Rezension: W. Lau. Schriftgelehrte Prophetie in Jesaja 56–66." *ThLZ* 120 (1995): 782–86.

————. "Zur Rezeption des Psalters im apokryphen Baruchbuch." *Neue Wege der Psalmenforschung. Festschrift W. Beyerlin.* K. Seybold und E. Zenger, eds. Herders biblische Studien 1. 361–80. Freiburg, 1994.

————. *Studien zu Tritojesaja.* BZAW 203. Berlin, 1991.

————. *Old Testament Exegesis: A Guide to the Methodology.* J. D. Nogalski, trans. SBLRBS 39. 2d ed. Atlanta, 1998.

————. "Tritojesaja im Jesajabuch." *The Book of Isaiah. Le livre d'Isaïe. Les oracles et leurs relectures.* J. Vermeylen, ed. BEThL 81. 361–406. Leuven, 1989.

————. "Weltgeschehen und Gottesvolk im Buche Daniel." *Wahrnehmungen Gottes im Alten Testament. Gesammelte Studien.* ThB 70. 262–90. Munich, 1982.

————. "Zu Zefanja 3:9–10." *BZ* 34 (1990): 90–95.

————. "Die getöteten 'Zeugen' und die verfolgten 'Tora-Sucher' in Jubiläenbuches 1:12. Ein Beitrag zur Zeugnis-Terminologie des Jubiläenbuches." Part 1: *ZAW* 107 (1995): 445–65; Part 2: *ZAW* 108 (1996): 70–86.

————. "Zukunft des einzelnen-Zukunft des Gottesvolkes. Beobachtungen zur Annäherung von weisheitlichen und eschatologischen Lebensperspektiven im Israel der hellenistischen Zeit." *Festschrift W. Richter.* 471–82. St. Ottilien, 1991.

Stegemann, H. *Die Essener. Qumran. Johannes der Täufer und Jesus. Ein Sachbuch.* Herder Spektrum 4128. 4th ed. Freiburg, 1994.

Steudel, A. "Eschatological Interpretation of Scripture in 4Q177 (4Q Catena^a)." *RevQ* 14 (1989): 473–81.

————. *Der Midrasch zur Eschatologie aus der Qumrangemeinde (4QMidrEschat^{a.b}).* StTDJ 13. Leiden, 1994.

Sweeney, M. A. "The Book of Isaiah in Recent Research." *Currents in Research: Biblical Studies* 1 (1993): 141–62.

[———. *Isaiah 1–39. With an Introduction to Prophetic Literature.* FOTL. Grand Rapids, 1996.]

———. *Isaiah 1–4 and the Post-Exilic Understanding of the Isaianic Tradition.* BZAW 171. Berlin, 1988.

———. "On Multiple Settings in the Book of Isaiah." SBLSP 32. 267–73. Atlanta, 1993.

Tigay, J. H., ed. *Empirical Models for Biblical Criticism.* Philadelphia, 1985.

Tomasino, A. J. "Isaiah 1:1–2:4 and 63–66 and the Composition of the Isaianic Corpus." *JSOT* 57 (1993): 81–98.

Tov, E. *Textual Criticism of the Bible.* Minneapolis, 1992.

[———. "Scribal Markings in the Texts from the Judean Desert." *Current Research and Technological Developments on the Dead Sea Scrolls.* D. W. Parry and St. D. Ricks, eds. StTDJ 20. 41–77. Leiden, 1996.]

[———. "The Text of Isaiah at Qumran." *Writing and Reading the Scroll of Isaiah. Studies of an Interpretive Tradition.* C. C. Broyles and C. A. Evans, eds. 2 vols. VTSup 70. 491–511. Leiden, 1997.]

Tracy, D. *Theologie als Gespräch. Eine postmoderne Hermeneutik.* Mainz, 1993.

Tucker, G. M. "Prophetic Superscriptions and the Growth of a Canon." *Canon and Authority. Essays in Old Testament Religion and Theology.* G. W. Coats and B. O. Long, eds. 56–70. Philadelphia, 1977.

[Ulrich, E. "An Index to the Contents of the Isaiah Manuscripts from the Judean Desert." In *Writing and Reading the Scroll of Isaiah. Studies of an Interpretive Tradition.* 2 vols. C. C. Broyles and C. A. Evans, eds. VTSup 70. 477–80. Leiden, 1997.]

[———, et al., eds. *Qumran Cave 4, Vol. 10: The Prophets.* Discoveries in the Judaean Desert 15. Oxford, 1997.]

Utzschneider, H. *Künder oder Schreiber? Eine These zum Problem der 'Schriftprophetie' auf Grund von Maleachi 1:6–2:9.* BEATAJ, 19. Frankfurt a. M., 1989.

———. "Die Schriftprophetie und die Frage nach dem Ende der Prophetie. Überlegungen anhand von Mal 1:6–2:16*." *ZAW* 104 (1992): 337–94.

Vanoni, G. "Anspielungen und Zitate innerhalb der hebräischen Bibel. Am Beispiel von Deuteronomium 4:29; Deuteronomium 30:3 und Jeremia 29:13–14." *Jeremia und die "deuteronomistische Bewegung".* W. Groß, ed. BBB 98. 383–97. Weinheim, 1995.

————. "'Die Tora im Herzen' (Jesaja 51:7). Oder: Über das Vergleichen." *Festschrift N. Füglister*. 357–71. Würzburg, 1991.

Vermeylen, J. *Du prophète Isaïe à 'lApocalyptique*. EtB. Vol. 1: Paris, 1977; vol. 2: Paris, 1978.

————. "L'unité du livre d'Isaïe." *The Book of Isaiah. Le livre d'Isaïe. Les oracles et leurs relectures.* J. Vermeylen, ed. BEThL 81. 11–53. Leuven, 1989.

Vosberg, L. *Studien zum Reden vom Schöpfer in den Psalmen*. BEvTh 69. Munich, 1975.

Vries, S. de. *From Old Revelation to New. A Tradition-Historical and Redaction-Critical Study of Temporal Transitions in Prophetic Predicition*. Grand Rapids, 1995.

Wahl, H.-M. "Die Überschriften der Prophetenbücher. Anmerkungen zu Form. Redaktion und Bedeutung für die Datierung der Bücher." *EThL* 70 (1994): 91–104.

Watts, J. D. W. *Isaiah 1–33*. WBC 24. Waco, 1985.

————. *Isaiah 34–66*. WBC 25. Waco, 1987.

Werlitz, J. *Studien zur literarkritischen Methode. Gericht und Heil in Jesaja 7:1–17 und 29:1–8*. BZAW 204. Berlin, 1992.

Wieringen, A. L. H. M. van. *Analogies in Isaiah*. Vol. A: *Computerized Analysis of Parallel Text between Isaiah 56–66 and Isaiah 40–66*. Amsterdam, 1993.

————. *Analogies in Isaiah*. Vol. B: *Computerized Concordance of Analogies between Isaiah 56–66 and Isaiah 40–66*. Applicatio 10A.B. Amsterdam, 1993.

Wildberger, H. *Jesaja*. BK X/1–3. Neukirchen-Vluyn, 1972–1982.

Williamson, H. G. M. *The Book Called Isaiah. Deutero-Isaiah's Role in Composition and Redaction*. Oxford, 1994.

————. "Isaiah XI 11–16 and the Redaction of Isaiah I–XII." *Congress Volume Paris, 1992*. VTSup 61. 343–57. Leiden, 1995.

————. "Isaiah 63:7–64:11. Exilic Lament or Post-Exilic Protest?" *ZAW* 102 (1990): 48–58.

Willi-Plein, I. *Vorformen der Schriftexegese innerhalb des Alten Testaments. Untersuchungen zum literarischen Werden der auf Amos, Hosea und Micha zurückgehenden Bücher im hebräischen Zwölfprophetenbuch*. BZAW 123. Berlin, 1971.

Wolfe, R. E. "The Editing of the Book of the Twelve." *ZAW* 53 (1935): 90–129.

Wolff, C. *Jeremia im Frühjudentum und Urchristentum*. TU 118. Berlin, 1976.

Wonneberger, R. *Redaktion. Studien zur Textfortschreibung im Alten Testament entwickelt am Beispiel der Samuelüberlieferung.* FRLANT 156. Göttingen, 1992.

Woude, A. S. van der. "Fünfzehn Jahre Qumranforschung (1974–1988)." *ThR* 55 (1990): 245–307.

———. "Fünfzehn Jahre Qumranforschung (1974–1988)." *ThR* 57 (1992): 1–57, 225–53.

Yee, G. A. *Composition and Tradition in the Book of Hosea. A Redaction Critical Investigation.* SBLDS 102. Atlanta, 1987.

Zapff, B. M. *Schriftgelehrte Prophetie–Jesaja 13 und die Komposition des Jesajabuches. Ein Beitrag zur Erforschung der Redaktionsgeschichte des Jesajabuches.* FZB 74. Würzburg, 1995.

Zenger, E. "Das Zwölfprophetenbuch." In *Einleitung in das Alte Testament.* Studienbücher Theologie 1.1. 3d ed. E. Zenger et al. 467–533. Stuttgart, 1995.

Zima, P. V. *Literarische Ästhetik. Methoden und Modelle der Literaturwissenschaft.* UTB 1590. 2d ed. Tübingen, 1995.

Zimmerli, W. *Ezechiel.* BK TWELVE/1.2. 2d ed. Neukirchen-Vluyn, 1969 (1979).

———. "Vom Prophetenwort zum Prophetenbuch." *ThLZ* 104 (1979): 481–96.

Notes

Chapter 1: The Prophetic Word and
Prophetic Book as a Historical Problem

[1]Concerning the question of prophetic message/prophetic book, see Kratz, *Kyros*, pp. 218–29; [Kratz, *Redaktion*]. See also his work in *TRE*, and Steck, *Prophetenauslegung* (below, pp. 117–63); Kaiser, *Grundriß*, §20; Jeremias, *ThLZ* 119 (1994); [*Rezeptionsprozesse*]. One must, of course, keep open the possibility that not every book necessarily goes back to a concrete prophetic figure. The book could also provide a materially controlled stylizing of the tradition process in this sense. Such is suggested for Malachi especially, but also for Jonah and Nahum.

[2]We use the term "prophetic book" for the presentation of prophetic statements recorded as a document or a scroll. It also includes third person reports. As such, this presentation goes beyond the occasional recording of an isolated logion which is dubious enough. Smaller literary collections thus fall under the term as well as the transmitted final form of a prophetic writing. It is not recommended that we differentiate between the size of the scroll or the degree of redactional revision and only use the term "book" after a certain point. This is not recommended because too much would be presupposed by that point. This critique applies to Collins, *Mantle*, pp. 16, 24–34. Carroll, *Jeremiah*, pp. 38f, abandons the term "book" all too skeptically. "Book" stands materially for scroll (see C. Dohmen, F. L. Hossfeld, and E. Reuter *ThWAT*, vol. 5, pp. 929–44). Anything else related to matters of the "prophetic book" requires clarification.

[3]*BK* 10/1–3, 1972–1982, especially 10/3, chapters 3 and 4.

[4]*ATD* 17, 5th ed., ATD 18, 1973, especially p. 3. See also Kaiser, *BEThL* 81, pp. 55–58; and *Grundriß*, §21, especially pp. 39–42.

[5]See recent discussion in Barstad, *JSOT* 57 (1993); Jeremias, *ThLZ* 119 (1994); Kratz, *TRE*.

[6]See Schottroff, *ZThK* 67 (1970): 293f, who is entirely correct as far as he goes. However, the conclusions deduced by Schottroff presuppose a far too simple image of the complex prophetic processes of tradition resulting in a fatal abbreviation of the necessary approaches. As a result, he states: "*From the outset, it is quite probable* that all of the *components* of the tradition complexes are transmitted to us by redaction *which can be plausibly explained as having developed from later presuppositions*. In fact, these components arose later, and owe their origin to redaction" (emphasis mine). This postulation is only a one-sided counterproposal against the long dominant search for the oldest original logia.

[7]The given literary entity increasingly steps into the forefront as the foundation and starting point for historical investigations beyond historically neutral, holistic endeavors in the sense of "new literary criticism" or "canonical criticism." See, as an example, Knierim, *Criticism*, 1985, p. 156. Approaches toward and results from such investigation of the given are nevertheless very different. The same is true of the readiness to continue from historically synchronic investigations to diachronic reconstructions. The following are mentioned as examples of the expressly demanded entry with that which is given: Smend, *Entstehung* (1978) for the Torah and the Deuteronomistic History. For the prophetic books, see Koch and co-workers, *Amos* (1976); Koch, *Propheten*, vol. 1, (1978, 1995, 3d ed.); Collins, *Mantle*, especially pp. 11–17. For Ezekiel, see Krüger, *Geschichtskonzepte* (1989), p. 294; and recently Feist, *Ezechiel* (1995). For Hosea, see Yee (1987); Missinen (1991). For works devoted especially to Isaiah, see Becker, *Isaias* (1968); Beuken, *Jesaja*, vol. IIA, B (1989, see my review of this work in *Bijdr* 52 (1991), pp. 439f; Rendtorff, *Einführung* (1983); Rendtorff, *VT* 34 (1984); Rendtorff, *Book of Isaiah* (1991); Clements, *JSOT* 31 (1985); cf. also Clements, *Int* 36 (1982); Steck, *Heimkehr* (1985); Steck, *Tritojesaja im Jesajabuch* (1987/89); Meade, *Pseudonymity* (1986); Vermeylen, *L'unité* (1987/89); Seitz, *Reading* (1988), pp. 13–22, 105–26; Seitz, *Divisions* (1993); Seitz, *Isaiah 1–39* (1993); Sweeney, *Isaiah 1–4* (1988); [Sweeney, *Isaiah 1–39* (1996)]; Evans, *VT* (1988); Matheus, *Singt* (1990), pp. 156–71; [Rofé, *Introduction* (1992/1997), pp. 11–55 provides important,

foundational observations about prophetic books (!)]; Carr, *JSOT* 57 (1993); [Reading (1997)]; Tomasino, *JSOT* 57 (1993); O'Connell, *Concentricity* (1994); [Gosse, *Structuration* (1997), pp. 8–26]. For a programmatic treatment with methodological reflection, see Laato, *SJOT* 8 (1994); [Laato, *History* (1996)].

⁸See the recent groundbreaking work of J. Jeremias in his studies to Hosea and Amos (see Steck, *Prophetenauslegung*, p. 208; above, p. 127), that are now collected in his book, *Hosea und Amos*. See also, Jeremias, *ThLZ* 119 (1994), 488–92; Jeremias, ATD, vol. 24/1 and 24/2 [and now Jeremias, *Tendenzen*]; Collins, *Mantle*, pp. 26ff; Koch, *Profeten*, vol. 1, pp. 39–41; Kratz, *TRE*, and already von Rad, *Theol AT*, vol. 2, pp. 53–57; Steck, *Rettung* (1973). Concerning the methodology, see Steck, *Exegesis*, pp. 63ff, 68–72, 80f, 90f.

⁹For explanations and rationale of the illustrative texts, we point to the exegetical investigations that we have published in the years 1985–1993 on the book of Isaiah: *Heimkehr*, and the collective volumes, *Studien zu Tritojesaja*, and *Gottesknecht und Zion*. See also *BZ* 1990, *ZAW*, 1990, *Abschluß*, *Preuß-Festschrift*, *Metzger-Festschrift*, *ZThK* 1993, *Prophetenauslegung*. The current work will present fundamental methodological options with the result held open. Therefore, we will generally take up the observations and questions about the expounded statements in Isaiah from the above mentioned investigations, not the suggested results. Illustrative observations to Jeremiah are taken from the work of K. Schmid, *Buchgestalten des Jeremiabuches*. The references to the book of Ezekiel below, p. 104, n. 131, derive from Peter Schwagmeier's Zürich dissertation in progress.

¹⁰See the works of Rendtorff (see n. 7, above, p. 11); Steck, *Heimkehr* and *Studien*, pp. 3–13 (programmatically related to Trito-Isaiah). See also Collins, *Mantle*, pp. 37–55.

¹¹The Trito-Isaiah investigations of Sekine and Koenen treat Isaiah 56–66 in this manner as do, generally, Emmerson, *Isaiah 56–66; Seitz*, ABD, vol. 3; and *de facto* Schramm, even though he is aware of the problem, *Opponents*, pp. 50–52. See also Lau, *Prophetie*; Aejmelaeus, *ZAW* (1995); de Vries, *Revelation*, pp. 126–29; Smith, *Rhetoric*, pp. 1–6. We continue to contest vigorously the idea that one can investigate Isaiah 56–66 independently of an investigation of Isaiah 1–66 with any really significant results.

¹²See the recent works on this topic in Steck, *Studien*, pp. 230ff, 245f, 179; Emmerson, *Isaiah 56–66*, p. 20; O'Connell, *Concentricity*, pp. 216–21.

¹³Concerning this statement, compare [now Coggins, *Deutero-Isaiah*, and the] current efforts which see Isaiah 40–55 in an original literary connection to Proto-Isaiah (Albertz, *Rendtorff-Festschrift*; Seitz, *Destiny*; Collins, *Mantle*, p. 42f; Williamson, *Book*) or to Jeremiah (Kratz, *ZAW* 106 [1994]).

¹⁴See Steck, *Heimkehr*, p. 79, n. 94; *BZ* (1990); *ZAW* (1990); *Abschluß; Gottesknecht*, pp. 190–207; Bosshard, *BN* (1987); and especially, Bosshard-Nepustil, *Rezeptionen von Jesaja 1–39 im Zwölfprophetenbuch*.

¹⁵See the rationale expressed quite similarly in Collins, *Mantle*, especially pp. 13ff.

¹⁶See below, p. 21 n. 16; p. 53, n. 54; and Steck, *Prophetenauslegung*, pp. 234–36 (see below, pp. 152–55); Stegemann, *Essener*, pp. 116–93; Schmid, *Buchgestalten*, pp. 35–42. There is insufficient evidence to support the conviction that biblical books were externally circulated over a lengthy period (Knauf, *Umwelt*, pp. 234–37; cf. Lohfink, *Bewegung*, pp. 340ff; Seybold, *Prophet*, pp. 182ff). The prophetic books also had no recognizable circulation outside the operation of the tradent school with its patterned examples. Cf. also Koch, *Profeten*, vol. 1, p. 48. Thus, the problem did not exist with respect to how the rereading processes were related to a wider circulation of versions of prophetic books as prophetic books developed (Lohfink, *Bewegung*, p. 348). See also Schmid, *Buchgestalten*, pp. 40f.

¹⁷This limitation lies at the close of the third century B.C.E. (Steck, *Abschluß*). It is, of course, not simply discernible with the Masoretic consonantal text (see the recent discussion of the MT text group in Tov, *Criticism*, pp. 21–79), as the finding of different versions alongside one another in Qumran shows (see chapter I below). Without undervaluing the continuation of interpretation until the vocalized version in the Masoretic codices of the Middle Ages, we nevertheless see no reason to push this limitation into this late period, since Qumran proves that the later Masoretic contributions no longer really concerned prophetic book formation. No one doubts the fact that the reception history operated on traditional editions of our text. See Koch, *Ausgang*, pp. 223f; Koch, *Profeten*, vol. 1., p. 46; Steck, *Prophetenauslegung*, p. 210f, n. 27 (see below, pp. 127–28).

¹⁸Investigations working ahistorically on that which is provided include "structuralism" (see J. Barton, *ABD*, vol. 6, pp. 214–17) and "rhetorical criticism" (see Th. B. Dozeman,

ABD, vol. 5, pp. 712–15). Other investigations belonging alongside these ahistorical investigations include the fashionable [and already out of date] approach of "reader response criticism," (see B.C. Lategan, *ABD*, vol. 5, pp. 625–28; Exum and Clines, *Criticism*, pp. 11–20, 24f [bibliography]) as well as additional contributions in the collection of essays in Exum and Clines. For application to Isaiah, see Conrad, *Reading Isaiah* (see Sweeney, *Currents* 1993, pp. 154ff; [and the individual essays in Melugin and Sweeney, *Visions*]). For a critique, see Knierim, *Criticism*; Culley, *Directions*. For the approach of "intertextuality," see, chapter 4. For the historical problem inside literary science, see for example, Margaret Davies, "Poststructural Analysis," *ABD*, vol. 5, pp. 424–26; Zima, *Ästhetik*; Eagleton, *Literaturtheorie*; Bassler (ed.), *New Historicism*; Adam, *Criticism*.

[19]For example, see the graphic signals in 1QIsaᵃ. See Olley, *VT* 43 (1993). [Tov, *Markings*; Steck, *Jesajarolle*, pp. 33–39, 124–55].

Chapter 2: From the Book to the Message: Procedural Steps

[1]See the references in Steck, *Kanon*, p. 21, n. 28; recently Tov, *Criticism*, pp. 155–63; and now Jones, *Formation*. This dissertation appeared in 1995, and impressively surveys the state of the manuscripts, starting with the entry point we describe in chapter 1. However, the determinations of the age of the various arrangements of the books in the manuscripts of the XII, which form the thesis of this dissertation, appear to us to be too hasty, despite the prudent rationale. Jones's work overvalues the "external evidence" (p. 41) of the manuscript findings, opts one-sidedly for the origin of the XII from a collection of individual books, and avoids synchronic and diachronic questions regarding the origin of the complex (!) sequencing of the text flow in the XII (see chapters 2–4 regarding the literary signals, the conceptual indicators, and the theological, linguistic profiles that appear in and behind the concrete path of the statements in the text sequence and in the book sequence). Jones criticizes literary critical and redaction historical endeavors concerning the given series of statements (pp. 14–23, 27) without taking a position on this area. Indeed, the question of the arrangements of the books in the manuscripts cannot be separated from the question of the origin of the text material. Limiting this approach may seem more objective, but it does not do justice to the content. Concerning the degrees of probability, see Jones, pp. 47, 126).

[2]For example, concerning Isaiah, see van der Kooij, *Textzeugen*; Koenig, *L'Herméneutique*; Barthélemy, *Critique*, vol. 2. For Jeremiah, see nn. 24 and 25. For Psalms, see the recent work of Koch, *Psalter*, and Flint, *Psalms*.

[3]See the listings in Fitzmyer, *Dead Sea Scrolls*, pp. 228–37; Gleßmer, *RevQ* 62 (1993): 173–80.

[4]1QIsaᵃ. See Skehan, *DBS*, p. 810; van der Kooij, *Textzeugen*, p. 109. Recently, Olley, *VT* (1993), treats this manuscript [and now Steck, *Jesajarolle*]. Concerning additional Isaiah manuscripts from 1Q, 4Q, and 5Q, see Skehan, *DBS*, pp. 810–12; van der Woude, *ThR* 57 (1990): 293f; and García Martinez, *Scrolls*, pp. 467, 477, 508; [Ulrich, *Index*; Flint, *Scrolls*; Tov, *Text*; Text Edition: *DJD* XV, pp. 7–143; plates 1–23].

[5]See the overviews in Skehan, *DBS*, p. 813; van der Woude, *ThR* 57 (1990): 294–96; García Martinez, *Scrolls*, pp. 467, 472, 477f, 509, 511. For Isaiah in Qumran, see now P. Jay, *RAC*, vol. 17, fascicles 132/133 (Stuttgart, 1995), pp. 770–75. For Jeremiah, see Schmid, *Buchgestalten*, pp. 13–15. For Ezekiel in Qumran, see Lust, *Ezekiel Manuscripts*; Brooke, *Ezekiel*, especially pp. 317–31, 336f. For the Book of the Twelve, especially in cave 4, see Fuller, *Minor Prophets*; Fuller, *Form;* [and Fuller, *DJD* XV, pp. 221–318 (4Q76–82)].

[6]Regarding the controversially discussed difference between the Hebrew and Greek Jeremiah versions, and their relationships and age, see Schmid, *Buchgestalten*, pp. 15–23, 305–27.

[7]For the different versions of the XII, see Fuller, *Minor Prophets*; Fuller, *Form*; and now Jones, *Formation*. Regarding 4Q76, see also Steck, "Abfolge," *ZAW* 108 (1976).

[8]See Steck, *Abschluß*, pp. 127–56, 167–78; *Kanon*, pp. 17–25. For the beginnings of the prophetic transmission in view of Hosea-Amos, see the groundbreaking work of Jeremias, *Anfänge*. Along with Lohfink (*SBS* 154, p. 30), Fischer, *Tora* (see the summary, pp. 117–24), has now further investigated the receptional accents in Isaiah starting with the תורה references by way of illustration. These references are provided from the position of the book in the larger "canonical" frame of the Nebiim in connection with the Torah. It is essential that one

form a historical (!) decision based upon possibly consciously placed signals that are still inside the corpora themselves and based upon findings in the slightly later intertestamental sources that document this combined perspective. See the following examples for the question of how the Torah and Nebiim were seen in a higher material unity after the second century B.C.E. and what "canonical reading" could have been at that time. For Qumran, see Steudel, *Midrasch*; for *Jubilees*, see Steck, *ZAW* (1995, 1996). See also discussion of the question below, p. 41, n. 39 and 106, n. 135 and 137.

9See preliminary indications in Steck, *Abschluß*, pp. 167–75.

10See G. T. Sheppard, *ABD*, vol. 1, pp. 861–66.

11See the groundbreaking work of Sheppard, *Interpretation* (1982), Clements, *Patterns*, as well as Steck, *Rezeption*, pp. 371ff, Kratz, *Identität*, and the references above in n. 14.

12With respect to the XII, see Wolfe, *ZAW* 53 (1935); Bosshard, *BN* 40 (1987) and *Rezeptionen*; Steck *ZAW* 102 (1990), and *Abschluß* (for Zephaniah-Haggai-Zechariah-Malachi); Jeremias, *Anfänge* (for Hosea-Amos) and especially Nogalski, *Precursors*; *Processes*; and *Intertextuality*.

13See Schmid, *Buchgestalten*, pp. 305–27. Cf. also the differences in the textual arrangement of Ezekiel 36–39 in the oldest Greek manuscript. See Pohlmann, in Kaiser, *Grundriß*, p. 83; and Ohnesorge, *Jahwe*, pp. 203–7.

14See the considerations in Steck, *Baruchbuch*, pp. 265–303. It is by no means certain whether the linguistically late insertion of Ezekiel 37:7a, 8b–10 really reflects the Maccabean period as stated by Bartelmus, *ZAW* (1985). Less extensively attested events from the third century B.C.E. also come into question. Also, the general resurrection of the dead in Daniel 12 is not a newly developed concept.

15See Steck, *Abschluß*, pp. 161–63.

16See above p. 15, n. 16 and Steck, *Heimkehr*, p. 84; *Studien*, pp. 270–77; *Prophetenauslegung*, pp. 234–36 (see below, pp. 152 ff). See Collins, *Mantle*, pp. 15, 28f; Koch, *Profeten*, vol. 1, p. 45. My colleague Dr. Krüger has suggested to me that the study of Old Testament tradition should also consider "The Late Babylonian Prophecy from Uruk" (Introduction and translation by K. Hecker, in *TUAT*, vol. 2 [Gütersloh, 1986], pp. 69ff). This work shows that this transmission material belongs to a library of a priestly family (!) from "the late Babylonian to the Seleucid period" (!) and that it was transmitted and consulted in this framework! Should one situate the growth of the prophetic books in the care of such longstanding scribal families?

17For the approach, cf. Baltzer, *Biographie*, Ackroyd, *Isaiah 1–12*; Koch, et al., *Amos*; and recently, Jeremias, *ThLZ* 119 (1994): 487, n. 13; Koch, *Profeten*, vol. 1, pp. 26–33. The initial endeavors from Sato, *Q*, pp. 69–77, do not withstand scrutiny of the state of the problem for Old Testament studies. The remainder has recently now been critiqued correctly with respect to the genre of Q: see Robinson, *EvTh* 53 (1993).

18Recently, others have correctly made this observation: Watts, *Isaiah 1–33*, pp. xxvii–xxix; Seitz, *Reading*, pp. 18–21, cf. pp. 116–23; Collins, *Mantle*, p. 55. See especially, Isaiah 58:1 and the discussion of it in Steck, *Studien*, p. 34 (n. 95), 177f. See also Isaiah 59:21 and the discussion in *Studien*, p. 28f (n. 70); *Gottesknecht*, pp. 168ff; *Prophetenauslegung*, pp. 240–42 (see below, pp. 160–62).

19See Seitz, *Reading*, pp. 112–16. Despite his comments (*Isaiah 1–39*, pp. xi–xii, 1–18), Seitz's desire to remain on the level of the given while writing a commentary to Isaiah 1–39, without a comparable incorporation of Isaiah 40–66, remains a contradictory venture. Sweeney, *CBQ* 56 (1994): 353, correctly raises a similar methodological objection against Werlitz, *Studien*.

20For the prophetic image of the late period, cf. Hartman, *Prophecy Interpreted*; Auld, *JSOT* 27 (1983); Barton, *Oracles*; Steck, *Israel*; *Abschluß*. For the image in Chronicles, see Schniedewind, *Word*; and especially for the image of Jeremiah, see Wolff, *Jeremia*.

21See the research overview in Sweeney, *Currents*, 1993. See also the recent works of Collins, *Mantle*, pp. 37–58; Seitz, *Isaiah 1–39*, pp. 1–18; [Becker, *Jesajaforschung*;] Koch, *Profeten*, vol. 1, pp. 197–205. The latter, however, too quickly disposes of Isaiah 40–66 and limits himself to the composition of Isaiah 1–39, as if one may be certain that this entity was a book by itself in this form. He then abruptly starts with the leap to the foundational cache and historical Isaiah. Is not a more precisely detailed investigation of the entire text required? Many questions are raised in light of textual assertions when one reads the characterizations (p. 199f) of Isaiah 24–27, 34 and even Isaiah 35 (which he sees as "presumably a later redactional song in Deutero-Isaianic style," p. 201). [In 1995, Koole, *Isaiah III,* 1–43, later attempts too quickly to explore the latest research regarding the book of Isaiah.] – Observations about the structure and internal coherence of Isaiah 1–66 have recently reappeared in the (precritical) commentary of Motyer, *Isaiah.* In this respect, see also Oswalt, *Book.*

[22]See references above, p. 12, n. 9.

[23]In addition to the references in n. 21, 26, 27, see also Steck, *Studien,* pp. 34–45, 217–28; *Gottesknecht,* pp. 17–172; *Abschluß,* pp. 29ff, 91–99, 112–26; *Preuß-Festschrift, Metzger-Festschrift.* See especially, Clements, *Int* (1982); Meade, *Pseudonymity;* Vermeylen, *L'unit;* Seitz, *Reading,* pp. 13–22, 105–26; Sweeney, *Isaiah 1–4;* Collins, *Mantle,* pp. 37–58. Also, see the recent individual observations in Jüngling, *Buch Jesaja,* especially pp. 393–99. Carr, *JSOT* 57 (1993), pp. 78–80, correctly indicates the limits of this reading for coherence of the final form. Nevertheless, these limits do not absolve one from asking the question which still awaits the foundational work. In spite of a corresponding effort, the attempt of Darr, *Vision,* is not what we conceive by a historical synchronic reading of the book of Isaiah that presumes coherence. This fact requires no further explanation. In contrast to the isolated lines of metaphors traced through the book, the book signals provided in the entire text must be the decisive point of reference. In her book, Darr does not refer to the current European research on Isaiah and does not contribute to the redactional-critical work that takes seriously the coherence of the final form. Instead, she offers only an exercise in reader-response theory that is not relevant for the present task.

[24]For Jeremiah, see Carroll, *Jeremiah.* However, Carroll spends too little time on Jeremiah as a book. Instead, now see Schmid, *Buchgestalten,* pp. 355–88. For Ezekiel, along with the commentary by Allen (1990, 1994), see the recent work of Pohlmann in Kaiser, *Grundriß,* pp. 89–99; and Hossfeld, *Buch Ezechiel,* pp. 445–51. For the Twelve, see the recent work of Collins, *Mantle,* pp. 59–84; Zenger, *Zwölfprophetenbuch,* pp. 467–72. Compare also, with considerable caution because of a theoretically ahistorical manner of reading, House, *Unity;* and recently Coggins, *Prophets.*

[25]See the recent work of Lau, *Prophetie,* treating the integration of Trito-Isaianic material into Isaiah and my review of that work in *ThLZ* 120 (1995).

[26]See the recent work of O'Connell, *Concentricity.* This work is very stimulating for the relationships in the flow of the immediate context, but it perceives with difficulty the intended flow of reading for the given material in Isaiah. It has this difficulty because the explicit concentric structure of blocks of sayings frequently must move beyond the structuring signals of the vocabulary (cf. the analysis of Isaiah 65–6, pp. 229–32). Also, the highly complex concentricity is frequently only reached by the selection and abstractions of the vocabulary's meaning. The thesis that an individual compiler created Isaiah 1–66 in the late 6th century B.C.E. must clarify, historically, how this person accomplished the complexity of the arranged shape and content in Isaiah materially.

[27]In addition to Miscall, *Isaiah,* see especially Watts, *Isaiah 1–33; Isaiah 34–66,* and the comments about these works by Sweeney, *Currents* 1 (1993): 145f. The larger concerns of Watts remain important because he orients himself thoroughly toward the chronological epochs in which the Isaiah of the book is concentrated in accordance with the book's flow. In addition to the inquiry into the meaning of the statements on the level of Isaiah 1–66, one should critically mention, above all, the principal consideration that the wording itself does not satisfactorily demonstrate the dramatic strategy and the detailed segmenting into epochs. – Even the drama concept should not be dismissed from the outset for prophetic books, but it requires more extensive evidence and assurances for the final form and the prior literary stages of these books. The idea of disclosures recorded as though taking minutes from the realm of YHWH's heavenly decrees, together with word and deed performances of the prophetic mediator of these disclosures (see below, n. 50), appears to us to be a sustainable working hypothesis. Based upon ancient Near Eastern conceptual findings regarding what a prophetic book presents and what it expresses in the form, this idea appears more promising than the drama model that stands in danger of overlooking the character of the book and transcriptional character of that which has been transmitted. In light of the drama model, it must be ascertained whether the change of speakers so obvious in Isaiah could not actually be explained more simply by material aspects within the framework of a comprehensive concept presented in the book (and the book's diachronic traces of growth). The "dramatic" element should possibly not be seen as literary, but as a phenomenon of the transmitted design of YHWH (the image of history revealed in the final effect within the book). For an

explanation of the change of voices, for example, see the illustrative examination of Isaiah 51:12–16 in Steck, *Gottesknecht*, pp. 60–72, 119f. By contrast, Vanoni, *Füglister-Festschrift*, wants to see 51:9–16 on the same level. The essays in *BN* 44 (1988), *BN* 46 (1986), and in the *Rendtorff-Festschrift*, which also appear in the collected essays of *Gottesknecht*, were not even worthy of consideration in his essay that appeared in 1991. Upon closer examination, his rebuke, p. 360, n. 12, falls back on him in light of the successive comments upon this text in Steck, *Heimkehr*.

²⁸See Sweeney, *Isaiah 1–4* [and *Isaiah 1–39*, pp. 31–61], who achieves an impressive characterization of Isaiah 1–66, especially, pp. 185–201. The internal organization of the final formation of the book that Sweeney puts forth is worth considering as an initial endeavor. This endeavor, however, suffers from the fact that the higher unity only appears to be a logical, higher level of generalization. It is only achieved by uncovered structurings, schemata, and through generalizations made by ignoring the concrete wording (its compositional signals, its exegetically uncovered aspects of meaning, and its positioning in the flow of the book). Thus, the higher unity is achieved by extensively overlooking the concrete reading clues. Sweeney correctly observes that the Isaiah of the book finally incorporates the perspective of the Persian period and no longer treats the Greeks on their own. However, dating Isaiah 1–66 to the end of the fifth century (p. 99, n. 224) on this basis is too hasty a decision. An investigation of several texts using detailed exegesis and a consideration of a history of theology, along with a comparison of Zechariah 9–14 (see Steck, *Abschluß*) argues against this decision. The liberation of the diaspora from Assyria and Egypt together with the intersection of the return path in Edom (Isa 35 as limitation of Isa 34) in the face of a universal judgment (!) leads to a later period seen from the end time (!) (See *Abschluß*, pp. 23, 73–111). See below, beginning p. 108, concerning the above-mentioned question.

²⁹See now Schmid, *Buchgestalten*, pp. 2–7, 217–20, 330–40.

³⁰For conversation with Laato, see also K. Nielsen, *SJOT* 8 (1994): 298–301; S. Ö. Steingrimsson, *SJOT*, 8 (1994): 302–5. [For the semiotic entry point of Laato, see Laato, *History*, pp. 301–97].

³¹The concluding passages of several books in particular have a decisively clarifying, explanatory goal because of the completion of Israel's salvation: Isaiah, Jeremiah (LXX), Ezekiel, Hosea, Joel, Amos, Micah, Zephaniah, Haggai, Zechariah, Malachi. Other books with striking connecting arcs between the beginning and end are explained as partial goals in the production of a series, as we presume in earlier discussion (1, 2), for example, for Jeremiah (MT). Was Jeremiah (MT) seen as sufficient, with its connecting arc of prophecy about the nations (Jer 1; 4–10; 46–51) in light of the transmitted material from Jeremiah, but seen as insufficient in light of the book's material message in the macro-structural context of the series requiring individual entities? Corresponding questions present themselves in connection to J. Jeremias regarding speeches against the nations at the beginning of Amos.

³²See Steck, *Studien*, pp. 231f; *Abschluß*, p. 26; also recently Tomasino, *JSOT* 57 (1993): 85.

³³For the framing inclusions between the beginning and ending chapters of Isaiah, see recently Sweeney, *Isaiah 1–4*, pp. 21–25, 196f; Beuken, *Closure*; Steck, *Studien*, pp. 41, 44f, 229–65; Steck, *Metzger-Festschrift*, p. 229; Gosse, *ZAW* (1992); Carr, *JSOT* 57 (1993): 71–75; [Carr, *Reading*;] Tomasino, *JSOT* 57 (1993).

³⁴Cf. Isaiah 11:9//1: 4,3: see Steck, *Preuß-Festrschrift*, pp. 106ff; Isaiah 33//Isaiah 1–2: see Steck, *Heimkehr*, p. 56 (with n. 35); Beuken, *EThL* 67 (1991); Bosshard-Nepustil, *Rezeptionen*, pp. 183–233; see Steck, *Studien*, scripture index to Isaiah 1–2.

³⁵See Steck, *Studien*, pp. 150, 157, 192f, 230f.

³⁶Cf., e.g., Isaiah 66:5–24 as a compromise of the nations' participation in salvation and their final judgment, which appear side by side in Isaiah 1–2; 33f and 40:5; 49–51; 60–63:6; and already Isaiah 12 after 11:11–16 (see Steck, *Studien*, pp. 42ff, 230f; Matheus, *Singt*, pp. 159–64; Prinsloo, *Isaiah 12*; Mathys, *Dichter*, pp. 181–200).

³⁷See Rendtorff, *VT* 34 (1984); Steck, *Gottesknecht*, pp. 73–91; Steck, *Studien*, pp. 257, 264.

³⁸Regarding Rendtorff's demonstration of pointed concepts, see the references in Steck, *Studien*, p. 44.

³⁹It is more than questionable that one can say as much as Lohfink does (*Gott Israels*, pp. 37–58) based upon such a narrow basis about "covenant and Torah with the pilgrimage of the nations (the book of Isaiah and Psalm 25)" without having processed a clarified image of

noteworthy material intentions of statements for the literary whole from the given book of Isaiah in a series of books. At best, there are first heuristic impressions which require more extensive treatment if the attempted "synchronic observation of the final text" (p. 45, n. 24) is to be considered a historical approach. If not, however, then everything in the canon can be related to everything else, and the relational possibilities would be legion. However, these possibilities lie outside the framework of our investigation, because they concern later hermeneutical levels beyond the genetic levels. See also the critique of Groß, *Neuer Bund*, pp. 94–96. For the question of *torah* in Isaiah, cf. now the observations to the current book in the frame of the "Nebiim" in the position of "*torah*" in Fischer, *Tora*.

⁴⁰For the question, see Steck, *Abschluß*, pp. 120–26, 167–75; and especially Bosshard-Nepustil, *Rezeptionen*, pp. 450–64.

⁴¹See Steck, *Studien*, p. 34 (n. 95), 178.

⁴²For this question, see Steck, *Abschluß*, pp. 112–26, 167–75, and especially Bosshard-Nepustil, *Rezeptionen*, pp. 450–64; Schmid, *Buchgestalten*, pp. 349–54.

⁴³Sirach 48:23f. For the Isaiah connection which Sirach presupposes, see Steck, *Studien*, p. 39, n. 115. [Concerning the question of Isaiah 40–66 as an "Isaiah" text, see the recent work of Seitz, *JBL* 115 (1996). Knauf, *BK* 53 (1998): 121, formulates something for the Pentateuch which also holds true for the prophetic books. "Tradition-literature is not literature by authors…It is a collection which is taught and transmitted in the name of authorities, not authors. The great prophetic books could contain very few words of the historical Isaiah, Jeremiah, or Ezekiel without being falsely titled, because the material in the collection does not come from the author, but from the authority in whose name one thinks and continues to think."]

⁴⁴See the connection to the Isaiah-manuscripts in Qumran (Isa 65f in 1QIsaᵇ; 4QIsaᵇ·ᶜ). Further, see 4Q174, col. VI (Isa 65:22f).

⁴⁵In its course, the framework constantly opens "windows" into the Assyrian and the Babylonian epochs. From these windows, one can glance in advance with Isaiah into the future until the final consummation. See Steck, *Prophetenauslegung*, pp. 217f, n. 40 (see below, p. 138). References back to the earlier epochs function correspondingly where the current salvation events of that time and, especially, where sayings about the final consummation constitute the theme.

⁴⁶For Isaiah 56–59, see Steck, *Studien*, pp. 169–213; *Metzger-Festschrift*. For Isaiah 65f, see Steck, *Studien*, pp. 248–65.

⁴⁷See Steck, *Prophetenauslegung*, pp. 215ff (see below, pp. 135–37). For the multiple validation of sayings, see also Sheppard, *SBLSP* (1992), p. 576; Seitz, *SBLSP* (1993), pp. 260–63.

⁴⁸For a discussion, see Steck, *Israel*, pp. 133–95 in summary form. For the comprehensive image that these prophetic books offer, see Koch, *TRE*, vol. 12, pp. 577–79 (with heavy schematization and without diachronic differentiation of the transmission). Also, see Steck, *Abschluß*, pp. 112–26; *Prophetenauslegung*, pp. 217–25 (see below, beginning p. 137). And with respect to *Jubilees*, see Steck, *ZAW*, 1995 and 1996. For the question of the Deuteronomistically shaped image of history in the late period, cf. now also Schmid, *Buchgestalten*, pp. 305–23. Particularly noteworthy in this context is the fact that, in distinction to the message, Schniedewind (*Word*, in summary form, pp. 231–52) lays out the task of the prophets in Chronicles: to "explain to the king how God has acted, is acting, or shall act in history" (p. 235).

⁴⁹In terms of concepts, this image concerns prophetic glimpses into the future into the long-term "plans" of YHWH. See examples and discussion in *ThWAT*: O. Steingrimsson, vol. 2, pp. 599–603; K. Seybold, vol. 3, pp. 254–56; H.-J. Fabry, vol. 5, pp. 777–80; and L. Ruppert vol. 3, pp. 735–51. For examples in Jeremiah, see Schmid, *Buchgestalten*, pp. 229–49, 305–23, 355–66. Nevertheless, in the final form of the books these concepts are not exposed in such a manner that they appear as leading concepts for the reception of the prophetic book as such. One could speak correspondingly about the concepts "work" and "way."

⁵⁰See Steck, *Prophetenauslegung*, pp. 217–35, especially 217f, n. 40 (see below, pp. 137ff, especially p. 137 n. 26. Cf. now, Koch, *Profeten*, vol. 1, pp. 21–26, with the designated superscription "Metahistory as hermeneutical key." Concerning Isaiah, see Koch, *Profeten*, vol. 1, pp. 249–60. Prophetic books do not simply leave their readership to flounder on the level of the wording (and its multiple complexities) and on the level of the divergent formulations. Rather, prophetic books want to be read from the background of the advance knowledge of

comprehensive divine planning indicated by the wording and construction. The prophetic books attain their inner coherence and material unity from this depth dimension. These elements are known to Jewish exegesis (see Rabinowitz, *Witness*, especially pp. 74f, 77f, 110–21), and they find echoes in historical prophetic research in recent times. See, for example, Carroll, *Prophecy Failed*, pp. 6–40; Clements, *Mays-Festschrift*; Clements, *Patterns*; Fishbane, *Interpretation*, pp. 506–43; Seitz, *Reading*, pp. 113–16; Seitz, *Isaiah 1–39*, pp. 17ff; Collins, *Mantle*, pp. 29–31; Jeremias, *ThLZ* 119 (1994): 492–94; De Vries, *Revelation*, especially pp. 8–20, 310–22. A typical illustration of this type of metahistorical perspective is now found in Schmid, *Buchgestalten*, pp. 355–76.

If we say that the primary intention of the final formation of prophetic books is orientation toward Israel in its time by the declaration of a prophetically conveyed, divinely-metahistorical knowledge of history, we do not propose to make these sources "apocalyptic." After the close of the Nebiim, the apocalypses of the late period of ancient Israel are thoroughly governed by particular influences of Wisdom's systematization of prophetic aspects concerning God's decree and foreknowledge. They have become God's comprehensive plan of history presented as a whole in advance (Daniel, *Ethiopian Enoch, Jubilees, Assumption of Moses*) or in retrospect (*4 Ezra; Syriac Baruch*). They are shaped by the correspondence of the worlds of heaven and earth, and they are particularly shaped by the escalation of legitimation by special revelation. Do these later efforts reflect a compensation for the failure of perspectives of imminent expectations related to the original time period within the Nebiim? However, it appears to us both intentional and functional that we encounter more continuity than is generally perceived between God's divinely decreed world that prophetic books disclose (perhaps following the concept of prophetic insights into the heavenly counsel of YHWH), and the visions, auditions, and heavenly trips of the apocalypses. For questions about the historical understanding of the prophetic books and of the theological and religio-historical environment, cf. above all, Koch, *TRE*, vol. 12, pp. 570–86 (bibliography); Koch, *Reiche*. For the role of the prophets conveying decrees, see the material, for example, in Holladay, *HTR* 63 (1970); Petersen, *Roles*; Meier, *Messenger*, cf. Steck, *Heimkehr*, p. 94, n. 25.

[51]See Rabinowitz, *Witness*, p. 77; Seitz, *Reading*, p. 122.

[52]This side-by-side placement of Isaiah 36–39 and 40 gives all researchers difficulty who want to demonstrate older connections between Proto- and Deutero-Isaiah. See the recent work of Seitz, *Destiny*, pp. 23–26; Seitz, *SBLSP* (1993); Seitz, *Isaiah 1–39*. See also Williamson, *Book*. However, we are still of the opinion that Isaiah 35 most readily serves as the first connection between First Isaiah and Second Isaiah. Also, the placement of Isaiah 35 after Isaiah 34 (which Seitz considers problematic) rather than after Isaiah 39 (*SBLSP* [1993]: 262–65); *Isaiah 1–39*, pp. 236–42) rests upon the fact that Isaiah 35 [corresponding to Numbers] wants to assure the final piece of the return path (!) from the diaspora from Assyria and (!) Egypt (11:11–16; 27:12f) in the Edomite territory destroyed in the universal judgment. Therefore, the side-by-side placement enables the material bridge between Isaiah 34 (universal judgment in Edom) and Isaiah 40 (a programmatic text about the return) through an immediate connection to Isaiah 34, made necessary by the content (see Steck, *Heimkehr*, pp. 58ff; *Gottesknecht*, pp. 86–89; *Studien*, pp. 20–27, 143–166). The theme is cultivated throughout the book in material gradations (Isa 11:11–16, liberation; 27:12f, gathering; 35, return path; 51:1–11, uniting the returning streams; 62:10–12, arrival, parallel 66:5–24). Still, we will here have to bypass the diachronic aspects that now would also have to include an investigation of Isaiah *1–62 in a dialogue (with Williamson, *Isaiah XI*; Williamson, *Book*; and Smith, *Rhetoric*) with respect to whether Isaiah 11:11–16; 27:12f; 35; 62:10–12 all belong to the same level of a "return redaction." Harrelson, *Barr-Festschrift*, now offers a less satisfying report on the state of the research upon Isaiah 35. Also, the new investigation of Mathews, *Defending Zion*, which draws only from my 1985 study on Isaiah 35, really oversimplifies the task of understanding Isaiah 34 and following in the development of Isaiah by her uncertainty, her imprecision over against the complexity of Isaiah as a whole, and the neglect of a conceptual profile.

[Concerning the insufficient diachronic method of Mathews and Childs, see also p. 83, n. 77 below. Similarly, Seitz (see the reference above) really mitigates the literary historical questions about Isaiah 35, as does Berges, *Buch Jesaja*, pp. 249–63, with an odd spiritualization of the sayings of the return trip. Concerning Isaiah 35, see the recent work by Kuan, *Jian Dao*, 1996, who too readily assigns Isaiah 35 to Isaiah himself. See also the recent work of

Miscall, *Isaiah 34–35.* One should here consider the transmission of Isaiah 35 onward. An isolated treatment of Isaiah 34–35 is not directed toward its own subject. Rather, it is directed toward an exegetical preparation. Finally, according to Williamson, and recently Berges, *Buch Jesaja,* pp. 242–48, Isaiah 33 (not Isa 35) should be seen as the initial bridge text between First and Second Isaiah. One can only contest this idea. Isaiah 33 does not lead directly to Isaiah 40:1–2 (neither stylistically nor materially). In Isaiah 33, Zion is not a person, in contrast to Isaiah 40:1. In Isaiah 33, Zion is innocent and already in salvation again.]

   [53]We would assign the essentials of this designed structuring to our "homecoming redaction" of the Isaiah corpus in Isaiah*1–62. This structure was preserved in the final formation but was modified, especially by Isaiah 66:5–24. See Steck, *Studien,* pp. 230ff, 279. For the diachronic elements of the Babylon-universal judgment sayings in Isaiah, see now Zapff, *Prophetie.* For the diachronic elements in Isaiah 33–39, see Bosshard-Nepustil, *Rezeptionen,* pp. 17–267. For the references back to the liberation from Babylon, e.g., in Jeremiah 30:8f to statements relating to the liberation from Assyria in Isaiah 8:21–9:6, 10:27, and 14:25, see Duhm, *Jeremia,* p. 239. Also, see now Schmid, *Buchgestalten,* pp. 161–64. For the succession of YHWH's judgment activity over a lengthy time span against God's people, Assyria, Babylon, and the nations according to their parallel occurrence in Isaiah and in the XII, see Bosshard-Nepustil, *Rezeptionen,* pp. 17–267, 269–431. For this element in Jeremiah, see Schmid, *Buchgestalten,* pp. 305–23.

   The homecoming redaction, which in our opinion is only slightly older than the final formation of Isaiah, offers three kinds of processes for the return of God's people. These processes were potentially differentiated and observed in phases in this redactional level. (1) From the older stage the process of return from Babylon is adopted as it was found in Isaiah 41–49:13. This process was understood as the return of the Babylonian *golah* (accomplished under Cyrus/Darius?) from all Israel (Northern Israelite and Judeans; see a different idea in Steck, *Gottesknecht,* pp. 87f and *Studien,* pp. 161, 279). The process took place under YHWH's direct leadership and was connected to the downfall of Babylon. It is also associated with YHWH's own return to Jerusalem. Thus the return redaction receives the arc of Isaiah 33//40:1–11//52:7–10(12). (2) Also from a prior literary stage, the process of the return of the children of Zion from the entire world is received as it appeared in Isaiah 49:14ff and 50:1–3 (and further in Isa 54 and 60). It was understood as the resettlement of Jerusalem (accomplished under Ezra and Nehemiah?). It happened at YHWH's initiative, but YHWH does not march with them. Rather, it happens through the escort of the nations honoring Zion. The Judeans play no role here (contra *Gottesknecht,* pp. 87ff; *Studien,* pp. 161, 279). (3) The return of those in Assyria and Egypt still to come (the Seleucid and Ptolemean kingdoms) is constructed through its own redactional formulations in Isaiah *1–62 that are attached to existing statements about YHWH's return of the universal diaspora (Isa 43:5f; 49:9–13). These statements correspond to the diaspora promises of Jeremiah (see recently, Schmid, *Buchgestalten,* pp. 274–76). This actual return first expected eschatologically happens in the power (51:9–11; 54:4–6), initiative, and gathering (11:11; 27:12; 35) of Zion's God, who marches with them and leads them home. Only this return is characterized as salvation from the universal judgment of the nations (Isa 10–13; 24–27; 34f; 51). It also has a correspondence in Jeremiah (see Schmid, *Buchgestalten,* pp. 310, 325f).

   These three processes are differentiated chronologically and in various aspects. They are seen together in the book's flow in three main texts. These three processes are seen in the framework of the movement to Zion in Isaiah 40:1–11 as the divinely initiated beginning of these processes of return. They are seen in Isaiah 51:1–11 as the combined vision of all returnees as YHWH's people before entering into the land, where Abraham and Sarah represent the earthly parents of this whole people. Abraham stands for the population of the land and Sarah stands for the population of Jerusalem with mother Zion (still different in *Gottesknecht,* pp. 89ff). And these three processes are seen in Isaiah 62:10–12 in the framework of the perspective of the arrival in Zion after Isaiah 51:12. It begins with the summons to the city inhabitants, who can already be found in Jerusalem (Isa 60). It has its goal in the statement of Isaiah 62:10–12 concerning the arrival of the Assyrian-Egyptian diaspora that then finally restores the whole people with Zion as its center (62:12). Later, Isaiah 66 expressly adds the distant diaspora.

   [54]See Steck, *Heimkehr,* pp. 83f, 102; *Prophetenauslegung,* p. 236 (see below, p. 152). Also, one should keep in mind that the literary measures of reception treat speech and discussion

processes between prophetic tradents and the population. One should also keep in mind that the literary measures of reception were also processed in the continuations (*Fortschreibungen*), e.g., in view of Isaiah 56–59 or Malachi (see Mason, *Preaching*).

⁵⁵See Steck, *Richter-Festschrift*. Concerning the manner of reception within wisdom, see the recent insights from Krüger, *ZThK* 92 (1995). He considers the compositional connection of disparate materials and the discussion processes thereby opened.

⁵⁶See recently, Schmid, *Buchgestalten*, especially pp. 201–17, 253–304, 323–27. For the historical images in Ezekiel, see Krüger, *Geschichtskonzepte*.

⁵⁷Compare, e.g., the "book" in Jeremiah 30–33 with the "book" in Jeremiah 36. See the discussion in Schmid, *Buchgestalten*, pp. 75–77.

⁵⁸For Zechariah 9–14, Malachi, see Steck, *Abschluß*, pp. 33–60, 61–72, 112–26.

⁵⁹See Steck, *Studien*, pp. 27–33, 34–35, 257–65; *Gottesknecht*, pp. 170–72; *Metzger-Festschrift*, p. 229.

⁶⁰See above, nn. 38, 40, 41. See also Kratz, *Kyros*, pp. 218–29; Steck, *Prophetenauslegung*, pp. 213–25 (see below, pp. 134ff); Collins, *Mantle*, pp. 30ff; Rabinowitz, *Witness*, especially pp. 110–21; [Rofé *Introduction*, pp. 20–25, 56–73.] Cf. also Barr, *JSOT* 44 (1989): 11f.

⁶¹The statements in 1QpHab 7:12f show clearly that the prophetic reception has in mind a metahistorical concept. Cf. also examples that relate to a particular day (e.g., in 4QpIsab/4Q162, 2:1 [reference from P. Schwagmeier]).

For the understanding of time in the prophetic transmission, see the reference above in n. 40. See especially Steck, *Prophetenauslegung*, especially 239f, n. 90 (see below, p. 158, n. 78), and recently Rabinowitz, *Witness*, Jeremias, *ThLZ* (1994): 490f; de Vries, *Revelation*, especially pp. 310–32, with particular insights into the details of developmental accents. However, in the broader redaction-historical perspectives to Isaiah, Jeremiah, Ezekiel, and the XII no less, de Vries as well as Collins greatly overshoot the boundaries of the material that is explained redaction-historically at present.

⁶²Our diachronically achieved suggestion for the intended meaning of the final formation of Isaiah, primarily conceived with Isaiah 56–66, is found in Steck, *Studien*, pp. 229–65. It is placed in a wider framework of the final formation of the prophetic books in *Abschluß*, pp. 112–26, 145–78.

⁶³In the phenomenon of "repetition" (*Wiederaufnahme*) observed by Kuhl (*ZAW* 64 [1952]), this expansion appears clearly visible inside the texts. Nevertheless, these repetitions do not want to be denoted by themselves from the growth of the text. The tradents do not accent them as an independent entity over against the prophets. In the minds of the productive tradents, this process serves the material unification of the expanded whole. It is self-evident that the phenomenon exposed by Kuhl using specific texts from Jeremiah and Ezekiel must also be examined in the wider framework of the book's development. Even the receptional references are not intentional signals of text growth. The discipline discusses these references under the catchwords "quote" and "allusion," although the donating prophet in these passages is not expressly quoted. Even in these cases no one else speaks besides the prophet of the book. The tradents do not bring themselves into play over against the prophet. These manifestations demonstrate material references to the extent considered necessary, but they do not require the legitimation of later tradents. The image presented in the books of episodic processes of revelation in the prophet's lifetime should not simply be conducted into the historical phenomenon of the textual growth of the existing book. In Jeremiah, these processes even appear as different records in the books (see Schmid, *Buchgestalten*, pp. 7–12, 91–94). Whether this image reflects literary development requires special investigation.

⁶⁴See, e.g., Rendtorff, *Einführung*, pp. 201–12; Kaiser, *Grundriß*, §21; Koch, *Profeten*, vol. 1, pp. 42ff; [Rofé, *Introduction*, pp. 12–20, 37–40.]

⁶⁵Cf. for example, the narrow compositional lines from Isaiah 11:11–16//62:10–12; from 40:1–5//52:7–10; from Isaiah 13//27; from Isaiah 34//63:1–6. These lines are not part of the final formation, as Isaiah 66 shows. Rather, they are earlier than the final shape.

⁶⁶For Isaiah 60–62, see Steck, *Studien*, pp. 119–39; *Gottesknecht*, pp. 161–69; *ZThK* 90 (1993). For Isaiah 65f, see *Studien*, pp. 248–65.

⁶⁷See Davies, *Destiny*, and Steck's treatment of that work in *Studien*, pp. 243, 246, and *Abschluß*, p. 29, n. 43; Groß, *Israel und die Völker*, Ruppert, *MThZ* 45 (1994).

⁶⁸The warnings from Koch, *Profeten*, vol. 1, pp. 47–49, against subjective, modernistic literary criticism should, of course, be taken to heart, as the following shows. We begin our

diachronic investigation more foundationally, namely with observations not just upon "every/each text(s)," but especially with observations upon the given book in its entirety.

[69]The character of the superscriptions and partial superscriptions requires more detailed explanation inside Isaiah, Jeremiah, Ezekiel, and especially in the XII, and their structuring and material function in the respective literary whole, for the historical synchronic reading of the final formation of the prophetic books as well as for their prior literary stages. For a discussion, see Gevarjahu, *Colophons*; Tucker, *Superscriptions*; Freedman, *Headings*; Wahl, *Überschriften*. For the XII, see now Nogalski, *Precursors*; Nogalski, *Processes*; Bosshard-Nepustil, *Rezeptionen,* pp. 409–31, 433–64.

[70]See the references in Steck, *Studien,* pp. 244ff, 193, 132f.

[71]See the relevant studies in his collection of essays, *Hosea und Amos.* The finding is summarized in ATD 24/2, pp. xix–xxi. For the character of the book of Hosea, see Jeremias, *Hosea und Amos,* pp. 41, 52f; ATD 24/2, p. xix.

[72]See J. L. McLaughlin, *JBL* 113 (1994): 714. Led by the purpose statements in Isaiah 66 and Isaiah 60–62, we see in Isaiah these advance structuring statements especially in the announcements of the return of the diaspora, which deviate in their formulation from those in Jeremiah and Ezekiel. These have their older position in Jeremiah and Ezekiel because of the Babylonian period. They were first explained in Isaiah as return from "Assyria" and "Egypt," or relatedly from the far regions of the world (Isa 11:11; 66:19), in redactions from the Hellenistic period.

[73]See now Schmid, *Buchgestalten.*

[74]See Steck, *Prophetenauslegung,* pp. 210ff, n. 27 (see below, p. 130, n. 11). For the question of literary criticism in prophetic books, with extensive methodological reflections upon the history of the discipline, see Werlitz, *Studien,* 7–92 (especially concerning Duhm's criteria for literary criticism in Isa 28–35), and Blum, *ZAW* 108 (1996). We have striven to connect literary criticism strictly with the given subject, and, in the prophetic realm, to disconnect it from the question of the proclamation of genuine/non-genuine material that still dominates many places. See also, Werlitz, *Methode,* pp. 28–41, 42f (under the reference to E. Zenger), 56–58. However, Werlitz does not provide sufficient consideration to starting with the given literary entity, either in his methodological reflection or even in the illustrative execution.

[75]See now Koch, *Profeten,* vol. 1, pp. 47–49. Koch correctly points out the foreign nature of ancient presuppositions for text transmission that must be considered. We protect this nature by the interdependence and oscillation of exegetical methods that control literary critical judgments. Cf. Steck, *Exegesis,* pp. 17ff, etc. As the following shows, it is proper for us to examine analytically the literary criticism on a specific text from the outset by using perspectives of the entire book. Literary fissures, tensions, and doublets (see also Vanoni, *Füglister-Festschrift,* p. 361), also appear in a literarily unified text. From the other side, redactional measures can specifically avoid such fissures, tensions, and doublets. So, we want to push into the foreground conceptual differences of content (meaning separately attested) or new accentuations (a text is thus not already secondary, [just] "because it presupposes another text," as Vanoni underscores). These differences must be exegetically controlled by the history of tradition and the history of theology. Koch's polemic against "a…'criticism of tendencies' according to ideological or theological ideas" (p. 48) is thus overcome by this methodological consideration. In addition, his criteria for literary disunity (disturbing fissures, tensions in the line of thought [!], or contradictions of a chronological, linguistic, or thematic type) are also based upon content.

[76]See Steck, *Gottesknecht,* pp. 64–72, 119f. In this manner, Schmid (*Buchgestalten,* pp. 113–27) explains the connectedness of Jeremiah 30:5–7, 18–21 and also the largely unified nature of Jeremiah 24 (*Buchgestalten,* pp. 253–69).

[77]See Steck, *Studien,* p. 13; *Abschluß,* pp. 21–24. See already, *Heimkehr,* pp. 68–80. Cf. the reference above in n. 9. [On the basis of an inaccurate rendering of *FAT* 4, pp. 47–59, Childs, *ZAW* 108 (1996): 368f, erroneously considers the efforts of an appropriate literary criticism oriented toward linguistic observations, religio-historical investigations, tradition-historical investigations, and theological concepts as we have suggested and practiced. Over against the related sayings, he neglects the very prominent metaphorical use of Lady Zion in Isaiah 49, preferring the magic word "metaphorical." He also pointedly denounces the "conceptual coherence" as "defined according to modern rational categories." Are the very simple systematizings, to which Childs himself tends to submit the multiplicity of statements in the

Old Testament, more closely related to the texts themselves? In the slender Yale dissertation of Claire Mathews, *Defending Zion* (however, see continuations in *SBLSP*, 1995), one can see what happens when careful observation of the text and historical inquiry are impeded. Diachronic indicators are put aside using terms like "metaphorical" or "poetic." In pp. 141–56, she must replace carefully considered historical arguments with qualifications like "far too literal" or "poetic images," versus "read literally," "arguments...overly subtle," "extremely literal reading," and "overly subtle nature." By contrast, we proceed from the foundation of diachronic inquiry in which a historical text about which we know nothing else (least of all how it was meant specifically or figuratively), must first be taken seriously, as precisely and as literally as it appears.]

[78]See Steck, *Gottesknecht*, pp. 173–90.

[79]Hermisson, *Einheit*, especially pp. 289–91.

[80]Kratz, *Kyros*.

[81]For the methodology, see Steck, *Exegesis*, pp. 129–41.

[82]In Isaiah, compare the ultimate metahistorical statements about teaching the nations on the temple mountain (Isa 2), the nations' attack against Jerusalem (Isa 17; 29), the nations' homage to Lady Zion (Isa 49; 60; 61), or various versions of the universal judgment of the nations in Isaiah. Or compare the various ideas regarding the extent and time of the returnees, or God's people in the completion of salvation in the Davidic kingdom: as the tribal people Israel/Jacob, as Israel and Judah, as the people of Zion, as the people of Jerusalem, as Judah. Or compare the people of God before the completion of salvation. They exist as a whole in a non-problematic status of obedience. They are divided into the righteous and the wicked. Sometimes they all have the chance to repent, and sometimes they have already definitively been divided into the wicked and the chosen pious ones. One should also ask how the homogenous, comprehensive concepts proceed to these ultimate perspectives, and whether diachronically diverse literary layers in Isaiah presented them.

[83]Compare, for example, the understandable continuing step (probably diachronically understandable) signified in Isaiah 60–62 over against Isaiah 49–52 (see Steck, *Studien*, especially pp. 119–39); *Gottesknecht*, pp. 47–145; *ZThK* 90 (1993). Also compare the continuing step signified in Isaiah 66 over against Isaiah 62:1–63:6 (see Steck, *Studien*, especially pp. 229–65).

[84]At this point, one should avoid prior affirmations that anticipate but by no means have performed the process of working through the prophetic books. A glance into the discipline shows how debated the attempts to explain the genesis of individual books are to this point. Thus, we also observe the three-staged suggestion that Collins (*Mantle*, pp. 24–34) proposed ("'pre-book phase'/redactor, 'book phase,'/writer, and 'revised book phase'// editor") as a possibility that, like all other possibilities, may not be generalized too early. The same should be said for the affirmations of de Vries (*Revelation*, pp. 241–69). One should especially guard against the misunderstanding that only one initial book formation existed that was later expanded only in particular places. (See the otherwise praiseworthy article of Schreiner, *Interpretation*, pp. 19–29; also Levin, *Verheißung*, p. 67.) One cannot exclude the fact that these later expansions also want to form a literary whole with a changed book profile of its own. See above, p. 7, n. 2.

[85]This is the traditional synthetic procedure in the prophetic book commentary proceeding from the analysis of the oldest logia. Still, this procedure has also recently been impressively transcended. See, for example, the text analysis and conclusions of Hermisson about Isaiah 40–55 (*Einheit*; BK) and of Jeremias for Hosea and Amos (see the hints above, p. 11, n. 8).

[86]So, for example, Barth, *Jesaja-Worte*; see also Steck, *Heimkehr*.

[87]So, for example, Steck, *Heimkehr*, and recently Seitz, *Destiny*; Williamson, *Book*.

[88]See especially, Rendtorff, *Einführung*, *VT* 34 (1984), and subsequent works; Seitz, *Reading*.

[89]As briefly suggested recently by Koch, *Profeten*, vol. 1, pp. 33–40. See also the works mentioned above, p. 39, n. 33.

[90]So, recently, Blum, *ZAW* 108 (1996).

[91]So Steck, *Heimkehr*, especially pp. 67–80, and subsequent works; Sekine, *Sammlung*; Koenen, *Ethik*; and recently Smith, *Rhetoric*.

[92]For example: Evans, *To See*; Rendtorff, *Jesaja 6*; Aitken, *Hearing*; Steck, *Metzger-Festschrift*; McLaughlin, *Bib* 75 (1994).

[93]See recently, de Vries, *Revelation*.

⁹⁴See Davies, *Destiny*, and Bosshard-Nepustil, *Rezeptionen* (with a broad redaction-historical horizon).

⁹⁵For the methodology, see Steck, *Exegesis*, §6; Nissinen, *Prophetie*, pp. 1–43; Kratz, *TRE*. Cf. also J. Barton, *ABD*, vol. 5, pp. 644–47. An extremely chaotic multiplicity of nuances exists in defining the concept "redaction" (see recently, Odashima, *Heilsworte*, pp. 71ff; Wonneberger, *Redaktion*; Collins, Lau, de Vries). For this reason, and in order to avoid any preliminary decision regarding the origin of the prophetic books, we conceive "redaction" broadly as all intentional measures directed toward conveying the written text, without characterizing the qualitative or quantitative degree. Also, intentional changes after the final formation of the book essentially fall into this definition. In this respect, the concept of the "continuation" (*Fortschreibung*) is identical with this broadly conceived concept of redaction (Zimmerli in particular has brought this concept into play). See Steck, *Exegesis*, pp. 77ff, with the cases (a)–(d) treated there. See Nissinen, *Prophetie*, pp. 37f, who distinguishes "continuation" (*Fortschreibung*) from "redaction." Unlike redaction, composition is essentially a diachronically neutral concept. It denotes contexts of various lengths, expressly structured (literarily and/or materially), in principle on every diachronic level. See Steck, *Exegesis*, p. 81, n. 80.

⁹⁶See Steck, *Exegesis*, pp. 68f, 80–84, 90. And concerning the criteria for processed redactional texts of literarily preexisting and included material, see *Exegesis*, §6; *Studien*, pp. v–viii, 119, 165f, 269–77; *Prophetenauslegung*, pp. 206–25 (see below, pp. 127ff); *ThLZ* 120 (1995); Kratz, *Kyros*, pp. 157–74; *TRE*. We only have possible logia recorded, and thus we can only go behind the transmission level hypothetically, but not without further criteria that are explicitly tangible textually. For this reason, the already difficult distinction between poetry and prose and, even more so, speculations based upon meter (that still remains unfathomable) are not self-evident criteria for original logia. The same is true for revelatory formulas. In principle, the same is also true for genres, which redactional texts know to use (as opposed to the overly hasty use by form criticism). Cf. now, Smith, *Rhetoric*, pp. 7–21. In prophetic textual material, one encounters only diversely perceived transmission. Its point of origin and the extent to which it can be traced linguistically to its origins must be ascertained with other criteria.

⁹⁷For such collections, see now especially the above mentioned insights from Jeremias (p. 11, n. 8). See also Jeremias, *ThLZ* 119 (1994): 487f; Kratz, *TRE*. See further Schreiner, *Interpretation* pp. 19–22; Steck, *Exegesis*, pp. 82ff, 90. *Prophetenauslegung*, pp. 207–09 (see below, pp. 127ff); Clements, *Mays-Festschrift*; Collins, *Mantle*, pp. 16, 24, 32; de Vries, *Revelation*, pp. 241–69.

⁹⁸Such would be the model propagated by Levin (*Verheißung*, pp. 63–69, 162–65) for the entire prophetic transmission and that Carroll (*Jeremiah*, 49f) and McKane (*Jeremiah*, pp. 1–lxxtwelve) propagate for Jeremiah (a "rolling corpus").

⁹⁹For the material aspects of book transmission in ancient Israel, see the compilation in Schmid, *Buchgestalten*, pp. 35–43. See also below, pp. 108–111.

¹⁰⁰For the Isaiah book, see especially Barth, *Jesaja-Worte*, Vermeylen, *Du Prophète*. For the prophetic corpus in general, see especially Collins, *Mantle*.

¹⁰¹See above, p. 85, n. 84.

¹⁰²See Steck, *Exegesis*, pp. 76f, 78f, 82f, 91.

¹⁰³Regarding these formulations, see Steck, *Exegesis*, pp. 86–89; *Prophetenauslegung*, pp. 209–34 (see below, pp. 128ff).

¹⁰⁴For the metahistorical perspective conveyed by prophetic books, see pp. 43–46 above.

¹⁰⁵See Steck, *Studien*, pp. 25ff, *Abschluß*, pp. 22f, 80–83; and *Gottesknecht*, pp. 90, 124, and 137.

¹⁰⁶Concerning Zechariah 10:3–11:3 as a new redactional writing in connection to Zechariah 9:1–10:2, see Steck, *Abschluß*, pp. 36f, 65f. For the dating, see *Abschluß*, pp. 71f, 73–76, 76–80.

¹⁰⁷See Steck, *Weltgeschehen*, especially the references on p. 279, n. 62.

¹⁰⁸Thus the suggestion in Steck, *Studien*, pp. 27–30, 34–44, 229–65; *Abschluß*, pp. 29f, 58–60. Now see Steck, *Autor*.

¹⁰⁹Barth, *Jesaja-Worte*.

¹¹⁰In addition to our own suggestions, compare the suggestions of Kratz (*Kyros*) regarding Isaiah 40–55, those of Bosshard-Nepustil (*Rezeptionen*) to Isaiah in the exilic period, and further back and those of Schmid to Jeremiah (*Buchgestalten*). Concerning the challenges

that lead to changes in the metahistorical image and thus to the productively literary rereadings of the prophetic books in the sense of continuing, explanatory, divinely prophetic declarations, see Steck, *Prophetenauslegung*, especially pp. 221–42 (see below, pp. 141ff).

[111]See the recent work of deVries, *Revelation.*

[112]See Kratz, *ZThK* 89 (1992); Steck, *Abschluß*, pp. 157–60; *Rezeption.*

[113]For later, non-messianic receptions of Isaiah 9:1–6 and 11:1–5 in Isaiah, see Steck, *Studien* (see the index); *Preuß- Festschrift*; and *Metzger-Festschrift.*

[114]As an example, to us, the first written layer of Deutero-Isaiah, which Kratz has processed, that is framed by Isaiah 40:1–5//52:7–10, appears to indicate these threads (see *Kyros*, pp. 148–57; cf. Steck, *Gottesknecht*, especially pp. 173–84). The situation is similar for the expansion of Isaiah *60–62 (see Kratz, *Kyros*, pp. 206–17; *ZAW* 105 [1993]: 409f. See also Steck, *Studien*, pp. 120–39; *Gottesknecht*, pp. 161–66; *ZThK* 90 [1993]). For signs of prior literary stages in Proto-Isaiah, see Barth, Vermeylen, and now especially Bosshard-Nepustil, *Rezeptionen*, pp. 17–267. In view of the parts of comprehensive literary wholes that we have called "Greater Isaiah" (*Heimkehr*, p. 9), one should still consider whether or not certain texts (Isa 11:11–16; 27:12f; 35 [see above, p. 50, n. 52, p. 51, n. 53]; 40:1–11; 51:1–11; 54:4–6; 62:10–12) show an Isaiah book that essentially extends from Isaiah *1–62 with its own material profile and structural divisions, even in the case of different chronological origins. This possibility should be considered despite the questions raised by Williamson, "Isaiah XI," *Book* (especially pp. 123–55, 176–83, 211–29) and Smith's inquiries about Isaiah 62:10–12 (*Rhetoric*, pp. 33–38), whose questions are driven by their own redactional theses. See Steck, *Heimkehr, Gottesknecht*, pp. 73–95; *Studien*, pp. 20–27, 143–66, 279; [*Autor*, pp. 244ff.]

[115]See the observations mentioned in the preaching discussion at the beginning of p. 65, especially Jeremias' observation about the book of Amos.

[116]Concerning Isaiah 13, 24–27, 34 within the framework of redactional proceedings in Isaiah in connection to our work, see Zapff, *Prophetie*; Bosshard-Nepustil, *Rezeptionen*, pp. 17–267. Regarding references back to the beginning of Isaiah, see Steck, *Studien*, Scripture Index to Isaiah 1f. Corresponding material can be shown in redactionally created macro-bridges and blocks in Jeremiah and Ezekiel.

[117]In the meantime, I have modified (see *Gottesknecht*, pp. 204f) the initially heuristically established argument for the division of layers in Trito-Isaiah, with respect to which text surfaces presuppose Proto-Isaiah and which do not (see Steck, *Heimkehr*, pp. 67–80; *Studien*, pp. 14f). I have done so in light of orientational, fixed arrangements of the prophetic books already in the Persian period (Steck, *Gottesknecht*, pp. 190–207; *Rezeption*). In *Isaiah 60–62, which expands upon Isaiah *40–55, references to Isaiah 40–55 dominate (the immediate context literarily and metahistorically), it is nevertheless worth considering that these chapters also bring ideas from Proto-Isaiah to an end. In addition to Kratz, *Kyros*, pp. 207–12, see now Jüngling, *Lohfink-Festschrift*. See also Bosshard-Nepustil, *Rezeptionen*, pp. 262–64), for the reference by 61:2 back to 34:8. From the other side, see Bosshard-Nepustil (*Rezeptionen*, pp. 253–64; cf. Steck, *Gottesknecht*, pp. 204f) for the reference by Isaiah 2:2–4 to Isaiah *60f. The fact that Isaiah *60f refers to Ezekiel (which was the next book at the time) is apparent (see Steck, *Studien*, pp. 93, 97–100, 101–5). However, the references to Jeremiah are particularly important (see Kratz, *ZAW* 106 [1994]). In addition to Isaiah 61:2 // Jeremiah 46:10; 50:28; and Isaiah 61:7//Jeremiah 16:18; 17:18, cf. now especially the connections taking up Jeremiah which Schmid (*Buchgestalten*, p. 291f) has noted between Isaiah *60f and Jeremiah *2–6; *13. All of this provides new approaches for the genesis and literary horizon of the statements in Isaiah *60f seen by us as continuations [*Fortschreibungen*]. The answer lies perhaps most readily in the fact that here one continues to write in the literary horizon of an older series of books (Proto-Isaiah–Jeremiah–Isaiah *40–55, Isaiah *60–62–Ezekiel). Duhm (*Buch Jesaja*, pp. 8ff) already expressed this opinion. It has now been revised and further considered in Zürich: see Steck, *Abschluß*, pp. 26f, n. 33; *Gottesknecht*, pp. 201–07; *Rezeption*, pp. 371ff; Bosshard-Nepustil, *Rezeptionen*, pp. 450–64; Kratz, *ZAW* 106 (1994); Schmid, *Buchgestalten*, pp. 159–61, 249f, 291–92, 311–19. The fact that in Isaiah *60f references to Isaiah *40–55 dominate is understandable in light of the literary and thematic proximity. The same is true for the fact that the elevated, or relatedly the predictive view is also directed to the neighboring complexes preceding (Jer) and following (Ezek). However, even the references to what was at the time the more distant literary beginning of the series (Proto-Isaiah) can be understood in this framework. The fact that these connections to Proto-Isaiah within Trito-Isaiah texts, which we considered as part of the three concluding layers of Isaiah, are massively elevated, depends upon

the placement of Second Isaiah directly behind First Isaiah that has now been undertaken and with the function which is now indicated where the larger Isaiah corpus is the "leading voice" of the entire series of prophetic books. This leading voice has already prophesied everything comprehensively (see Steck, *Studien*, p. 34, n. 95; *Gottesknecht*, p. 205).

[118]For the features and character of these book texts, see the references in n. 115 preceding. In Collins, *Mantle*, and Koch, *Profeten I*, these book-redactional formulations, which one knows from Joshua-Kings and even the gospels, are not yet given the necessary attention that would contribute much to the illumination of the prophetic book and its development.

[119]Concerning Lau, *Prophetie*, pp. 7–21, and recently Aejmelaeus, *ZAW* 107 (1995): 32f, although briefly and without taking up the problem of potential growth of the book.

[120]Cf. Donner, *ZThK* 87 (1990). For Trito-Isaiah, see especially the literature in Steck, *Studien*, p. 4.

[121]The English linguistic essays in Broich/Pfister, *Intertextualität*, are foundational. See further references in van Ruiten, *Begin*, pp. 10–25; Vanoni, *Anspielungen*. For the use of biblical texts, see, e.g., the essays in the *van Iersel-Festschrift*; Nielsen, *SJOT* 2 (1990); Fewell, ed., *Reading*; as well as the literature in Laato, *SJOT* 8 (1994): 279, n. 21. For use in prophetic books, see Laato, *SJOT* 8 (1994); [also Laato, *History*], see pp. 20–65 above. For concrete examples, see van Ruiten, *Begin*; Vanoni, *Anspielungen*; Carroll, *Intertextuality*. For the problem of quotes, see especially Fox, *ZAW* 92 (1980); Savran, *Telling*; Schultz, *Search*. When using the approach historically on prophetic books, one should not consider potential relationships. Rather, one can only consider those relationships signaled in the book, those specifically marked by the tradents for the readership and thereby intentional relationships. One must determine whether these relationships aim toward external points of knowledge, toward points of a written record in a state of tradition (see Steck, *Exegesis*, §8), or toward internal points of the existing literary entity in a referential connection to other literary entities in an authoritative series of writings. Of course, literary entities can produce effects of reception among the readerships because of their deviating experience, intellectual matrix, etc., that are not documented in the text. These effects are thus not expressly intended by the tradents. Nevertheless, this phenomenon (cf. Clines and Exum, *Criticism*, pp. 19ff, 21 [bibliography], for deconstruction; and 18f, 24f [bibliography], for "reader response criticism") is not decisive for an *intentional* book formation, which we are exploring in this essay, in contrast to an observable openness to the freedom of the divine realization of the word, reaching into the specific formulations (see above, pp. 20–65; Steck *Prophetenauslegung*, pp. 215–25 [see following, pp. 135ff]).

[122]See already Steck, *Studien*, p. 10. Quotations are a noetic category, but not an ontic category that is itself suitable to the subject. For the discipline, the perspective of the orientation on quotes (heuristically conceived) would be far too limited for the text orientations in the course of the prophetic transmission. In so doing, significant relational phenomena are not even recognized, such as complementary texts and contrasting texts that are also suggested by close, commonly based formulations in light of the flow of reading inside the same writing (or series of writings). Recent works by Lau (see the critical evaluation in Steck, *ThLZ* 120 [1995]) and Aejmelaeus show as much for Trito-Isaiah. In this framework, the limit of the foundational statistical tabulation by van Wieringen, *Analogies*, also becomes apparent. The evidence of text-receptional processes does not simply correspond to the statistical exactness of exact proof of common formulational constellations. However, there are material reasons why there are so few quotes in the prophetic transmission inside of the same authoritative, known literary context by the recipients. See Steck, *Prophetenauslegung*, pp. 225–34 (see below, pp. 145ff). One must also differentiate between the use of a writing and the quotation of a writing before the second century B.C.E. It is only necessary to quote in the strict sense after the conclusion of the Nebiim as the Qumran findings show. See Steudel, *Midrasch*; Bernstein, *DSD*, 1994. [The investigation of Sommer, *Prophet*, is very unsatisfactory from a historical exegetical perspective and requires a thoroughgoing methodological critique. Cf. also other works by Sommer, *Allusions* and *Scroll*. Macrostructurings of the text flow, cross references, and repetitions in the book itself show that continuous reading of the book over the entire text flow can be intended in the growth of the prophetic books. Later, the Qumran findings in 1QIsa (see Steck, *Jesajarolle*) also show the continuous reading of books in the interpretative presentation of the texts, in *pesharim*, and by material incorporation as in 4QTanch.]

[123]One can observe repeatedly that corresponding context references can also travel over prominent individual words in continuation texts within the prophetic transmission. An

example of a corresponding procedure within another realm of transmission, the realm of the Psalms, may illustrate the procedure. Psalm 147 is apparently a psalm literarily formed for its position at the end of the psalter (before Ps 148, 150). See Kratz, *ZThK* 89 (1992): 13–25, 35–40. The song begins with Jerusalem (147:2), resulting in the attachment to the end of the preceding psalm (146:10; see also עוד in 146:9//147:6), the supporting statements (147:7–9) are determined by corresponding material in the immediate context and supplied by the text flow of the psalter (Kratz). Text-genetically, Psalm 147 is oriented especially on Psalm 33 (see the thorough study of Vosberg, *Studien*, pp. 91–99; Kratz, *ZThK* [1992]: 14–16), along with Psalm 34, the תהלה psalm of Book 1. When at the end of the psalter, a תהה must be formed with respect to the final realization of salvation, Psalm 33 serves as the preeminent donating text (cf. Ps 147:1//33:1f). Petitions from the preceding literary context of Psalms are taken up as now having been heard while serving to praise the realization of salvation in the present (cf. Ps 147:2a, 13//51:20; 147:2b//106:47 and Isa 56:8; Ezek 39:28). The text production in Psalm 147 results from the fact that it always proceeds from psalm statements. These statements are seen together with statements from the prophets (and Torah) in order to confirm that these statements are now fulfilled in a manner worthy of praise, or are still to be fulfilled. Coinciding concepts and formulations from materially corresponding contexts are the essential hermeneutical pathway by which Psalm 147 comes to its own formulation from reference text to reference text. These concepts and formulations also make apparent the text-genetic background of the formulations of Psalm 147 for professionals knowledgeable in scripture. Seen in this way, several things are explained, for example, the peculiar thematic sequence of statements in 147:4–5 between 147:3 and 147:6. The formulation in Psalm 147:3 is provided from the pathway (cf. Ps 51:20//147:2a) from Psalm 51:19 and 34:19, prophetic statements (Ezek 6:9; Isa 61:1; Ezek 34:16; cf. Isa 30:26; Jer 33:6). Psalm 147:4–5 should apparently accentuate God's salvific power for the downtrodden pious ones (147:11). The statements arise by looking at Psalm 34:20b (cf. Ps 147:3//34:19) *via* נצל and by looking further at Psalm 33:16b (cf. also the use of the contrast from Ps. 33:17a in Ps 147:10 over against 147:11 and the adoption of Ps. 33:18 in Ps. 147:11), and by looking *via* רבאכח at Isaiah 40:26–31. This text, together with Genesis 13:16 and 15:5, authoritatively influences the formulation of Psalm 147:4f and apparently is read in such a way that it refers to YHWH's power, as demonstrated on the stars, that strengthens God's people. It is important for the reception of Psalm 147 that YHWH, in his power, can count all the stars (147:4a, cf. Isa 40:26aß,b). Therefore, insight is at YHWH's disposal that is itself not numerable (147:5b, cf. Isa 40:28b). In the background stands the idea that Israel will be saved by this strength of YHWH demonstrated on the stars (Isaiah 40:26) so that it will be gathered completely (147:2, using כרס Ezekiel 39:28), whereby Isaiah 40:26 and Ezekiel 39:28b are materially identical. In light of the realization of salvation granted to God's people, Psalm 147 wants to praise YHWH, who purposefully makes the statements of the psalter come true and at the same time fulfills the promises made to the ancestors and the prophets.

[124]Donner, *ZThK* 87 (1990); Lau, *Prophetie*.

[125]In this respect, the commentaries by Beuken to Isaiah 40–55 and 56–66 are especially impressive. See other works by Beuken, *Closure*; *Isaiah 34*; and *EThL* 67 (1991).

[126]Summary of these redactional formulations can be found in Steck, *Studien*, p. 279.

[127]See the references in n. 9 above, p. 12. [In his *Habilitationsschrift*, *Das Buch Jesaja*, Berges does not make the laudatory effort of using a closely investigated text complex within (!) Isaiah to deduce the consequences for the development of the entire Isaiah corpus. Instead, Berges sets about to do nothing less than determine the "composition and final form" of the book as a whole, a task that is not possible at this point. Berges provides this image by compiling divergent, partial contributions of other researchers, and all too often provides inadequate justification. The image anticipates a state of the discipline that is capable of consensus, but that has yet to be processed. His image does not prove satisfactory. Careful observations and conclusions about Isaiah are generally found in Jüngling, *Buch Jesaja*.]

[128]See Steck, *BZ* 34 (1990); *Abschluß*; *Gottesknecht*, pp. 190–205; *ZAW* 108 (1996). Jones, *Formation*, continues the inquiry behind the text transmission.

[129]See Bosshard-Nepustil, *Rezeptionen*. The work suggests that one must reckon with an exilic "Assyria/Babylon Redaction" in the complexes of *Proto-Isaiah and the *XII respectively. Bosshard-Nepustil bases his suggestion on established book-redactional texts and redactional measures in *Proto-Isaiah and subsequently *Jeremiah followed by redactional texts in the *XII oriented toward *Proto-Isaiah and *Jeremiah. This redaction continues divine

judgment from Assyria through Babylon. Both text realms establish redactionally created, metahistorical flows of reading in older text material in *Isaiah and *Jeremiah respectively from Hosea, Amos, Micah, and Nahum by *Joel, *Habakkuk, and *Zephaniah. Correspondingly, the work suggests an attached early postexilic "Babylon Redaction" in both text realms. This redaction continues the metahistorical flow up to the judgment against Babylon. Again, the XII, in its extent at the time, is oriented to the sequence of texts of the great prophets, in fact in the sequence First Isaiah–Jeremiah–Lamentations–Second Isaiah.

[130]See Schmid, *Buchgestalten.* In a summary that the author has placed at my disposal, the following phenomena are highlighted: "In the MT version of the book of Jeremiah one can mention the following examples of book-wide redactional structures that now overlap one another. These structures point toward a successive reshaping of the Jeremiah book as a book. (1) In its current formulation and literary position Jeremiah 24 structures the entire text flow that follows in Jeremiah 26–44. If one holds Jeremiah 24 with the text complex of Jeremiah 26–44, then both sides contain a positive (24:5-7//29-33) and a negative (24:8-10//37-44) dimension. Also, in Jeremiah 24:5-7, 8-10 and in Jeremiah 26–44, the same identifications are undertaken. One finds the central (first) exile in YHWH's broader salvific plan (24:5-7//29-33 cf. 24:1//29:2!) in one part, while one finds those remaining in the land have fallen in judgment and the Egyptian refugees in the other part (24:8-10//37-44). The vision of the fig-basket in Jeremiah 24 suggests references toward the front to Jeremiah 1:11f by its stylization as a vision. Thus, it can serve as the middle of the book. This division is supported by references backward from 44:27 to the beginning of the book in 1:12, on the one hand, and to the book's middle in Jeremiah 24 on the other hand. (2) The linguistically closely related texts of Jeremiah 25:12 and 29:10 structure the complex of Jeremiah 25–50f as a large double inclusion. Just as Jeremiah 25:12, carefully placed at the end of Jeremiah 1–25, anticipates Jeremiah 50f, so Jeremiah 29:10 reciprocally and materially refers to Jeremiah 30ff. In this form, the book of Jeremiah essentially prophesies Babylon's seventy-year world rule. In Jeremiah 1–25:12, this rule announces the resulting situation in negative terms for Babylon (25:12f//50f) and in positive terms for Israel (29:10//30ff). (3) Inside the series of texts that belong together linguistically and materially (30:1-3; 31:27-34) Jeremiah 31:28 has a book structuring function. Jeremiah 31:28 overtly takes up the series of infinitives from Jeremiah 1:10 and the interpretation of the vision of the almond staff in 1:12, but then looks at Jeremiah 25 (see 25:6, 29) because of the surplus רעע (hif) over against Jeremiah 1. Jeremiah 31:28 inclusively refers to Jeremiah 1 and 25, which for their part correspond closely to one another. Jeremiah 31:28 knows Jeremiah 1–25 as the judgment part of the book of Jeremiah and contrasts its salvific part in Jeremiah 30ff with Jeremiah 1–25. (4) At prominent points, Jeremiah 25:27-38 and Jeremiah 45:4f broaden the judgment sayings against the nations in Jeremiah 25 and 46–51 on the one hand, and toward a complete universal judgment on the other hand. Thus, the Jeremiah book in its current form is directed as a whole toward this perspective of world judgment."

[131]See the references above, p. 26, n. 24. In a summary that he has made available to me, based upon his dissertation in process, Schwagmeier (see above, p. 12, n. 9) illustratively mentions the following structural elements that point to an intentional construction of the text as a book:

"(1) First, the large blocks of visions in Ezekiel 1–3, 8–11, and 40–48 are conspicuous by their internal networking and explicit references back to preceding texts in the book. Thus, the second and third block each refer explicitly back to the first block in 1:1ff with the formulation 'When I looked to/at the river Chebar' in 10:15 and 43:3aß. In addition, chapters 40–66 is bound backward to the vision of 8–11 by 43:3a. Thus, the return movement of the *kabod* in 43:4f (cf. 44:4) should be read as corresponding to the departure in 10:4f, 18f; 11:22f. However, by the form of the dates in 40:1, chapters 40–66 are bound on the one hand to the first vision in 1:1ff and on the other hand to 33:21...For the last-mentioned passage, the ties to 40:1 are struck materially by the explanation of the date as the fourteenth year after the capture of the city...These multiple references to 33:21 in the current context show that the passage has special weight as the resolution of 8–11 in the framing system formed in three blocks. All together an interwoven system of references back to the vision blocks thus arises (cf. also מראות 1:1; 8:3; 40:2). References to 33:21 also play a particular role in forming the structure for the vision complex of 40ff. Thus, the formulations pointing backward clearly show that a flow of reading is intended for the text, as does the entry of the *kabod* after Ezekiel 11.

(2) At the same time, the three vision blocks do fit the book into a successively chronological dating system passing through the book (1:1–2; 8:1; 20:1; [24:1]; 33:21; 40:1). This framework presents the book as the history of the prophetic reception of the continuing word of God and visions.

(3) This system is broken by the block in Ezekiel 25–32 with its dates deviating from successive chronology. It divides the book into the 'threefold eschatological scheme.' The speeches against the foreign nations are arranged materially and geographically rather than chronologically. They are positioned in the book (24:1ff; 33:21) in the time of the downfall, between the siege and the fall of Jerusalem. This positioning attains formally that which is expressed materially in 25–32 by the numerous adoptions and applications of material especially from Ezekiel 15–24: the correspondence and negative surmounting of Israel's fate by the downfall of the nations. (At the same time, the position of 25ff draws upon the report of the catastrophe of Jerusalem in the 'salvific portion' of the book and thus even formally becomes the opening for the announcement of salvation in 33:21ff.) The block is worked into the system by the prophet's silence and the accentuation of that silence by 29:21 (cf. 24:26f // 33:21f) – though not consistently (see #4 below). As a result, Ezekiel (corresponding to 3:5f) does not carry out speeches against the nations that he has received. Just as the thoroughgoing chronological system is interrupted for material reasons with 25–32, the block in its current form manifestly intends to insert another structural marker for the book.

(4) This structural marker is the silencing of the prophet announced in 3:26. This marker also intends a flow of reading with its material development. Thus, the announcement and execution of the accentuation of the prophet's silence follows 3:26 in three stages: 24:26f offers this announcement; in 29:21, the silence continues; and in 33:22 it finally finds its resolution…This structural system is adapted into the sequential dating system already mentioned by affiliation with 1:1ff performed by 3:22f. It is adapted into the dating system by positioning after 24:1ff and by the formulation of 33:21f. However, 29:21 creates an exception based on the dating of 29:17 (!), which makes no sense when read chronologically. This passage allows one to step into diachronic analysis of the book."

[132]See Steck, *ZAW* 107 (1995).

[133]See Steck, *Studien*, pp. 144–66; *Gottesknecht*, pp. 73–91, 166–68; and recently Rendtorff, *SBLSP* (1991); Williamson, *Book* (see index to Isa 35).

[134]See Steck, *Studien*, pp. vi–vii, 9–12.

[135]In addition to our own investigations of Isaiah and the Twelve, see especially Nogalski, and Jeremias. In addition, see the dissertation completed under Jeremias (1993) by N. Ho Fai Tai, *Traditionsgeschichtliche Studien zu Sacharja 9–14*; Bosshard-Nepustil, *Rezeptionen*; Kratz, *ZAW* 105 (1993) and 106 (1994); Schmid, *Buchgestalten*. For Jones, *Formation*, see p. 17, n. 1. [In contrast to the foundational critical discourse of Nogalski (*Processes*, especially pp. 182–280), Schart's (*Entstehung*, 275–77, 291–97) remarks show that he does not adequately account for the conceptual argumentations concerning the material incompleteness of Zechariah 14 and the correspondence of Zechariah 14 only with (!) Malachi 1:1–3:21 to Isaiah 66. These argumentations appear in Steck (*Abschluß*, especially pp. 43–60), and are already presupposed by Bosshard (*BN* 40 [1987]) and Bosshard/Kratz (*BN* 52 [1990]), see below p. 120, n. 2. We need not here treat the less detailed inquiries of Schart (see also Schart, *VF* 43 [1998]: 28f).]

[136]See Steck, *Rezeption*. The question of why a series of prophetic books was formed in the Persian period would be a subject worth investigating. May one consider an "eschatologically" oriented counterbalance to "theocratically" shaped Persian royal writings, especially the Behistun inscription that was circulated? By contrast, this counterbalance affirms how YHWH, the God of heaven in Jerusalem, ruled the world from long ago with effective prophetic disclosures and actions, and how YHWH called the king of Assyria, Nebuchadnezzar, and Cyrus into office.

[137]See the findings in the works mentioned in p. 106, n. 135, and for the particular influence of the concluding chapters of Deuteronomy exposed in the Torah, see the work by Gosse, *ZAW* 107 (1995); see above, p. 18, n. 8; p. 41, n. 39; and Utzschneider, *ZAW* 104 (1992).

[138]See Steck, *Prophetenauslegung* (see below, pp. 152ff); Schmid, *Buchgestalten*, pp. 376–88.

[139]See van der Kooij, *Textzeugen*, p. 114; Schmid, *Buchgestalten*, pp. 35–43. See also above, p. 15, n. 16 and p. 21, n. 16.

[140]See the references above in n. 16 and 35.

[141]See especially Hermisson, *ZThK* 86 (1989): 129–31.

[142]See especially Tigay, *Models*, pp. 1–20, 21–52; Laato, *SJOT* 8 (1994): 272–74. However, a direct empirical example for accepting the accumulated growth of prophetic books until the final formation is not provided outside or inside ancient Israel (see Steck, *Prophetenauslegung*, pp. 210f, n. 27 [below, p. 130]). However, see divergent text versions in Old Testament manuscripts (see Jones, *Formation*, pp. 43–78).

[143]See now Stegemann, *Essener*, as well as the article by W. Stegemann, *ThLZ* 119 (1994): 387–407, 403. The *War Scroll* is particularly noteworthy. Its various versions show revision and continued shaping of the text. See Stegemann, *Essener*, pp. 145–47; van der Woude, *ThR* (1990): 254–57. The texts appear in translation in García-Martínez, *Scrolls*, pp. 95–125; Maier, *Qumran-Essener*, vol. 1, pp. 125–56; vol. 2, pp. 242–44, 554–70.

[144]See also Schmid, *Buchgestalten*, pp. 35–43, as well as pp. 90 and 107 above. The changes in the different versions of the *War Scroll* of Qumran mentioned above are diachronically instructive. [The same is true for the *Community Rule*. See Metso, *Development*.]

[145]We adopt this manner which Smend, *Entstehung*, p. 141, conducted for "both possible starting points" for clarifying the history of the prophetic book.

[146]See the references above in p. 64, n. 62. For the hermeneutical concept toward the Torah and *Nebiim* in Jubilees, see Steck, *ZAW* 108 (1996).

[147]See Steck, *Abschluß*.

[148]Cf., e.g., H. Chr. Schmitt, in *ZAW* 104 (1992), pp. 310ff; Hengel, *"Schriftauslegung,"* pp. 15ff, n. 57, pp. 27ff, n., 94; p. 34; Sweeney, *Currents*, 1993, p. 147.

[149]See Steck, *Abschluß*, pp. 22f.

[150]See Steck, *Abschluß*, p. 119. For example, it is not permissible to proceed from the path of an apparent consensus for dating Trito-Isaiah and then to collect apparently contemporary material outside' and inside the Old Testament to compare with the statements of Trito-Isaiah about internal Israelite tensions, as is done by Ackerman, *Tree*, pp. 101–63, 165–212, and Schramm, *Opponents*, especially pp. 53–80, 174–90. This material would only be relevant for dating Trito-Isaiah if it were characteristic of one specific time, thus excluding other dates. There are commonalities between Ezra-Nehemiah and Isaiah 56–66 (see *Studien*, especially p. 35f with n. 102, pp. 246ff with n. 111) and criteria for showing that *Ezra-Nehemiah also used material from Trito-Isaiah (see Kratz, *Translatio*, p. 214 with n. 274; *Kyros*, p. 190; especially Ezra 7:27f//Isa 60; cf. also Steck, *Rezeption*, pp. 371f). The literary relationship between Isaiah and Ezra 9ff; Nehemiah 8–10 should be seen in this light. However, this relationship is not yet explained. To this extent, even the latest attempt for dating Isaiah 56–66 by Smith (*Rhetoric*, pp. 187–204) operates with too much that is unknown. Whether Isaiah 56–59, 63–66 characterize a literary image of the metahistorical Persian epoch or derive historically from the Persian period should be differentiated in the investigation.

[151]For the parallelism of conceptual modifications in Isaiah and the XII, see Steck, *Abschluß*. In this sense, one can also find carefully considered suggestions for dating the growth of a prophetic book in Kratz, *Kyros*; Bosshard-Nepustil, *Rezeptionen*, and Schmid, *Buchgestalten*. There, see also pp. 45ff, 197–201 for questions about methodological principles.

[152]For the dating of Zechariah 9:1–10:2, see Steck, *Abschluß*, pp. 35f, 65f, 73–76, and in the most recent introductions to the Old Testament, see Kaiser, *Grundriß*, p. 153f; Zenger, *Zwölfprophetenbuch*, p. 528f.

[153]See above, pp. 65–85.

[154]See Steck, *Studien*, pp. 163ff; *Abschluß*, pp. 23, 27, 63–69, 80–83.

[155]See Steck, *Abschluß*, pp. 73–111.

[156]See Steck, *Prophetenauslegung*, pp. 213–25 (below, pp. 134ff) and pp. 20–65 above.

[157]Contrary to Lau, *Prophetie*, pp. 285ff, n. 113; Aejmelaeus, *ZAW* 107 (1995): 46f.

[158][Concerning the inquiry from the written material to the preliterary, orally transmitted material see also Rofé, *Introduction*, pp. 41–73.] Accepting that communicative prophetic logia directed toward individuals and/or the population stood at the beginning requires further clarification and differentiation in several respects in the sense of the approach to prophetic research highlighted in this essay. As mentioned at the beginning of this essay, one must continually keep in mind that written, redactional text material was stylized to imitate and to assimilate these logia, especially in later phases of the transmission of prophetic books. Also, one should consider that the vision reports apparently stood at the beginning of the transmission in the case of Amos (see recently, Jeremias, ATD 24/2, pp. xvi–xvii). In the case of Jeremiah, one might consider that the beginning of the transmission is a composition from formerly orally delivered pronouncements of judgment and complaints especially

in Jeremiah 4–6, 8–10. These pronouncements were directed against the current validity of the ruling Zion theology (see Schmid, *Buchgestalten*, pp. 330–40 in conjunction with investigations by Levin, Pohlmann, Biddle). The case of Ezekiel should be considered similarly (see K.-F. Pohlmann, in Kaiser, *Grundriß*, p. 100f). Do these beginnings of the work and the transmission have something to do with an original character of prophetic intercession (see recently, Jeremias, ATD 24/2, p. 98)?

[159]See the references above, p. 89, n. 96.

[160]In our view, Isaiah 65f is an example of the book-redactional use of formulas. See Steck, *Studien*, pp. 217–228. Introduction and conclusion by these types of formulas to which the summonses to hear also belong, however, is no self-evident clue to older, small units. Rather, one must examine whether or not these formulas concern book-redactional measures for dividing (and subdividing). See the statistical findings in Meier, *Speaking*; and for the structuring of the literary layer, see for example, Neumann, *VT* 23 (1973); Neumann, *Wort Jahwähs*; Koch, *Amos*.

[161]See Jeremias, *ThLZ* 119 (1994).

[162]ATD 24/2, p. xxii. See also Jeremias, ATD 24/1, p. 19. See also Pohlmann for Ezekiel in Kaiser, *Grundriß*, p. 85. See also Römheld, *ZAW* 104 (1992): 29f.

Chapter 3: Prophetic Exegesis before and after the Boundaries of the "Canon" as a Starting Point for the Inquiry

[1]We wrote this essay in honor of Gerhard Ebeling, for whom it was originally developed and delivered. See Ebeling, *Evangelische Evangelienauslegung*.

[2]For the material foundation of this study, see also the references to our own works above, p. 12, n. 9. The redaction-historical approach to Zechariah 14 and Malachi also belong to it. The parallelism of Zechariah 9–Malachi 3 with the final phases of the Isaiah book was shown to me in the lines of the Trito-Isaiah thesis (cf. Heimkehr, p. 79, n. 94; Bosshard, *BN* 40 [1987]: 55–62). Bosshard (*BN* 40 [1987]) then considered this parallelism in conjunction with the entire book of the XII. Then, Bosshard and Kratz worked out the details for Malachi more closely (*BN* 52 [1990]), while my own treatment of Zechariah 9–14 and Malachi and to the parallel rhythm in the final phases of the growth of Isaiah and the XII according to *BZ* 34 (1990) and *ZAW* 102 (1990) was then published somewhat later in a more far-reaching investigation of the prophetic canon (*Abschluß*, pp. 30–72). Critical questions about Malachi as a continuation text (*Fortschreibungstext*) should therefore also be directed to me (Meinhold, *TRE*; Lescow, *Maleachi*, especially, pp. 145–91), since I provoked this perspective. However, these questions do not necessitate a fundamental revision of our view of the late phases of Isaiah and the XII.

[3]Cf. Stadelmann, *Ben Sira*, especially pp. 188–270; Skehan and Di Lella, *Anchor Bible*, pp. 451–53; Schnabel, *Law*, pp. 52–54, 57–69.

[4]Cf. now Steck, *Abschluß*, pp. 136–44. Even though Sirach introduces these prophets as persons in his hymn to the fathers, a literary entity clearly stands behind the "Twelve Prophets" for him. Therefore, it is suggested that literary entities preceding the XII in this order also stand behind the prophets "Isaiah," "Jeremiah," and "Ezekiel" who were previously mentioned. Despite Sirach's attested knowledge of the sequence of the order of books in the Nebiim, the hymn to the fathers is oriented toward a historical sequence that explains why Isaiah does not appear after the conclusion of 2 Kings, but already in the time of Hezekiah.

[5]Compare the following concerning the Hebrew book of Daniel from the Maccabean period in Steck, *Weltgeschehen*; *Arbeitsblätter*, no. 24a; Kratz, *Translatio*, pp. 16–42.

[6]For Daniel 9:2, see Kratz, *Translatio*, pp. 260–79, especially 265–67.

[7]See Steck, *Weltgeschehen*, pp. 272–90.

[8]Koch, *Bedeutung*, pp. 191ff; cf. also Fishbane, *Interpretation*, pp. 482–89.

[9]Koch, *Bedeutung*, p. 196.

[10]Koch, *Bedeutung*, pp. 200ff. Cf. also Steck, *Abschluß*, p. 149.

[11]Cf. the recent works of Feltes, *Gattung*; Brewer, *Techniques*, pp. 187–98, including the older literature mentioned there. Cf. also Koch, *Bedeutung*, p. 200; Koch, *Rezeptionsgeschichte*, pp. 147ff; Kratz, *Kyros*, pp. 220–22; Fabry, *Schriftverständnis*; [cf. Fabry, *Methoden*; Fabry, *Qumran*, especially pp. 236–38; Brooke, *Isaiah*, 618–32 (bibliography)]. Also, see the thorough discussion

of the relationship between special revelation and exegesis by van der Woude, *ThR* 57 (1992): 23–30.

[12]See the overview in Fitzmyer, *Scrolls*, pp. 14, 12, 46–48; cf. 62f. In addition, the so-called "thematic Midrashim" like 11QMelch and 4QFlor/4Q174 (cf. Brooke, *Exegesis*; van der Woude, *ThR* 57 [1992]: 30–32, 41–45) and especially 4Q177 are significant for the type and meaning of the use of scripture in Qumran. For 4Q174 and 4Q177, see the recent work of Steudel, *RevQ* 14 (1989): 473–81 and extensively in *Midrasch.*

[13]See Albertz, *ZNW* 74 (1983), and the recent work of Koch for example, *Rezeptionsgeschichte*; also Koch, *Ausgang.*

[14]In addition to the reception of the prophets in apocalyptic texts, one should mention especially the prophetic Targum. Cf., e.g., Patte, *Hermeneutic*, pp. 49–81; Alexander, *Translations*; Koch, *Rezeptionsgeschichte*, pp. 147ff.

[15]Cf. the attempt in Steck, *Abschluß*, pp. 145–50, 167–78. Concerning the preparation of the Nebiim by the only slightly older collection of a prophetic corpus, see *Abschluß*, pp. 112–26. The reception of the prophets in Sirach, Daniel 9, and Qumran demonstrates conclusively that the provision of the meaning of the shape of this collection in the subsequent period no longer continues (cf. also Koch, *Ausgang*, p. 222ff, n. 16).

[16]For the adoption of reception historical approaches into historical exegesis, see Dohmen, *TThZ* 96 (1987); Steck, *Exegesis*, p. 79; Koch, *Rezeptionsgeschichte*; Koch, *Ausgang*, p. 223f with n. 21. Compare these works with the suggestion of a differentiation over against the "history of the effect" (*Wirkungsgeschichte*) and a delimitation of against a text's constitution of meaning solely by the reader (see Kratz, *Kyros*, pp. 227ff).

Chapter 4: Prophetic Exegesis of the Prophets in the Growth of the Prophetic Books

[1]See the references in Barth, *Jesaja-Worte*, pp. 303–5.

[2]Zimmerli, BK XIII/1, p. 2; Zimmerli, *ThLZ* 104 (1979); cf. von Rad, *TheolAT*, vol. II, 1987, 9th ed., pp. 47–57.

[3]See Nissinen, *Prophetie*, pp. 33ff.

[4]For the history of research, cf., e.g., Barth, *Jesaja-Worte*, pp. 301–5; Nissinen, *Prophetie*, 17–43; Steck, *Heimkehr*, pp. 81ff. With respect to Deutero-Isaiah, see Kratz, *Kyros*, pp. 1–15; with respect to Trito-Isaiah, see Koenen, *Ethik*, pp. 1–7; Steck, *Studien*, pp. 3–9.

[5]Cf. Jeremias, ATD 24/1, 2 and the studies mentioned in ATD 24/1, p. 10 (see Steck, *Exegesis*, p. 82, n. 82). See also Jeremias, *ZAW* 100, supplement (1988); *Childs-Festschrift*; *Kaiser-Festschrift*; *Deissler-Festschrift*; *Scharbert-Festschrift*; *Richter-Festschrift*; *Wolff-Festschrift*; *Reventlow-Festschrift.* These studies have now been combined, along with others, in the collection of essays *Hosea und Amos.*

[6]See Steck, *Exegesis*, §6 concerning the literary horizon of insertions of various breadths.

[7]Possibly even the cluster model favored one-sidedly by Levin and others. Cf. Steck, *Studien*, p. 269f, n. 1; Schmid, *Buchgestalten*, pp. 25–35, 193–96, 376–88.

[8]Concerning the character of these redaction texts that have been created from the outset for the larger entity of a book (or even a series of books), cf. Steck, *Studien*, pp. v–viii, 119, and the references provided there. See also, pp. 270–77, and the discussion in the works mentioned above on p. 12, n. 9; and p. 120, n. 2. See also the methodological discussion in *Exegesis*, §6. Further, see Nissinen, *Prophetie*, pp. 22–43, for the redactional characteristics of Emmerson and for a distinction between "continuation" (*Fortschreibung*) and "redaction." However, see above, p. 88, n. 95.

[9]Concerning the source of these mistakes in exegesis delimited by pericopes, see Steck, *Studien*, pp. 269–71; *Abschluß*, p. 22.

[10]An impressive example of one who does not do this is Nogalski, *Precursors*; *Processes.*

[11]Koch (*Ausgang*, pp. 223ff) correctly considers a text's reception history even "after composition and recording,"…"even when the wording is unchanged." In our case, one must keep in mind a prophetic writing's path of reception even after it is concluded. It is not contradictory to add that aspects of reception remain valid for the redactional reception of existing literary stages, even while the formation of the transmission is still fluid. For this reason, we also perceive redaction history as the history of literary reception. Discovering a writing as a writing is the first step for the redaction-historical approach. As such, a potentially intentional, planned material unity should appear today in the flow of reading. In the

transmission of ancient Israel, no parallel versions, or changed versions, have yet been found prior to Qumran. This fact requires literary-critical research. One finds binding literature of transmission that demands inquiry into prior stages of redaction-historical syntheses, which are rooted in the transmission finding. This literary-critical research needs to consider redactional horizons. It cannot be founded upon the exegete's impression of breaks from a perspective limited to pericopes. Rather, it is founded upon conceptual unity or disunity, upon style, genres, circumstances of the time, and problems for the placement of a text in the literary whole.

[12]Over against the reception process in the same book, or similarly in a series of prophetic books, Kratz (orally) notes that the reception processes also lead to a new writing that represent a phenomenon of a particular type. Examples include the Chronicler's History, with its reception of Genesis–2 Kings (see now Kratz, *Identität*), and the book of *Jubilees* as a reception of Genesis-Exodus. Do these types of processes presuppose that the writing being cited already possessed quasi-canonical form and therefore required reception? Did the receptional writings seek to document the writings being cited in their true sense or did they seek to replace it?

[13]*Jesaja-Worte*. See also the references in Steck, *Heimkehr*, pp. 82, 84.

[14]See Bosshard, *BN* 40 (1987); Bosshard and Kratz, *BN* 52 (1990); Steck, *Abschluß*; *Gottesknecht*, pp. 190–207; *Rezeption*, pp. 371ff; Nogalski, *Precursors*; *Processes*; Bosshard-Nepustil, *Rezeptionen*. However, see also the methodologically important essay by Sheppard, *Int* 36 (1982) which poses the question of "canon conscious" redactions in conjunction with Seeligmann.

[15]See the references above, p. 120, n. 2.

[16]See the references above, p. 12, n. 9.

[17]See above, p. 111, n. 158. Also, the statements formed as the prophets' own words express the question about the current presence of YHWH, or they serve to concretize YHWH's revelation.

[18]See Steck, *Wahrnehmungen*, p. 306; *Heimkehr*, p. 93f.

[19]The circumstance is significant for the tradents' conviction that the prophetically formulated coming event can realize additional, analogous processes beyond the original chronological reference. For example, announcements of the end of the Northern Kingdom are also related to the end of the Southern Kingdom. Statements about the threat from Assyria relate to the Babylonians, and oracles against Babylon and the Edom are expanded into a comprehensive human judgment of the end. Lines of thought from Isaiah 40:1–11, especially 40:5, are continually reused and redirected (cf. Steck, *Studien*, in the index to Isaiah 40).

[20]This condition is also already encountered in different phases in the work of the same prophet. The current correspondence of guilt for the coming judgment is sought. Compare the different exhibitions of guilt in Isaiah's work in the Syro-Ephraimite War, in Isaiah's so-called early period and his late period. For an example from the tradents, cf. the connection and change between Amos 2:6f and 8:4–7 which Jeremias (*Richter-Festschrift*) has demonstrated, the finding in Isaiah 56–59 mentioned below, p. 142, n. 37, or the reinterpretation of the Jeremiah transmission by the composition about repentance in Jeremiah *3:1–4:2 (cf. Schmid, *Buchgestalten*, pp. 277–94). The chance for a change of meaning is found in an initial phase that is later reworked as a result of the late period of Isaiah's work, over against the definitive announcements of judgment in Isaiah *6–8. This chance also appears in the early period and the late period. For the tradents, see, for example, the finding that Jeremias has demonstrated in the *Kaiser-Festschrift*.

[21]See also Carroll, *When Prophecy Failed*, for this question.

[22]In conjunction to the fundamental explanations of von Rad, cf. also Barth, *Jesaja-Worte*, pp. 307–9; Zimmerli, *Prophetenwort*; Jeremias, SBS 100, pp. 93–95.

[23]See the explanations of Barth, which remain influential, in *Jesaja-Worte*, pp. 277–309.

[24]ATD 24/2, p. xix.

[25]See also Koch, *Profeten*, vol. 1, pp. 21–26, 249–60.

[26]Compare Koch, *Profeten*, vol. 1, throughout (but especially, pp. 249ff). By "Metahistory," Koch understands the theory of "*Übergeschichte*." "*Übergeschichte*" is a particularly loaded and misunderstood concept, one that we prefer to avoid. "*Übergeschichte*" means "a comprehensive movement flowing through times, that encompasses and drives forward not just Israelite people, but everything deemed necessary between them and God's reality lying in the background." (p. 250). The reality concentrated in the dimension of depth is seen as a process and an event of meaning intentionally driven forward by YHWH. "*Übergeschichte*"

is "as a whole, only accessible to God as a context of meaning. However, '*Übergeschichte*' provisionally reveals the events by an authorized speaker of Israel" (p. 257). See the extensive treatment above pp. 43–61, in the first part of this book concerning our use of the concept "metahistory" as the perspective of the center of action in the decision-making world of YHWH, and as the divinely achieved depth of meaning in the background of the history of events, experience, and expectations. Prophetic observation uncovers this dimension of depth, and it continues to grow and change materially by divine impulse. The later one goes, the more it happens that a comprehensive metahistorical image of history is provided from the available state of the transmission by the continuation and unification of written prophetic transmission (see below, pp. 139–40). This image of history can later be revealed in advance as the comprehensive divine plan and the comprehensive chronological order in apocalyptic texts with respect to its ontic *prae* (prior existence) by God (cf., e.g., *1 Enoch* 85–90). See above, p. 49, n. 50. For the prophets and prophetic transmission, the notable reduction, concentration, and selection of the historically diverse experiences and expectations are connected with this alignment of the metahistorical perspective and this divine event of meaning in the flow of historical elements (see also Barton, *Oracles*, pp. 199–202, 214–34). However, they are also connected to the finding that was not written at the time. Concerning the authoritative understanding of time, see p. 158, n. 76. When seen as a whole, the intention of the tradents is apparent in this comprehensive image that determines the flow of a prophetic book or even a series of prophetic books. Specifically, it cannot be expressed definitively because of the growing transmission image and the combination of previously separate writings into the text sequence. Nevertheless, one can demonstrate that in the text flow, "windows" with eschatological outlook continually break through. These windows already allow one to see the goal and final completion of this historical image. These windows limit the validity of their historical perspective and function as a network for different prophetic corpora by cross references placed in parallel to one another. Also, for the sake of the reader-reception, at many points the statements of a book (or series of books) that are literally positioned at the end devote special attention to the material determination of purpose.

[27]For this phenomenon, cf. Sæbø, *JBTh* 3 (1988); Sheppard, *Int* 36 (1982); Schmid, *Buchgestalten*, pp. 355–76; and especially Steck, *Abschluß*, pp. 116–19 and 167–77.

[28]For the metahistorical image of history in the concluding formations of prophetic books, an image taken as a whole from the state of prophetic transmission, cf. Steck, *Abschluß*, pp. 112–26 (especially 120–26) and 167–77. Nevertheless, as presented above, this view is rooted in the presupposition and the prior history that reach back to the beginning of written prophecy. Cf. also, *Abschluß*, pp. 117ff; *Studien*, pp. 275ff.

[29]Kyros, summary on pp. 175–91; see also Steck, *Gottesknecht*, pp. 155–60, 204.

[30]See discussion in Steck, *Studien*, especially 233–42; *Abschluß*, pp. 67, 91f, 197.

[31]Cf. the references for Proto-Isaiah in *Gottesknecht*, p. 197, n. 110. For Micah, see Jeremias, *ZAW* 83 (1971).

[32]Cf. *Gottesknecht*, pp. 194–207 with references to the now completed study published as a dissertation in OBO 154 of Bosshard (see above, p. 12, n. 14; p. 130, n. 11).

[33]Cf. *Gottesknecht*, pp. 196ff.

[34]Cf. *Gottesknecht*, pp. 196–207, especially 205f.

[35]Cf. discussions in *Gottesknecht*, pp. 47–59, 96–125, 199f.

[36]Cf. Kratz's summaries in *Kyros*, pp. 206–16; Steck, *Studien*, pp. 49–139, especially 129–39; *Gottesknecht*, pp. 161–66. For the connections with Jeremiah *2–6*, *13, cf. Schmid, *Buchgestalten*, pp. 284–92.

[37]Compare the formulational references with respect to the assertions of guilt in Isaiah *56–59 to the book of Isaiah, Jeremiah, and Ezekiel. Isaiah *56–59 represents a late redactional insertion that extensively expands upon the admonition that precedes in 55:6f. See Steck, *Studien*, pp. 169–213; *Metzger-Festschrift*.

[38]See the discussion *Gottesknecht*, pp. 149–72.

[39]Compare the material in Steck, *Heimkehr*, *Studien*, pp. 20–44; 143–265. Regarding the question of dating, see *Studien*, pp. 163ff; *Abschluß*, pp. 23, 63–111.

[40]Compare the concluding stages of the written prophetic transmission that are documented in *Abschluß*. However, note also the thoughts about a previously processed "eschatological scenario" in Petersen, *Prophecy*, pp. 16–19.

[41]Cf. the discussion in Steck, *Heimkehr*, *Studien*, pp. 143–66; *Abschluß*, pp. 196ff (references to "Continuation [*Fortschreibung*] I in the book of Isaiah"); *Gottesknecht*, pp. 73–91, pp. 166ff. See also the first part of this volume, pp. 43–61.

[42]Cf. Steck, *Studien*, pp. 217–65; *Abschluß*, p. 197 (references to the book of Isaiah, Continuation [*Fortschreibung*] III, and the *XII).

[43]Cf. Steck, *Heimkehr*, pp. 84–94, especially p. 92. See also *Studien* and *Gottesknecht.*

[44]See the discussion in Steck, *Studien*, pp. 143–66.

[45]See the discussion in Steck, *Gottesknecht*, p. 166, and the references listed there.

[46]See the discussion in *Gottesknecht*, pp. 170ff, and the references there.

[47]Cf. Steck, *Heimkehr*, pp. 87–91, especially p. 88.

[48]Concerning this difference, consult the important introductions by Fishbane, *Interpretation*, pp. 282–91, especially 289–91, and above all, pp. 458–99, even though we do not always share Fishbane's view of the text's genesis. Moreover, see the brief but admirable identification of the character of prophetic transmission in Mason, *Books*, pp. 6–11. See also Utzschneider, *Künder*, pp. 9–17; Kratz, *Kyros*, pp. 218–29.

[49]In addition to the material in Fishbane, *Interpretation*, and in Steck, *Exegesis*, §6, as well as the Zürich works already mentioned (p. 12, n. 9; p. 120, n. 2; p. 124, n. 11; and p. 131, n. 14), consult the following with respect to their type of instructive investigations: Sheppard, *Wisdom*, pp. 100–19; regarding Sirach and Baruch, cf. also pp. 120–60. See also Utzschneider, *Künder*, pp. 42–44. Materially, the references naturally proceed far beyond a simple referential function. For example, these types of pointed statements from the rereading demonstrate the interchangeable nature of salvific ideas for various salvific objects (e.g., Zion ideas interchanged with the returnees) or the formation of salvific ideas by terminating guilt and judgment sayings in the referential texts.

[50]Concerning Donner, *ZThK* 87 (1990): 288f, Fishbane, *Interpretation*, pp. 286–91, 525–43, already correctly demonstrated this point by recognizing the finding here as not "anthological" or even as "midrashic." See also Sæbø, *JBTh* 3 (1988): 126f.

[51]Cf. the groundbreaking study of Seeligmann, *Voraussetzungen*, pp. 152–76 with accentuation of its difference to "correct exegesis" (p. 176). Cf. also the continuing work of Willi-Plein, *Vorformen*, pp. 1–14, especially 8–14; Barth, *Jesaja-Worte*, pp. 308ff; Utzschneider, *Künder*, p. 13.

[52]Cf. also Rendtorff, *Einführung*, pp. 255–57.

[53]Koch, *Ausgang*, recently accentuates the anachronistic distortions created if the original meaning, historical critically achieved, confronts later receptions of the same text and if one does not pay attention to the understanding of prophetic transmission at the time of reception (!).

[54]The discipline frequently speaks of "exegesis" (*Auslegung*) in view of literarily growing prophetic tradition. Cf., e.g., Willi-Plein, *Vorformen*, p. 2; Smend, *Entstehung*, p. 141; Donner, *ZThK* 87 (1990): 288; Utzschneider, *Künder*, pp. 12–17 (who references Hertzberg [p. 14], but correctly warns against understanding a single cause); Kratz, *Kyros*, pp. 218–29; Jeremias, *Richter-Festschrift.*

[55]Fishbane (*Interpretation*, pp. 166–70, 538) uses the concept "explication" differently. In conjunction with Seeligmann, Barth, *Jesaja-Worte*, pp. 308ff, prefers the concept of "adaptation" for the rereading process. In so doing, "adaptation" marks that which the tradents do as historically questionable according to our understanding. How the tradents see what they do is a very different question. See also Kratz, *Kyros*, pp. 218ff and pp. 152–63 below. The same is true for the concept "productive new interpretation" (Barth) or "interpretation" (Utzschneider). For the historical and hermeneutical questions that arise, cf. Steck, *Studien*, pp. 274ff; *Abschluß*, p. 61, n. 109.

[56]Compare the following: Barth, *Jesaja-Worte*, pp. 308ff; the important essay on this topic by Hermisson, *KuD* 27 (1981); the recent work by, Koch, *Ausgang*, pp. 223ff; and Kratz, *Kyros*, pp. 218–25. The aesthetics of reception (*Rezeptionsästhetik*), to the degree that they concentrate the constitution of a text's meaning upon the productive reader, are, of course, not really suitable historically for the processes of prophetic rereadings in light of the orientation toward the validity of the referential passages in the metahistorical sense. They are theologically questionable as well. Cf. Steck, *Heimkehr*, pp. 94–99; *Exegesis*, pp. 2, 3–23, 153–69. For the onset of the given material in "active readings," see Utzschneider, *ZAW* 104 (1992).

[57]Cf. Steck, *Studien*, especially pp. 113–39; *ZThK* 90 (1993). The expansion of the series of the three Servant of YHWH Songs shows that the fourth is similar. See the discussion in *Gottesknecht*, pp. 34–43.

[58]Consult the scripture index in Steck, *Studien.*

[59]See Steck, *Studien*, pp. 113, 152f, 184, 188f, 209, 259f.

[60]See Steck, *Gottesknecht*, pp. 149–72.

[61]See the example noted on p. 142, n. 37.

[62]Concerning this redaction historically constitutive aspect, see Steck, *Heimkehr*, pp. 82–84; *Studien*, pp. v–vi, 269f, and throughout; *Abschluß*, pp. 22ff, and throughout; see also the foundational treatment in *Exegesis*, §6.

[63]In many respects, the final redaction of the book of Isaiah that we have suggested would be an important example. Cf. Steck, *Studien*, pp. 217–65; and Utzschneider, *Künder*, pp. 44–74, 75–87.

[64]Cf. the discussion in *Abschluß*, pp. 30–72.

[65]Concerning these rules, cf. Willi-Plein, *Vorformen*, pp. 5–8; Feltes, *Gattung*, pp. 88–117; and Brewer, *Techniques*, pp. 11–23, 226–41. Concerning the question of their partial significance in the Qumran texts, see Feltes, *Gattung*, pp. 129–241; and Patte, *Hermeneutic*, pp. 299–308. Concerning the question of prior forms of these rules as prophetic books develop, see especially Willi-Plein, *Vorformen*, but also Steck, *Studien*, pp. 274ff. Especially, the exegetical aspect גזרה שוה should be discussed (see Brewer, *Techniques*, p. 18; Chernik, *JQR* 80 [1990]).

[66]See the discussion in Utzschneider, *Künder*, pp. 12–17 and his thesis, p. 17 (cf. p. 75). For many reasons, we cannot follow Utzschneider's criteria for what is prophetic in scribal prophecy: "The address that is presented and that occurs to specific readers in a particular time in the medium of the written nature" (75).

[67]As an example, see Steck, *Metzger-Festschrift*.

[68]Cf. also Utzschneider, *Künder*, p. 17.

[69]Cf. Steck, *Studien*, pp. v–vi, 26f, 270–77; *Abschluß*, pp. 61–63, 167–70. The conceptual nature of "deutero-prophetic" and "prophetic traditionists" is perceived differently by Petersen (*Prophecy*, pp. 13–19) because of the neglect of the redaction historical perspective.

[70]For the following, compare Steck, *Heimkehr*, pp. 82–91; *Studien*, 26f, 270–77; *Abschluß*, pp. 61–72, 105–11, 112–26, 145–56, 167–78. See above, pp. 13–16. For the question in connection to J. A. Sanders and M. Smith, see the recent work of Jones, *Formation*, pp. 72–75.

[71]See the discussion of Otto, *SJOT* 5 (1991).

[72]Compare the comments with respect to Sirach by Stadelmann, *Ben Sira*, pp. 271–309, especially pp. 293–98.

[73]See the attempts in Steck, *BZ* 34 (1990); *Metzger-Festschrift*.

[74]Compare Fishbane, *Interpretation*, pp. 78–88 (especially pp. 84–88, 288); Utzschneider, *Künder*, especially p. 74.

[75]Concerning convictions of tradition from the prophet who continues to speak out of the tradents and their measures, see the utterances in Barth, *Jesaja-Worte*, especially p. 238, and Fishbane, *Interpretation*, throughout (summary, pp. 525–43); Fishbane, *JBL* 99 (1980). See especially Steck, *Heimkehr*, pp. 87–91; *Studien*, throughout (summary, pp. 270–77); Steck, *Abschluß*, throughout (e.g., p. 62); *Metzger-Festschrift*, as well as the references below to Isaiah 59:21.

[76]A peculiar understanding of time is essential and constitutive for prophetic transmission. This understanding is connected to prophetic statements. It has recently been investigated and presented in various ways. Compare Steck, *Heimkehr*, pp. 91–94 (and the references there on p. 92, n. 22). See also recent work of Koch, *Profeten*, vol. 1, pp. 247–60. In particular, Hermisson, *KuD* 27 (1981), formulated important insights that the current essay covers from our viewpoint. The prophetic transmission preserves "dimensions…in continuing validity in which YHWH's present time and YHWH's activity are experienced and can be experienced again. They claim theological insight into a time-bound, historical shape that cannot be encountered in anything other than this shape. However, even in so doing, they nevertheless claim *more* than just a time-bound message relating only to the prophet's time. Such is the claim of the validity of prophetic texts beyond their own time" (pp. 98ff). Concerning the metahistorical image of history that the prophets demonstrate and the chronological reference of prophetic texts toward "the entirety of Israel's time," see the important discussions by Hermisson in *KuD* 27 (1981): 104–10 (especially 107–10). In light of Barth, *Jesaja-Worte*, p. 238, one should maintain that in these (developing) transmissions (or books), the prophets providing the name do not speak as persons actually present in the later period. Rather, they constantly speak as persons from their own, delimited time (superscriptions). This observation is significant for the contour of the statements of the rereading and for the meaning of the rereading in the flow of reading for the entire writing. However, it is clear from the contents and the position of the continuations (*Fortschreibungen*) and redactions, that the prophets providing the name speak from their historical standpoint (in our opinion) not only in their own time, but also in the times down to and including the respective present

time of the tradents. They speak to the onset of destruction and the completion of salvation. They also speak with YHWH's words that possess and maintain their validity in this comprehensive metahistorical framework whether with respect to past time, or to by-gone material with continuing effects, or with respect to the current time, or to that which remains in the future. The tradents are not of the opinion that prophetic transmission would be equally updated in every time period.

[77]Cf. Ebeling, *Evangelienauslegung*, pp. 9, 359–69.

[78]See Steck, *Abschluß*, pp. 13–24, 106–11. One should consider the prophetic reception in the Priestly writing, the wisdom transmission, and especially in the Chronicler's History.

[79]See the recent discussion in Jeremias, ATD 24/2, p. ix, cf. xix, xxii.

[80]See above, p. 126, n. 16.

[81]Cf. Steck, *Studien,* pp. 28ff, 30f, 182, 185, 193–95, 207f; *Abschluß*, p. 87; *Gottesknecht*, pp. 70–72, 166–69; *Metzger-Festschrift*; Gosse, *ZAW* 101 (1989). Now, see also, Rofé, *Piety*. Concerning the operative image of the chain of prophets after Moses, see *Abschluß*, pp. 130–34, and now Fischer, *Tora*, pp. 45ff, n. 13, pp. 81ff, 117–20. The observations about Isaiah 59:21 directed to the final form of Isaiah by Lohfink (SBS, p. 56, but cf. p. 30) ignore the problems that these assertions raise in the immediate context, in the context of reading the entire Isaiah corpus, or in a larger literary framework.

[82]In the immediate context, cf. 55:3 (covenant/people, ולם). See also 42:6 (cf. 42:1// 59:21: spirit; 42:7//58:6–12); 49:8 (cf. 49:8f//58:6–12); 54:10 (מוש cf. 59:21 שלום, 57:2, 19, 21; 59:8); anticipating 61:1 (spirit).

[83]See the discussion in Steck, *Exegesis*, p. 23.

[84]Compare the methodological approach in Steck, *Exegesis*, pp. 12f, 154f.

[85]We cannot properly approach the systematic theology questions concerning God and time in the framework of the concluding thoughts of this essay. See the recent discussion of Dalferth, *Gott und Zeit*, and Moxter, *Gegenwart*. Concerning the problem of time and the question of historical conveyance in theological hermeneutics, see the recent work of Tracy, *Theologie*, especially chapter 4; Jeanrond, *Hermeneutics*, especially chapters 5 and 7.4.

[86]See the discussion in Fishbane, *Interpretation*, throughout, and his categories of *traditum* and *traditio*. See also the recent work of Utzschneider, *Künder*, especially pp. 78–80. One should not miss Koch, *Rezeptionsgeschichte*, and Koch, *Ausgang*.

[87]See Steck, *Heimkehr*, pp. 94–99. For the concept of the material movement or the movement of meaning expressed in the course of the transmission process, see also Steck, *Exegesis*, pp. 79ff, 164–66.

[88]See Steck, *Heimkehr*, pp. 94–99; Kratz, *Kyros*, pp. 219–29; Koch, *Rezeptionsgeschichte*. The document of the Papal Commission on the Bible ("Die Interpretation der Bibel in der Kirche") offers an impressive discussion of this approach. In the exegetical realm we would accentuate more strongly, in light of the "final text" (pp. 100ff), that the historical movement of the revelation canonized in the final text runs toward the final form without increased rank. For its part, over against the earlier stages of the text, the final form is a historically stipulated form of reception with its own accents but also its own limits. For example, the original meaning preserved in the transmission of Isaiah 6 has the same, if not greater, weight as its limited reception in the final formation of the book of Isaiah. The connection to the subsequent New Testament witness in the tradition process and the current situational challenge could help one decide which of the meanings of a text transmitted within the Old Testament should come into play.

[89]See the references in p. 174, n. 87.

[90]See the discussion in Steck, *Metzger-Festschrift*; *Gottesknecht*, pp. 166–72.

[91]See the methodological discussion in Steck, *Exegesis*, pp. 1f, 3–14, 153–66, and the example discussed on pp. 199–202.

[92]See the recent discussion in Moxter, *Gegenwart.*

[93]See the discussion in Gese, *Hermeneutik*, especially pp. 67–81. In our essay, it is appropriate to think about the dialectic between validity and temporality that characterizes the inner-biblical transmission process.

[94]*Jesaja-Worte*, p. 309.

Scripture Index[*]

[*]The index was compiled by James D. Nogalski with the aid of Melanie Greer Nogalski.